ID0975250

As Long As
We Both Shall Eat

Rowman & Littlefield Studies in Food and Gastronomy

General Editor: Ken Albala, Professor of History,
University of the Pacific (kalbala@pacific.edu)

Rowman & Littlefield Executive Editor:
Suzanne Staszak-Silva (sstaszak-silva@rowman.com)

Food studies is a vibrant and thriving field encompassing not only cooking and eating habits but also issues such as health, sustainability, food safety, and animal rights. Scholars in disciplines as diverse as history, anthropology, sociology, literature, and the arts focus on food. The mission of **Rowman & Littlefield Studies in Food and Gastronomy** is to publish the best in food scholarship, harnessing the energy, ideas, and creativity of a wide array of food writers today. This broad line of food-related titles will range from food history, interdisciplinary food studies monographs, general interest series, and popular trade titles to textbooks for students and budding chefs, scholarly cookbooks, and reference works.

Appetites and Aspirations in Vietnam: Food and Drink in the Long Nineteenth Century, by Erica J. Peters
Three World Cuisines: Italian, Mexican, Chinese, by Ken Albala
Food and Social Media: You Are What You Tweet, by Signe Rousseau
Food and the Novel in Nineteenth-Century America, by Mark McWilliams
Man Bites Dog: Hot Dog Culture in America, by Bruce Kraig and Patty Carroll
A Year in Food and Beer: Recipes and Beer Pairings for Every Season, by Emily Baime and Darin Michaels
Celebraciones Mexicanas: History, Traditions, and Recipes, by Andrea Lawson Gray and Adriana Almazán Lahl
The Food Section: Newspaper Women and the Culinary Community, by Kimberly Wilmot Voss
Small Batch: Pickles, Cheese, Chocolate, Spirits, and the Return of Artisanal Foods, by Suzanne Cope
Food History Almanac: Over 1,300 Years of World Culinary History, Culture, and Social Influence, by Janet Clarkson
Cooking and Eating in Renaissance Italy: From Kitchen to Table, by Katherine A. McIver

Eating Together: Food, Space, and Identity in Malaysia and Singapore,
     by Jean Duruz and Gaik Cheng Khoo
Nazi Hunger Politics: A History of Food in the Third Reich, by Gesine Gerhard
The Carrot Purple and Other Curious Stories of the Food We Eat,
     by Joel S. Denker
Food in the Gilded Age: What Ordinary Americans Ate, by Robert Dirks
Food Cults: How Fads, Dogma, and Doctrine Influence Diet, edited by
     Kima Cargill
As Long As We Both Shall Eat: A History of Wedding Food and Feasts,
     by Claire Stewart

As Long As
We Both Shall Eat

A History of Wedding Food and Feasts

Claire Stewart

ROWMAN & LITTLEFIELD
Lanham • Boulder • New York • London

Published by Rowman & Littlefield
A wholly owned subsidiary of The Rowman & Littlefield Publishing Group, Inc.
4501 Forbes Boulevard, Suite 200, Lanham, Maryland 20706
www.rowman.com

Unit A, Whitacre Mews, 26-34 Stannary Street, London SE11 4AB

British Library Cataloguing in Publication Information Available

Library of Congress Cataloging-in-Publication Data
Names: Stewart, Claire, 1964– author.
Title: As long as we both shall eat : a history of wedding food and feasts /
    Claire Stewart.
Description: Lanham : Rowman & Littlefield, [2017] | Series: Rowman &
    Littlefield studies in food and gastronomy | Includes bibliographical
    references and index.
Identifiers: LCCN 2016038463 (print) | LCCN 2016057129 (ebook) |
    ISBN 9781442257139 (cloth : alk. paper) | ISBN 9781442257146 (electronic)
Subjects: LCSH: Marriage customs and rites. | Weddings. | Food habits.
Classification: LCC GT2690 .S74 2017 (print) | LCC GT2690 (ebook) |
    DDC 392.5—dc23
LC record available at https://lccn.loc.gov/2016038463

Printed in the United States of America

Contents

Introduction to the Menu

The study of food and culture incorporates the disciplines of sociology, anthropology, folklore, history, and economics. An examination of these spheres reveals some unlikely intersections, and among the undeniable and significant connections that bind them all together are the customs surrounding the consumption of food. An investigation of societal food traditions offers unique insight into a particular culture. Changing food habits can parallel and indicate shifts in cultural norms and may symbolize more meaningful changes that rest latent or unspoken in given societies. An analysis of the presentation of food and drinks served at celebrations, particularly at wedding feasts and banquets, may especially serve as an indicator of the social status of those who host the particular event.

For some people, food can be used as an expression of a desire for social betterment. Food, then, is unique in that it is literally taken into the body; yet the circumstances surrounding its consumption are also a reflection of this pursuit of societal advancement. The subliminal messages food embodies get reinforced by the celebration of milestones, and weddings are the most important of these social landmarks. Humans mark special occasions—religious events, birthdays, anniversaries, and even funerals—with feasting. No occasion is held in higher regard than the wedding, and no cultural marker is as universal as the wedding feast. Champagne and other luxury items regularly served at weddings broadcast the social status of individuals (and also of the larger community).

French philosopher and social critic Roland Barthes addressed how food surpasses its function as a means of mere human survival. Barthes wrote that food is a mirror of total experiences, a summation of conditions, and can serve as a "signal" of those experiences. For example,

Barthes wrote that coffee had become a "circumstance, not a substance."[1] Coffee was formerly so valuable it engendered wars. Its appeal was originally derived only from its ability to stimulate the nervous system. Present-day coffee consumption has morphed what was once an "item" into "an action," and this "action" is an indicator of status, copious leisure time, and conspicuous consumption. Likewise, sparkling wine is used to make the toast at weddings; yet its use is mostly symbolic, with the glasses often left undrunk. Champagne has become an "action" that American weddings demand.

Contemporary weddings especially employ food and drink as a "signal" that the hosts have achieved economic success, and wedding receptions can serve as an example of Barthes's idea of food as a way to announce social position. And champagne can serve as an extreme example of signaled luxury and a readily identifiable marker that an event is special.

The marketing and consumption of champagne mirrors the evolution of modern weddings. Consumption of this ancient beverage was eventually molded into a cultural phenomenon fueled by advertisers and a universal desire to experience and exhibit sumptuousness. In a brilliant marketing move, nineteenth-century champagne vintner Eugene Mercier commissioned the largest wine barrel in the world. A dramatic eighteen horses and twenty-four white oxen pulled the cask, containing the equivalent of two hundred thousand bottles of champagne. Its three-week trek to Paris, destined for the Paris Exposition of 1889, was reported all over the world, "keeping both champagne and Mercier in the public eye."[2] Mercier's giant barrel of champagne was a popular tourist attraction, though not quite as famous as its competitor for attention, the Eiffel Tower, which also debuted at the fair.[3]

BEYONCÉ'S BUBBLY

A modern version of champagne marketing involves music mogul Jay Z and his wife, music star Beyoncé. In 2006 Frederic Rouzaud, manager of the company that produces Cristal champagne, made less than complimentary remarks when asked how he felt about the popularity of the product within rap culture. The hip-hop community, including Jay Z, citing racism, responded with a boycott.[4]

Jay Z featured Armand de Brignac brand champagne in his 2006 music video for "Show Me What You Got." In the James Bond–esque video, he sits at a casino table and waves away Cristal when it is offered, instead accepting a locked briefcase of Armand de Brignac. Prior to the video, the brand was virtually unknown in the United States and sold under another name; it went for the equivalent of $60 per bottle in Europe.[5] Just after the release of the video, a spokesperson for Sovereign Brands, producers of Armand de Brignac, insisted there was no business relationship with Jay Z, and the appearance of the champagne (dubbed Ace of Spades) was not an instance of product placement. It was also reported that Jay Z had discovered the product in a New York wine store, although it was not available at the time in the United States.[6]

In 2014 a company press release announced that Jay Z had just purchased Armand de Brignac; yet Jay Z biographer Zack O'Malley Greenburg reports that the rapper had purchased the enterprise years before and had in fact been using his music to promote sales for some time.

Both Jay Z and Beyoncé have injected references to the product into their songs, linking it to their romance and heightening their depiction of their lavish and romantic lifestyle. In 2015 Beyoncé and Nicki Minaj recorded "Feeling Myself," in which they cavort in a hot tub filled with perfectly good Armand de Brignac. This wastefulness caused a minor social media stir, as the once $60 product now had a manufacturer's suggested retail price of $300. Beyoncé was taken to task by some of her more prudent fans, accused of being cavalier with such an expensive item, but clearly the wastefulness was the point.

Like the efforts of the producer who wheeled his giant barrel of wine across the French countryside, this was an especially successful advertising campaign, rejuvenating and repositioning a once obscure champagne. In the case of Armand de Brignac, we can see how a classic luxury wedding item, one that already signifies romance and enjoys celebrity endorsement, has increased in value even more when pitched by a real-life celebrity couple.

COFFEEHOUSE

Barthes wrote "Toward a Psychology of Contemporary Food Consumption" in 1943, long before the advent of contemporary coffee culture, well before Starbucks and Dunkin' Donuts existed. One can imagine that Barthes would find the sale of $7 mocha lattes and iced caramel macchiatos pithy examples of his thesis.

Regardless of whether the possession of coffee was once a form of economic dominance for those who could afford it, it eventually grew to be the symbol of prosperity that it is today. As the story of champagne illustrates, this dynamic of conspicuous consumption can be applied to items far beyond coffee. Clearly, consumers desire a seat at a Starbucks table and are willing to pay an exorbitant fee for it; yet this same mind-set can be applied to the desire to serve trendy artisanal foods at a wedding at prices far beyond what is necessary to prove cultural superiority.

As Long As We Both Shall Eat: A History of Wedding Food and Feasts, a culinary history of weddings, unearths the connections between food and bridal culture. While focusing primarily on American weddings, this book does touch on international marriage customs and food traditions from foreign countries that have been assimilated into the American mainstream. Modern wedding traditions are generally rooted in the cultures of the United Kingdom and Western Europe; thus the foods and customs of these cultures may seem disproportionally represented.

Popular culture's depiction of life is not necessarily an indicator of reality. Race, class, and religion have always dictated how people celebrate rites of passage. The media have generally reported on the middle class and the elite, thereby recording their practices as the norm. Bridal magazines concerned themselves only with the affairs of well-heeled white Christians for far too long, and their weddings are thus well documented. And yet a proper overview of wedding customs requires digging beyond what has been construed as the behavior of the mainstream. It would be impossible to touch on the customs of every ethnicity, religion, or region, however, so I have narrowed my focus to that which is most common in the United States. I have also taken particular interest in customs that are indicative of a significant time in American history.

Why are wedding celebrations important? The answer lies in reproduction, which ensures the survival of a species. At a time when chastity was essential for an unmarried woman, accusations of impropriety could be catastrophic, bringing ruin to her family and leading to the disinheritance of her future children. A memorable wedding, then, ensured that a disgruntled husband or his disappointed family could not later refute a marriage.

People have always celebrated rites of passage with the consumption of food, so, in a time when there were few written records, a wedding feast could emblazon in peers' memory the knowledge that an official, sanctioned ceremony had indeed taken place. Families have often spent more than they could afford to marry off their children. The act of *projecting* wealth was meant to *attract* wealth, serving as a type of rehearsal of and magnet for a better way of life. In a time before rented limousines and elaborate flower arrangements, families could proclaim their affluence by serving extravagant food. A nuptial feast could also announce that the newlyweds, a new amalgamation of combined family positions, were taking their place in the social hierarchy.

In order to illuminate the role that food plays in American weddings, this book first gives an overview of cookery traditions, providing an outline for the history of cuisine and its importance in society. It next gives a rundown of how weddings have been celebrated throughout history, with a summary of ritualistic practices that include cuisine. I take a peek at some famous nuptials (and a few notorious weddings as well). I then move into a discussion of prewedding celebrations, considering bachelor and bachelorette parties, wedding gifts, and bridal showers. Next I review the important role that etiquette has played in bridal practices, highlighting how standards of good behavior have changed and what this shift in societal expectations says about current culture.

This book examines various religious traditions that incorporate the foods employed in wedding rituals and surveys how geography and immigration have led to regional differences in wedding banquets. I examine the "wedding toast" and alcohol use, as well as the manner in which Prohibition gravely affected the hospitality industry. And, of course, the wedding cake gets its own chapter. Honeymoons are included as an important topic, along with an overview of how greed and capitalism have shaped the business of weddings.

In the course of my career as a professional chef, I have cooked for thousands of weddings, working in restaurants and hotels catering dozens of weddings per weekend. I use this experience to spike the research that substantiates what I know anecdotally to be true.

I hope this book will find its way to curious brides and grooms, as well as students of American foodways and food lovers. I particularly hope this book will reach my brethren, those chefs, servers, salespeople, and wedding planners who make a living within the wonderful, rich, interesting world of weddings in America.

A Brief History of Wedding Feasts

FEASTS

Historically, feasts were held to mark political victories, commemorate battles, and celebrate and publicize marriages. For the elite host, providing entertainment was a grave responsibility. Food was a vehicle for providing amusement, and in this the rulers of Renaissance Europe were experts. In fifteenth-century France, Philip, Duke of Burgundy, hosted a feast that featured an enormous pie, out of which cavorting musicians marched. Royal banquets often featured "subtleties," a form of "tabletop pastry construction," made from hardened pastry dough or sugar, some as large as life-size elephants or whales, and often rendered inedible by a covering of gold. Flambéing, or setting food ablaze, was fashionable, and displays called "past times" included elaborate pies whose crusts, once cracked open, released live snakes, or frogs, or even dancing dwarves.[1] This "theater of the table" was entertainment even for onlookers who gawked at the display of food with no hope of ever partaking in it.[2]

The medieval calendar was divided between feast days and fast days, so for hungry peasants, a noble's wedding day would surely be an added feast day. Few could hope to dine at palace tables, but everyone benefited from a royal wedding. Platters were filled with leftovers and marched through the streets. In this way, nobility demonstrated their wealth and also their generosity.[3]

FOREVER WILL YOU HOLD YOUR PEACE

Despite the many ways of celebrating matrimony across the globe, symbols of fertility are abundant in marriage rituals and are often signified by food. Plants that break open or contain seeds are common motifs, and honey, salt, eggs, nuts, and rice, as well as pomegranates (with their abundance of seeds), prevail in wedding customs in countless cultures. Orange blossoms are also popular, as orange trees bear fruit and flower at the same time. Rosemary was once a traditional bridal bouquet item, signifying "remembrance"; yet it was also commonly carried at funerals. Dill was meant to inspire lust and, after its use in bouquets, was added to the offerings in the wedding feast. Some modern brides carry lemongrass in their bouquets, the shoots resembling green stalks of corn, a practice dating to ancient Roman wedding ceremonies.[4] Bouquets have traditionally included herbs, whose scent was thought to ward off the bubonic plaque. Of course, rice thrown at the happy couple is an old tradition.

Throughout history, the acquisition of food has required exertion, and when lives were led under especially precarious circumstances, marriage and reproduction held particularly powerful consequences. Childbearing has always been a risky endeavor, and in sixteenth-century England, one in eight children died in infancy, whereas one in four did not make it to their tenth birthday.[5] As only the fortunate lived beyond forty, the specter of death was present at every marriage and every birth. With death terminating many marriages, the average length of a couple's union was just over thirteen years in Elizabethan England. As a result, roughly half of all marriages were remarriages.[6]

Marriage for love is a relatively modern phenomenon, especially among the wealthy, with marital unions among the elite best described as contracts that allowed for the exchange of benefits.[7] Affection and physical attraction were more common when no lands or titles were at stake. By the seventeenth century, parents had conceded much of their authority over whom their children married, now exercising veto power more than choosing spouses. This meant that marriages were serving less and less as a means to gain position and alliances for families and becoming personal choices made by the bride and groom.[8]

ENCORE BRIDES

According to tenth-century Welsh law, a woman could divorce her spouse if he had leprosy, if he could not achieve orgasm, or if he had "fetid breath." The law was specific about the division of property, with the man getting the swine while the woman took the sheep and milk pails.[9] The ability to acquire food, then, was crucial in the realm of divorce proceedings, with a husband left able to breed pigs and a wife to procure fresh milk and make cheese.

In Elizabethan England, an older widow was indulged and revered; yet a young widow, particularly if attractive, needed to keep up appearances of propriety. Her perceived threat came with the understanding that she was surely not a virgin and had therefore known the pleasures of the flesh. Widows in this era were stereotyped as lusty and monitored by their communities, likely out of suspicion.[10] But perhaps they were monitored for other reasons too.

In the sixteenth century, widows were able to inherit their deceased husbands' position as an apprentice, and women consequently were active in many trade guilds, most notably those of bakers and printers. Girls were allowed to join guilds, and the right to formal apprenticeships enabled women to find a measure of economic power. Positions within a trade guild were rarely vacant, and widows could claim membership rights and continue in the vocation.[11] The widow could also pass these rights to her *new* husband, so here we see how attractive a mate a young widow was—conceivably young enough to bear children and also able to furnish a ready-made occupation. Marital practices in Elizabethan England were progressing in terms of fairness between the sexes, but this would soon change with the incursion of Puritanism in both Old and New England.[12]

Puritan women in the United States wed in their early twenties and gave birth to an average of six children. Because of early deaths, couples often entered into second marriages out of a mutual need for child care and farm labor. Love as a driving force behind marriage did not become prevalent until at least the 1600s. In *A History of the Wife*, researcher Marilyn Yalom makes the point that the blended families of today pale in comparison to the restructured families of early America.[13]

One unusual type of second marriage occurred when a widow remarried wearing little or no clothing (or a simple dress—i.e., a "smock"). A bizarre New England law allowed a man to escape liability for a new wife's debt from her previous marriage if she was not clothed properly at the second wedding. So-called smock marriages were recorded in Maine, New York, Pennsylvania, and Rhode Island, and there are scores of stories of brides exchanging vows concealed in a cupboard or hidden unclothed behind a door.[14]

ANNOUNCEMENTS

Before the information age, it was feasible for a prospective bride or groom to have already been secretly married or to be hiding circumstances that would make him or her an unacceptable mate. The marriage "bann" developed as a way to allow time for decisive information to find its way into the ears of the community, perhaps preventing a disastrous alliance. An announcement of an impending marriage was read aloud on three Sundays, either in church or somewhere public like the town market. Publicizing the impending ceremony served as a way for anyone who protested to voice opposition before the rite occurred. This prevented claims of illegitimate children in the future should a party already be married, thereby invalidating the second marriage. Banns also curbed accusations that the union was impulsive or hastily coerced. After the banns had been read over at least three weeks, a couple would generally assemble at the church door to recite their vows. Weddings did not begin to take place inside churches until the sixteenth century.[15] Later, in the New World, couples nailed their announcements to the church door rather than have their banns read aloud. Puritans, who did not hold with flashiness, held civil proceedings, with the town magistrate regulating the waiting period after a bann.[16]

In present-day Great Britain, the Church of England still requires marriage banns, although there is a movement to modernize the practice, and a "common license" offers a civil alternative. A mandatory waiting period after a trip to the courthouse to get a marriage license is a version of the same practice in America. Engagement announcements in modern newspapers or social media serve a similar function.

CROWD SOURCING IS NOT NEW

British penny weddings, traced to sixteenth-century Scotland, were an early form of contributory celebration, in which guests paid admission to attend bridal feasts. Profits from the "bride ale" sold at the festivities helped newlyweds set up a home.[17] These gatherings got so rowdy and so large (and profitable) that English law eventually regulated the amount of beer that could be brewed and limited the number of attendees.[18] English wedding guests often paid a small fee (a penny), brought food, or paid admission as part of attending receptions, and often the entire town, and even strangers, showed up. Villagers were alerted to the occasion by the placement of a bush outside the party site or sometimes a branch over the door of a house where the gathering was to be held. The festivities, which featured prizes, games, and athletics, as well as enthusiastic drinking and dancing, often went on for days.

Jacklyn Geller, in *Here Comes the Bride*, writes that social climbers noted that the elite had guest lists and carefully plotted itineraries, while the lower classes hosted boisterous, improvised marathons of revelry. A striving middle class, increasing in number and wishing to mimic high society, began to appropriate the staid wedding repast, which had become a standard by the 1800s.[19] Those with "new money" aimed to display their wealth, and the "servant problem" made it difficult to host large events at home. The increased availability of palatial banquet rooms, fancy catering halls, and restaurants provided an opportunity for the affluent to brandish their wealth; these venues also provided a target to which others could aspire.[20]

KNOWING YOUR PLACE

> A quiet wedding took place yesterday morning at 11 o'clock at the Church of the Heavenly Rest, Fifth-avenue and Forty-fifth street, the contracting parties being Miss Sarah Josephine Rieck, daughter of Mr. J. C. Rieck, of No. 23 East Sixty-fifth street, and Mr. Francis Eugene Grant. After the ceremony an informal reception was given to the relatives and intimate friends of the bride and groom at the residence of the bride's parents.
>
> —"Fashionable Weddings," *New York Times*,
> November 23, 1881

The above is a typical description of an Eastern "society" wedding of the 1880s (if you weren't "society," you weren't making the *Times*). The columnist later noted that there were no bridesmaids and no best man. The bride's embroidered dress, her pearls and lace, the corsage, the veil, and her hair ornaments were described in detail, followed by a list of who exactly attended the wedding.[21]

The matrimonial model favored by the elite was a church wedding followed by a dignified "collation" (light meal) at the bride's family home. Particularly in the Victorian era, care was taken to mark gatherings as "quiet" and "intimate," lest they be judged vulgar. Tasteful marriage announcements were but one way to sort the social classes, clearly delineating where the participants stood on the social ladder—and where they lived, home address and all.

The forced gentility of Victorian life was grappling with the industrialization that threatened standards of culture. As telephones and electric light reshaped households, industry was producing standardized goods, which in turn begat a desire for yet more goods. Even a simple wedding like the one just described called for multiple commercial transactions. Researcher Barbara Penner asserts that as early as the 1850s, weddings were increasingly "choreographed," and merchants (florists, engravers, jewelers, and seamstresses, for a start) were necessary for the affluent to host even the most restrained of society weddings. Household staff and family members could sew or prepare for a party, but they could not engrave invitations or create elaborate floral displays. Etiquette writers, hitting their stride in producing manuals for navigating the changing social terrain, judged that the sanctity of marriage should be free of the indignities of advertising and commerce. Clergy in particular backed humble nuptial celebrations, contending that grandiosity created an excitement that "overstimulated" brides and grooms, who would be disenchanted when the routine of married life inevitably set in.[22]

> Never examine minutely the food before you. You insult your hostess by such a proceeding, as it looks as if you feared to find something upon the plate that should not be there.
>
> —Florence Hartley, *The Ladies' Book of Etiquette and Manual for Manners*, 1872

Outward displays of wealth or affection were considered "untoward," so for the stalwart elite, showiness of any kind was distasteful, and this applied to mealtime, with the enjoyment of food considered lusty and somehow debased. The convention that high society did not condone the use of wedding fare as a way to demonstrate status, then, perhaps goes back to food's lowly primary function—ensuring survival. Delicate Victorians did not like to be soiled by the earthy origins of food. So they instead exhibited their breeding with genteel endeavors like floral arrangements, needlework, and properly worded calling cards. *The Century Cook Book* (1895), for example, despite being a cookbook, sternly warned that food could not express refinement. The book outlined the responsibilities of hosting a meal but warned that it "should always be remembered that the social part of the entertainment is on a higher plane than the gastro-nomic one. A fig for your bill of fare, give me a bill of your company."[23]

THE NEW CENTURY

Since today, as always, simplicity and dignity are marks of good breeding, the bride recognizes that the most sacred event of her life—her wedding—should embrace these two virtues.

—*Good Housekeeping* 80, no. 6 (June 1925): 80

The reader is further advised that only tea and coffee, with "dainty open-faced sandwiches, cakes and ices," should be served at receptions. If a more "elaborate" menu was necessary, a salad could be included.

Society's desire for restraint continued into the new century. The call for moderation rode out the indiscretions of the Jazz Age (at least in the confines of the bridal industry), while food maintained its tepid station. A wedding cake recipe was obligatory in nearly every mainstream cookbook between the 1900s and the 1960s. Yet it was generally a fruit cake, with most recipes nearly indistinguishable from one another.

WARTIME

The food rationing that so restricted lives during both world wars also ratcheted up the call for simplicity, and "even the smartest weddings" were toned down. They featured special "war cakes," containing no butter or white sugar (no icing!) and were made with barley flour and dried fruit.[24] The pressure to display nationalism was keenly felt, and the wealthy, who could always get any food if willing to spend the money, were especially compelled to exhibit patriotism. One columnist, between reporting on "wheatless afternoon teas" and the splendid qualities of the maligned prune, bragged, "There have been no slacker marriages in New York soci-ety." Slackers, men who married in order to sidestep military service, had thankfully not contaminated the upper echelons. The media romanticized the soldier groom and called upon the public to offer "patriotic hospital-ity" to the best of its abilities at wartime weddings.[25] Red, white, and blue ribbons festooned table settings, and if a cake could not include frosting, it could be decorated with a ceramic eagle and tiny flags and swords.

The Biltmore

is a Member of the

UNITED STATES FOOD
ADMINISTRATION

Eat Plenty—Eat Wisely—But Without Waste

Food will decide the war

SAVE THE WHEAT
SAVE THE MEAT
SAVE THE FATS
SAVE THE MILK
SAVE THE SUGAR
SAVE THE FUEL

For
Your Soldiers at the Front Need Them All

IMPORTANT INFORMATION
SEE OVER

Rationing menu, Biltmore Hotel, 1918. *Source:* "The Biltmore," Buttolph Collection of Menus, New York Public Library Digital Collections, http://digitalcollections.nypl.org/items/c37c22b3-227d-835e-e040-e00a18066b39.

If possible, have the reception at home. That is your natural setting.

—Enid Wells, *Living for Two:*
A Guide to Homemaking, 1939[26]

Brides magazine (originally titled *Brides, So You're Going to Be Married*) debuted in 1934, at the height of the Depression. Its voluminous pages swelled with advertisements for honeymoon cruises to Havana, French champagne, and the "paper trousseaux," all out of reach of most citizens. If not the actual products, such magazines sold the ideal of the white wedding, and new definitions of the dream wedding were crystallizing in the nuptial psyche.

The Bride's Bureau, inside the massive Detroit department store J. L. Hudson's, advertised that its wedding consultant, Miss Carolyn Chase, could help a bride choose (and presumably buy) invitations, luggage, silver, and furniture; she could even arrange honeymoons. Miss Chase had "perfect knowledge of the proprieties and canons of good taste," a selling point for something needed by an insecure bride faced with all the new intricacies of a changing wedding culture.[27]

In the antebellum South, for instance, girls became brides as young as fourteen or fifteen, and after age twenty they risked being considered "stale."[28] The age of those marrying rose, then lowered during wartime. *Saturday Evening Post* article "War Brides," from June 12, 1943, claimed that, like their mothers in World War I, young women were arranging "hurry-up weddings" while their men were on brief furloughs. As during the Great War, there was a rash of very young brides. In the early 1950s, one-third of women getting married were only nineteen years old, and the average age for grooms was just twenty-two.[29]

These brides did not want to miss their big moment, and they did not want to get married in "practical suits" like their sacrificing mothers. According to Mrs. Alexandra Potts, the expert bridal consultant interviewed by the *Saturday Evening Post*, 90 percent of service men queried wanted to see their brides in a wedding train and veil. And brides definitely wanted photos of themselves wearing that veil in the pockets of their new husbands overseas. Readers were assured, however, that the champagne should still flow, albeit domestic bubbly in reduced circumstances.

WORLD WAR II AND FOOD PORN

During wartime rationing, cookbooks and magazines overflowed with recipes featuring meatless meals, ground meats stretched with bread crumbs, or inexpensive offal cuts such as liver, kidney, and tongue. "Victory gardens" were enthusiastically tended in order to save food reserves for the military. Rosie the Riveter and her colleagues worked hard to feed their families, grocery shopping in a time that required visiting multiple stores.

There was no infrastructure to provide child care, and many homes still used wood-burning stoves, despite the modern kitchens featured in magazines. Household refrigerators did not become common in private homes until after World War II, and cookbooks, throughout the postwar era, continued to have separate instructions and advice for those with iceboxes as opposed to "mechanical refrigerators." Just as during the Depression, the image of inaccessible luxuries fed consumers' aspirations, especially in the wedding industry.[30]

In 1941, while food rationing was at full tilt, *Gourmet* arrived, a magazine improbably dedicated to "good living." *Gourmet* breezed around the idea of food shortages and seemed to target affluent sportsmen needing instruction on how to prepare the spoils of their hunts. Addressing readers as people of means with access to such affluent pastimes generated a type of early food porn, a desire to experience the unattainable.

Rationing did not just apply to food. War Production Board Regulation L-85 limited the material used to make clothes. It also dictated the length of skirts, color choices, and even cuff size, forbidding "fabric on fabric" in order to conserve supplies. The manufacture of stockings was completely discontinued, as nylon and silk were needed to make parachutes. But the new bridal salons knew very well that the government made an exception for bridal gowns (and maternity clothes). Wedding dresses could be big and frilly with as much fabric as the bride could afford.[31]

Weddings became increasingly elaborate after World War II, with couples eager to flaunt liberties hard won through wartime sacrifices. To shop was to protest communism, binding democracy and capitalism together.[32] New technology that cranked out inexpensive personalized matchbooks, stirrers, and cocktail napkins buttressed a zeal for consumer goods. The diamond industry invested heavily in promotion, somewhat rewriting history as it proclaimed that double-ring ceremonies dated to "the time of the pharaohs," hence representing a lost tradition that the most masculine of men could reclaim.[33] Soon wedding rings for men had become a new norm. *Modern Bride* magazine appeared in 1949, just in time to help reconstruct perceptions of the ideal wedding and provide yet another shopping venue. Talk of etiquette, decoration, and fashion, however, would continue to eclipse enthusiasm for the food served at weddings.

Couples during the Vietnam era also planned weddings, of course, and the bridal business was careful to include military wives in its demographic. The industry was already accustomed to walking a tightrope in order to appeal to the mainstream, a particularly dicey undertaking considering that its target audience (the young) very possibly reviled the military. Columnists gave advice for how to properly address a thank-you note to a military officer, provided instruction on how to correctly introduce various ranks of soldiers, and recommended reception theme music appropriate for each military branch.[34] No talk of war there, and nothing to offend; yet also no direct reference to young soldiers risking their lives overseas. In 1966, when an activist yelled "murderer" outside the church when President Lyndon Johnson arrived at his daughter Luci's wedding rehearsal, it was not an isolated occurrence. If Johnson heard the remark, he did not react. He was undoubtedly accustomed to the protesters, who actively used Luci's wedding coverage to further their cause.[35]

The women's movement was also blazing, so bridal magazines adapted here as well, bringing in "lady doctors" to write health columns and featuring "working women" in photo spreads. By 1965 readers were able to get advice on "modern married sex" and read about birth control. But 1960s youth did not buy magazines, and the bridal industry suffered. The marriage rate dropped (couples started living together rather than taking vows), and Tricia Nixon's White House wedding in 1971 was considered decidedly "square."[36]

Trudging on, *Brides* offered scenarios highlighting various types of people and their corresponding style of entertaining, giving readers a chance to find their counterparts to identify with within its pages. "Menus for a Newlyweds First Get Together," from summer 1968, supposed some readers would identify with Jan and Carlton, "traditionalists" who prepared salmon steaks and green beans. Or perhaps readers were more like Mary and Bill, a "working couple," who lived in an apartment in the city and served a less formal menu, with raw vegetables and dip.[37] The magazine grouped dresses, honeymoons, and reception menus by budget, with the chance for any bride to find someone like herself within the magazine.

The wedding menus in the April/May 1967 issue of *Brides* encapsulate a perfect storm of 1960s food. "Luncheon" would include shrimp cocktail and cold sandwiches, and "Hot Seated" would call for tomato aspic and creamed chicken in pastry shells. "Cocktail Only" was tiny meatballs, chicken livers wrapped in bacon, and deviled eggs. The "Buffet Supper" would have beef stroganoff, noodles, and stuffed tomatoes. The big daddy was the "Seated Dinner," and here the menu would turn French, with consommé madrilène, filet mignon, and soufflé potatoes.

FOOTBALLS OR SANDWICHES?

Popular cookbooks and bridal magazines from the late 1940s to the 1960s scarcely mention wedding food without referring to sandwiches. A *Good Housekeeping* of October 1947 is characteristic, relating detailed instructions for how to make checkerboard, pinwheel, and domino sandwiches ahead of the main event. A June 1949 issue devoted pages to the art of sandwich production—"let your home freezer be the caterer!"— and both the May and June 1950 issues recommended chicken salad (branded a "wedding reception mainstay"). These were clearly "party" sandwiches, however, with some ambitious concoctions, featuring snipped dates, liver pate, curried mayonnaise, or apple butter with orange rind.[38] It was suggested that a bride might choose to ask her friend to "lend a maid" to help replenish trays. The intent may have been to appeal to a 1950 reader who would wish to employ a maid if she did not already have one, a reader without the income to throw a catered hotel reception, as the wealthy would have done, but who aspired to refinement. *Vogue's Book of Etiquette* recommended serving "coffee and chocolate, as well as every known kind of sandwich."[39] A June 1925 *Good Housekeeping* article suggested serving "Chicken Salad in a Cracker Pen," in which individual cheese straws (which had to be made first) were arranged in a triangle and held in place by yellow baby ribbons, fastened with a bow. The "pen" was then filled with chicken salad, a few pickles, some salted almonds, and a mint sprig. Maybe those sandwiches were not as easy to make as the writers imagined.

"Sandwich Weddings" were popular in the 1950s and 1960s, especially for immigrants or those with sizeable guest lists. Large halls were rented, which held an outsize crowd and allowed family members to defray reception costs and help with food preparation. "Football Weddings" could include hundreds of guests, all vying for sandwiches "thrown" back and forth as a favored flavor was hunted. These often boisterous parties were usually held in neighborhood halls, often linked to an ethnic or church group, or at a social club like the Elks or the American Legion.[40]

As first-generation Americans moved up the economic ladder, they tended to move their social events away from community centers and into commercial halls, where they could host more ambitious festivities. Couples chasing the American dream were ready to purchase wedding "packages" and all the accompanying goods and services that exhibited success.

Wedding hall, Leo and Mary Maffei, 1953. *Source*: Author's collection.

No matter how formal your wedding, a modest menu is always appropriate.

—*Brides* 33 (April–May 1967): 147

GROOVY

Wedding receptions in the 1960s may have seen guests dancing the monkey or the mashed potato in miniskirts, but the food was probably not a highlight and not nearly as progressive as the music and fashion of the time. The decorum called for by wedding authorities had indeed relaxed in many areas, especially in terms of etiquette, a discipline that was taking a beating from the so-called hippie culture. O. P. from Teaneck,

New Jersey, for instance, wrote to an etiquette columnist to complain that her fiancé, who had long hair, was going to "look ridiculous in a top hat in their formal wedding" (she was told it was OK to forego the hat if he would not cut his hair).

The November 1969 issue of *Brides* included an African American couple in its style pages. This "groovy but grown up" couple was irreproachably sophisticated in wool flannel and beige velvet suits, complete with a byline that told readers, "Through a handful of rice or through an earful of rock sounds, this with-it young couple just won't sit still!" The beauty advice section, however, called for "inspiration from Japan for a delicate brunette," showing Asian hair styles modeled on decidedly non-Asian models.[41] Some change was in the air, however, as the same publication (*Brides*, May 1969) presented wedding fashions worn by those of various faiths, including previously invisible Jewish, Russian Orthodox, and Baptist couples, the latter featuring an African American couple and clergy.

The same issue sounded rumbles of the Battle of the Sexes, showing a Caucasian man posing with his new bride in *his* "going away" outfit. He got to sport a full-length, raccoon-fur maxi coat by Halston. Alas, the same reformist attitude would see this groom sharing marketing space with a fleet of enthusiastic tampon ads and a Massengill ad that posited, "To douche or not to douche?"

The May/June 1981 issue of the *Saturday Evening Post* satirized a 1960 wedding, spoofing a "kinky" barefoot couple, their vows exchanged amid a haze of sandalwood incense and lute music. A bridesmaid sported a T-shirt that read, "Send the Pigs to War, Not Us," and the bride's mother trusted that valium would help her endure the proceedings. The article goes on to report how in 1981, however, couples had reestablished respect for wedding traditions. Their parents had weathered the hippie culture and resigned themselves to "keep communication lines open," and a happy medium existed. Young people could now appreciate a good limousine ride to the church like their parents had, although a limo driver could no longer be counted on to change to white-walled tires if driving for a wedding.[42]

The general sense of nonconformity in the 1970s (and a drop in the marriage rate) led to a flagging bridal industry. The magnificent wedding of Lady Diana Spencer and Prince Charles in 1981, however, enthralled the world. After 750 million television viewers watched Diana emerge from a glass coach, wearing a twenty-five-foot train and diamond tiara, the wedding business was back with a bang.[43]

FOOD GETS ITS DUE

New industry personalities emerged from cable television and the Internet, setting a new and permissive tone in wedding decorum. Starting in the late 1990s, a curious bride could troll the web for answers to any wedding question at all; the key to wedding success no longer lay in the hands of stern etiquette experts or columnists who preached restraint. The availability of information and the speed at which it could be shared unleashed a new level of empowerment for those planning their big day.

Reality television gave us bridezillas, an exaggerated portrayal of an entitled generation raised in a world where members of the losing team also get trophies. Vicki Howard, in *Brides, Inc.*, writes that an indulgent tone in wedding media emerged, one that assured couples that they were special and that their wedding could be a means to exhibit their oh-so-unique personalities.[44] This was a significant shift from a time when being "correct" was a priority and proper behavior demonstrated economic success.

Soon, we would have the "antibride," who inverted the counterculture newlyweds of the 1960s and set about redefining wedding traditions. A new "kooky" couple rose out of the new millennium. This couple could be of the same sex and of any race or religion; the bride might be eight months pregnant, or wear tennis shoes under a gown, or sport a sleeve tattoo. This generation has grown up watching cooking shows and shopping at Whole Foods. Its members regularly take photos of their entrees at restaurants. These people will not be denied the opportunity to use their big day, with a captive audience, as a vehicle for exhibiting their "personality." No matter the forced sense of informality evidenced by online RSVPs and cocktails served in mason jars, this couple will spend an enormous amount of energy plotting the meal to be served on their wedding day.

ॐ *2* ॐ

Famous and Infamous Feasts

ROYAL WEDDINGS

Nancy Miller Weds Former Maharajah in Gorgeous Rites, Admission in High Caste and Adoption as a Princess Precede Religious Marriage. Ceremonies Last All Day. Bride and Bridegroom in Brilliant Silks and Dazzling Jewels— Elephants Parade. Bride to Have Operation, She Will Be Taken to Europe Soon for Removal of Appendix. Mother Approves Union.

—Associated Press, *New York Times* page-one headline, March 18, 1928

This incredible headline only hints at the wild story of the maharajah of Indore, Tukoji Rao Holkar, an Indian sovereign whose third wife was Nancy Ann Miller from Seattle, Washington. The first two wives were still around, as polygamy was then an acceptable practice within the Indian aristocracy. Miller converted to Hinduism in order to marry, her promotion to princess finalized by a ritual eating of meat (Marathas, unlike many Hindus, are not vegetarians). Miller was smeared with turmeric in a traditional prewedding ceremony and wed barefooted in Indian robes before 10,000 people.[1]

The groom had been in some hot water earlier, and his marriage to an American Caucasian Christian did him no favors with his relations. Two years prior he had abdicated, sullied by a scandal when he allegedly ordered the kidnapping and forced return of his favorite "dancing girl," who had retired from her palace duties.[2]

In a similar vein, yet one more palatable to American appetites, the 1956 wedding of Hollywood actress Grace Kelly to Prince Rainier III of Monaco caused a storm of publicity. When, during their wedding rehearsal, crowds outside the Monte Carlo church got unruly, scuffling photographers were arrested in one of a series of media melees. On April 16, 1956, the *Pittsburgh Press* reported that Rainier was "aghast" at the commercialism attached to the event. The prince was surprised both by the media furor and by the opportunists hocking wedding-related souvenirs. The columnist Art Buchwald attended the affair and reported on the feast of lobster and foie gras, telling of the champagne that flowed to celebrities and Europe's nobility alike.[3] For an American populace recovering from the deprivations and sacrifices of wartime, Kelly's fairy-tale wedding fueled a bridal industry intent on selling fantasy.

WHY IS THAT CALLED BREAKFAST?

The Victorian English term "wedding breakfast," common in the United States until late in the twentieth century, referred to the celebratory meal eaten after the ceremony. "Breakfast" was once a catch-all term for anything from a significant meal to a simple buffet not necessarily eaten in the morning. The term was favored by the upper classes and soon appropriated by the so-called lower classes, who read of it in etiquette books. Etiquette books began to flourish in the mid-1800s in response to tensions in a society adjusting to a new identity and shifting norms.[4]

At the beginning of the twentieth century, a wedding breakfast for English royalty would have included a minimum of sixteen courses. When Lady Elizabeth Bowes-Lyon married the Duke of York in 1923 (they would become King George VI and queen consort of the United Kingdom), their wedding meal featured only eight courses, and the feast lasted about one hour. When the future Queen Elizabeth II and Prince Philip wed in 1947, they served four courses and were on their way within twenty minutes.[5] On September 10, 1911, the *New York Times* reported that when John Jacob Astor IV, then one of the wealthiest men in America, wed Madeleine Force, the bride and groom spent fifteen minutes at their wedding breakfast before leaving for their yacht.

Prince Philip of Schleswig-Holstein-Sonderburg-Glücksburg was born in Greece, and he and his wife, Queen Elizabeth II, are third cousins. His great grandfather was King Christian IX of Denmark, but his great grandmother, like Elizabeth's, was Queen Victoria.[6] Reports of his engagement to Elizabeth in 1947 publicized his ties with Germany at a time when an agitated royal household was already trying to downplay its Germanic roots. All four of his older sisters had married German nobility, and three were devoted Nazis. Philip even had a nephew named Karl Adolf in admiration for Hitler. A 2015 British documentary reissued photos of his sister Sophie seated across from Hitler at Hermann Goering's wedding and of his sister Cecile's funeral (she died young in a plane crash). The funeral photo shows a sixteen-year-old Philip flanked by swastika-clad relatives being met by mourners performing a heil Hitler salute to his family.[7] Philip's surviving three sisters were not invited to his royal wedding.

Philip became a British subject, joined the Church of England, and adopted Mountbatten as his last name (his mother was Princess Alice of Battenberg; *berg* means "mountain" in German). By the time of his marriage, Philip had become a respected military officer who had fought against the same forces that his sisters had embraced.

The story of Prince Philip's family is mind-boggling. His grandfather, George I of Greece, had been assassinated, and his father, Prince Andrew of Greece and Denmark, had been imprisoned for treason and was widely known to be bisexual. Andrew left a scandalous trail of both male and female lovers before he was exiled to Monaco.

Philip's mother, Alice, lived out her final years at Buckingham palace, where she died in 1967 after many years in a Greek convent. She founded and financed a religious order with the sale of the diamonds from her royal tiara (several of the diamonds she also gave to Philip in order to supply an engagement ring for Elizabeth). Alice had been born deaf (did you know Prince Philip used sign language as a child?) and was humiliated throughout her marriage by her husband's many scandals. She was diagnosed a paranoid schizophrenic, and Sigmund Freud himself prescribed X-raying her ovaries in order to "calm her hormones" (one could speculate that, having delivered five children, she may have suffered from postpartum depression). Alice claimed to have had sex with the Buddha as well as Jesus and was dispatched to a sanitarium while Philip was just a child.[8] She eventually entered religious life, becoming a Greek Orthodox nun, albeit one who chain-smoked and enjoyed a game of canasta.[9] Alice can be seen in video footage at Elizabeth's coronation, wearing her long grey nun's habit. Only recently was it discovered that she risked her life sheltering Jews in Nazi-occupied Athens during the war. Israel posthumously honored her as Righteous Among the Nations, the highest honor given to non-Jews who risked their lives during the Holocaust.

In 1898, when Chef Gabriel Tschumi was sixteen, he started working as a kitchen apprentice at Buckingham Palace. Chef Tschumi cooked
through the reigns of Queen Victoria, Edward VII, and George V. In his
1954 book *Royal Chef: Recollections of Life in Royal Households from Queen
Victoria to Queen Mary*, he lamented the downsizing of menus through the
ages. The quantity of food prepared every day at the palace had initially
shocked him. He wrote that in Queen Victoria's day, the morning meal
was "as big a meal as the main meal of the day in Switzerland" and that
lunches regularly included ten to twelve courses.[10] His memoirs open a
fascinating window into the psyche of the mid-twentieth-century British
mind-set (so closely related to the American one). Queen Mary, despite
her wealth and luxurious trappings, tracked the number of pears and
mangoes sent to her, pursuing the royal chef as to the fate of a particular
missing piece of fruit if she felt she had been fleeced.[11]

At the time of Elizabeth's 1947 wedding, food in postwar England
was still somewhat scarce, and the couple judiciously served partridge,
one of few meats not rationed during the war. The newlyweds received
five hundred tins of canned pineapple from the people of Queensland,
Australia, as well as a piece of fabric woven personally by Mohandas
Gandhi. Queen Mary, the bride's grandmother, reportedly thought the
fabric was a loincloth and "was not amused."[12]

When Victorian-era etiquette writer Cora C. Klein differentiated between a wedding breakfast, luncheon, and dinner, she characterized luncheons as the simplest. The following is her 1899 description of a "light"
lunch: "The menu is lighter than for a dinner, and generally consists of
sherbets, oyster patties, scalloped oysters, sweet-breads, sandwiches, sal-
ads, ices, cheese sticks, fruit, ice cream, cakes, bonbons, salted almonds,
olives, and black coffee, served in such number and order of courses as
best suits the hostess."[13]

THE WHITE HOUSE

After a full day of work in June 1886, President Grover Cleveland married
Frances Folsom; it was the first and only time a U.S. president wed in the
White House. The newlyweds spent six days honeymooning in Deer Park,
Maryland, hounded by the press. Enamored by the glamor of the beautiful
Frances, twenty-seven years the president's junior, eager reporters spied on
and stalked her with binoculars. When they were caught lifting the cover

of dishes sent from the kitchen to the newlyweds, the president wrote an outraged letter to the *New York Evening Post* accusing journalists of offending any and every one who claimed to be of "good breeding."[14]

Representative Nicholas Longworth of Ohio wed Theodore Roosevelt's daughter Alice in the White House in 1906, creating a whirl of publicity despite the president's attempts to keep the nuptials a private event. Alice was a celebrity prior to the wedding hoopla, known for "antics like smoking on the White House roof, carrying a snake in her purse, and betting at horse races."[15] Souvenirs commemorating the wedding of "Princess Alice" abounded, and her boisterous nature reveled in the attention. Legend has it that the cake knife given her proved too dull, so she seized the decorative sword of a nearby aide and carved out the first slice of wedding cake. Alice reported later that the sword incident had not been quite that dramatic, to which the press responded that, had its members had access, they would have reported the incident accurately, and rumors of her impetuousness would not have been embellished.[16]

The 1953 marriage of debutant Jacqueline Bouvier to junior senator John F. Kennedy was an American version of a royal wedding. *Life* magazine presented intimate photos of the outdoor reception on the estate of Bouvier's stepfather, which was palatial enough to host the fourteen hundred reception guests. The beautiful couple is shown in conversation, heads bowed over the remainders of a fruit cocktail, served in a hollowed-out pineapple. *Life* did not reveal that Jackie's father was too intoxicated to walk her down the aisle, requiring her stepfather to stand in.[17] Yet "Black Jack" Bouvier may have been able to clean up and carry out his duty that day. There is conjecture that Jackie's socialite mother conspired with family patriarch Joe Kennedy to exclude him, and one of Jackie's autobiographers wrote that the bride never forgave her mother for engineering her father's humiliation.[18]

In 1960, Julie Nixon (daughter of then President Richard Nixon) married Dwight David Eisenhower (grandson of former president Dwight D. Eisenhower) in New York City, opting out of a White House wedding altogether. In 1971, however, Julie's sister Tricia went whole hog, her Rose Garden nuptials broadcast live on television. The only scandal there involved the recipe for her wedding cake.

The White House press office issued a recipe for the lemon sponge cake, its measurements scaled down for household use. Acting on tips from disgruntled bakers across the country, the *New York Times* demonstrated that repeated attempts to produce the cake were unsuccessful. During the "Great Wedding Cake Controversy," journalists spent an entire night (and longer) editing statements from "cake" reporters. When a typesetter was asked what they were waiting for, he replied, "Would you believe a late breaking recipe?"[19]

When retired White House pastry chef Heinz H. Bender died in 1993, his *New York Times* obituary recounted his participation in the cake debacle. His wife recalled that phones had rung off the hook, as ovens opened across the country to reveal "hot soup that was supposed to be a cake."[20] Although Bender had worked in the White House for eleven years, a chef to three presidents (Nixon, Gerald Ford, and Jimmy Carter), his name would forever be associated with a recipe he did not create.

President Lyndon Johnson's young daughter Luci (she was only eighteen when her engagement was announced) was a sassy media darling, known for her Watusi dance moves and a "flair for drama." The press reported on every detail of her 1966 wedding plans, revealing her diet regimen to get into a size eight dress, and published photos of her chosen china and crystal patterns. The family decided against televising the wedding ceremony, which stirred a backlash against her. To a public given front-row seats to all of Luci's wedding plans up to that point, being denied access just when it mattered felt somehow traitorous. According to researcher Karen M. Dunak, the First Family was considered a "public entity," and the machinations of the wedding coverage show the complexity of carrying off a private event for people considered "public property."[21]

BACK TO THE PALACE

In 1981, the world was captivated by Prince Charles's shy bride, Lady Diana Spencer, whose big confection of a white dress defined the fashions of the 1980s and revived the appeal of wedding culture. The wedding breakfast at Buckingham Palace, however, featured a meal that may sound stingy now. First there were fish quenelles (light dumplings) and then chicken breast with buttered broad beans, new potatoes, and creamed corn. Then a salad was followed by a dessert of strawberries with clotted cream.[22] A nice menu, for sure, but not extravagant and not a statement of originality intended to impress connoisseurs. Those who flew on the Concorde the day of the royal wedding, however, fared better than the royals. Passengers, printed commemorative menus in hand, dined on salmon in puff pastry, beef filet wrapped in bacon, and asparagus, finishing with a cheese course.[23]

In 1986 Lady Sarah Ferguson married Prince Charles's brother Prince Andrew. Their dignified wedding breakfast featured stuffed eggs (deviled eggs to Americans), an entree of lamb with mint sauce, new potatoes, broad beans, and spinach with mushrooms.[24] Strawberries with cream were again the dessert. One might wonder at the lack of originality.

All would not prove to be happily ever after, as attested by the early deaths of both Diana and Grace Kelly in separate car accidents. To boot, in 1990, one of Princess Grace's six bridesmaids, Judith Balaban Quine, penned a tell-all book, writing that one of her fellow bridesmaids was living in a homeless shelter.[25] Prince Andrew and Sarah divorced after a scandal that involved toe sucking.

In 1981, a maid who came to be employed by the royal family for more than thirty years treated her mother to a visit to Buckingham Palace on the eve of Prince Charles's wedding to Lady Diana. This enterprising mom, accompanying her daughter on her domestic rounds within the palace, snatched a piece of toast left on Prince Charles's breakfast tray. The royal toast sat on her fireplace mantle for twenty-five years. She sensed the market for royal paraphernalia might be hot with the marriage of Prince William and Kate, so she brought her prize to an auction house in 2011. The toast was auctioned for the equivalent of $361.[26]

A slice from the eight-tier cake of Prince William and Kate Middleton sold at auction in 2014 for $7,500. The fruit cake had been packed in a commemorative tin embossed with the date and a card from the queen on official stationery. Slices of cake packed in monogrammed boxes are a traditional wedding favor; yet a number of enterprising souls took theirs to Julien's Auctions of Beverly Hills.[27] Julien's Auctions also sold a helping of twenty-seven-year-old cake from the wedding of Prince Charles and Princess Diana for just over $6,000.[28] That royal couple's cake weighed over 220 pounds and stood six feet tall; it was made four months prior to the wedding in order to develop the brandy-infused flavor.

The estate of Leonard Massey, the deceased former first chauffeur to Her Majesty, Queen Elizabeth II, included a portion of the wedding cake of Princess Anne and Captain Mark Phillips. That imperial cake stood five feet, six inches, tailored to match the exact height of the bride. The serving from Anne's 1973 cake was the oldest in the collection, and despite being labeled "not fit for human consumption," it sold for $320. A slice from the divorced Prince Andrew and Sarah Ferguson's 1986 cake also fetched $320. A piece from the 2005 wedding of Prince Charles and his second wife, Camilla, fetched $768. The enterprising chauffeur also had cake from Charles's first wedding, to Lady Diana, which sold for \$1,600. The royal driver had rounded out his collection with a sliver from Prince William's cake, which garnered \$1,600.[29] It is said that Diana's cake, abundant with brandy, may still be edible should someone care to partake.

LOVESICK

In 2010, 150 people were hospitalized after a wedding feast in Vadodara, India. May and June are especially popular months for weddings in India, corresponding to warm weather and outdoor celebrations, which cause refrigeration challenges.[30] Are you thinking this is only a foreign concern?

In 1982, an astonishing one thousand people got sick in one weekend in Minneapolis, and health authorities traced the outbreak to a batch of butter-cream icing made by a local bakery. The bakery had supplied cakes to six separate weddings.[31]

In 2005, food poisoning struck up to 2,700 people in Massachusetts, when a single bakery supplied contaminated cakes to forty-six weddings at three locations. Wedding guests, served a dose of norovirus with their cake, were horrified to learn the bakery was a hotbed of unwashed hands and unclean equipment. Cakes made with fresh strawberry filling, which required the most hand contact, proved the most toxic.[32]

What other event could be such an ideal vehicle for the rapid spread of illness? At weddings, people eat together, dance, shake hands, cry, and kiss. Pathogens require what humans require. Germs want heat and moisture and need just a little protein to procreate.

In 1994, after a wedding feast in Nepal, twenty people died after ingesting contaminated lard used to make bread. The bride and groom had not eaten the bread and did not get ill, but two hundred more of their guests were sickened, and fifty were hospitalized.[33] *Food Safety News* reported a 1990 wedding that sent thirty-one guests to the doctor, all sickened by salmonella derived from the hollandaise sauce served with an eggs Benedict brunch in Kentucky.

A 1995 wedding in Suffolk County, New York, was the site of twenty-six cases of sickness caused by contaminated Caesar salad. The dressing had been made with raw eggs, indeed the traditional method. But maybe the preparation was not up to the 6.5-hour nonrefrigerated lapse in time as the food waited to be served?[34] Hello salmonella!

Unwashed raspberries caused illness at a wedding in New York in 1997, and raspberries were also to blame for an outbreak in 2000. Eight days after her Pennsylvania wedding, a bride notified the health authorities. Fifty-four people had been sickened by parasites in the raspberry-cream filling of the wedding cake.[35]

In 2011 a cholera outbreak was traced to a wedding reception in the Dominican Republic, at which 57 percent of the guests (twenty-four people) and 38 percent of the workers (sixteen people) had been sickened.[36] Findings showed that the contamination arose from cooked shrimp on ice and beverages served with ice, as well as food that had come in contact with the decorative ice sculptures featured on the buffet. Health inspectors found that the food had been placed out at 7:00 p.m. but not consumed until 10:00 p.m.[37] More important, the kitchen workers employed improper hand hygiene, the root of so many foodborne illnesses.

Food poisoning is estimated to affect roughly one in six Americans a year, and surely there is underreporting as not all people with diarrhea or stomach distress seek medical care.[38] It is no surprise, then, that more than one law firm specializes in food poisoning incidents, and Marler Clark is one of the largest, with over $600 million in satisfied claims, many the result of wedding-related incidents. The Centers for Disease Control and Prevention advise that, statistically, people are more apt to get sick at catered events than in restaurants, which makes sense, but not because of volume. In a banquet, all guests are getting the same food at the same time, so if an item is compromised, chances are good that the majority will feel any negative reactions. In a restaurant, a food item may be acceptable for a certain period; yet once pathogens have been allowed to reproduce, the food becomes toxic. This is one reason why some people get sick and others don't. Chefs will tell you that their kitchens are not lone breeding grounds for foodborne illnesses, however. Their food may be carefully chilled and the kitchen staff highly trained. But one busboy with unwashed hands, one hostess with bad hygiene, or one infected bartender who dives into the common ice machine . . . just one of these scenarios can be the root of an outbreak, which the chef will likely take the rap for. And people wonder why chefs have attitudes?

꧂ *3* ꧂

The Last Hooray

*B*achelor parties are often portrayed as a final farewell to the supposedly carefree single life. A night of revelry before a wedding could also serve, however, to demonstrate that the bride or groom values, or is valued by, his or her circle of friends. It may remind participants that friendships will continue, and a wild night may embed the memory of kinship.[1]

STAG PARTIES AND HEN NIGHTS

Bachelor parties are an ancient tradition, generally planned by the groom's best man or male relatives. These parties have come a long way since the Spartans hosted drinking parties to toast a fellow soldier the evening before his wedding day.

Throughout history, revelry and excess have marked prewedding celebrations. While contemporary American culture assumes a certain level of overindulgence at wedding receptions, this has not always been the case for prewedding events. Decorum and self-restraint ruled wedding etiquette for much of history. Bachelor parties, however, have long been known for ribald behavior.

> The Phi Delta Phi fraternity cut up high jinx Saturday night in Cinncinaughty. They out Seeleyed the Seeley dance in New York by having the couchee-couchee danced by Moorish girls only in smile and anklets.
>
> —*Bourbon News*, January 15, 1897

Herbert Barnum Seeley, grandson of P. T. Barnum, hosted one famous bachelor party in honor of his brother Clinton. In December 1896, a police captain got word that there would be "a display of immodest dancing" and raided the dinner at Sherry's, an exclusive New York party venue. "Little Egypt" was booked to dance the couchee-couchee (later known as the hoochy coochy), but the police burst into the dressing rooms of the other dancers before she could perform. Despite uproar and lots of shrieking, the police found no evidence of indecency. The Seeleys were outraged and protested that their privacy had been violated. The ensuing court hearings drew large crowds, and when the dancers were called as witnesses, it seemed that there actually had been some wild goings-on.[2] After the police had left, Little Egypt and her crew performed her "peculiar gyrations, while nearly nude on a tabletop."[3] Men pawed at the ankles of the dancers and cut performers out of their costumes as they cavorted. And in the middle of the controversy was one underage girl whose father had procured her employment at the event but later squealed to the police because he was insulted by the low pay on offer.[4] One woman even popped naked out of a whipped cream pie.[5]

> The groom sometimes gives a dinner the night before he is married, but certain unspeakable orgies—or a certain unspeakable orgy—has altered the fashion, happily, for furious entertainment of a drunk and ribald sort.
>
> —A Woman of Fashion, *Etiquette for Americans*, written in 1898, two years after the infamous Seeley dinner

Outlandish bachelor party behavior, of course, is egalitarian, and when set to marry Princess Elizabeth, Prince Philip held his stag party at the tony Dorchester Club in London. An eager press had been invited, but it was meant to observe the protocol of the day, which respected the privacy of the royals. The prince's group must have been having some kind of fun, because eventually the flash bulbs of the journalists' cameras were torn off and stamped on the ground, with the groom's party moving on to the closed doors of the Belfry Club.[6]

> The table for the groom's dinner doesn't need any special décor, other than nice appointments and attractive flowers, arranged low, so they don't get in the way of conversation.
>
> —*Brides* 4, no. 3 (Spring 1937): 92

Cover page for the menu for a fortunate soul named Ralph, who was soon to arrive on the SS *Hymen*, 1913. *Source*: "Hotel Sherman," Buttolph Collection of Menus, New York Public Library Digital Collections, Rare Book Division, http://digitalcollections.nypl.org/items/5165e8f0-517d-0132-151b-58d385a7bbd0.

Ralph having engaged passage on the S. S. "Hymen," this Dinner is tendered him as a cheerful farewell before his leaving the Monks Brigade, together with the best wishes for a long, long joyful voyage.

Hotel Sherman
Saturday, September 6, 1913

Chicago

The menu for Ralph's bachelor party, whose host surely was literary, as the captions reference the poetry of Alexander Pope as well as Shakespeare's *Merchant of Venice* and *Twelfth Night*, 1913. *Source*: "Hotel Sherman," Buttolph Collection of Menus, New York Public Library Digital Collections, Rare Book Division, http://digitalcollections.nypl.org/items/5165e8f0-517d-0132-151b-58d385a7bbd0.

Menu

The Feast smells well

Cherrystone Clam Cocktail
I'll be with you in the squeezing of a lemon

Celery   Queen Olives
Cum grano salis.   *She is drowned already, sir, with salt water.*

Strained Gumbo, en Tasse
A delicate odor
As ever hit my nostril.

Broiled Whitefish, Matire d'Hotel
Potatoes Parisienne
Pressed Cucumbers
Eat of the fish

Breast of Capon, Virginia
Fresh Peas Grand Mere
And spread the sacred treasurers of the breast.

Hearts of Lettuce Salad, St. Laurent
I warrant there's vinegar and pepper in 't.

Raspberry Ice
Mignardises
Then farewell heat and welcome frost.

Demi Tasse
And for my soul I cannot sleep a wink.

Martini Cocktail
Chateau Yquem
G. H. Mumm's Extra Dry
Liqueurs
Apollinaris
Bock & Co. Cigars
Condax Padishah Cigarettes

Middle America was scandalized in 1949 by actor Jimmy Stewart's bash at the famous Hollywood restaurant Chasen's, where Alfred Hitchcock routinely left $200 tips for the coat-check girl, Liz Taylor ordered chili sent to the set of *Cleopatra* in Rome, and Shirley Temple had a certain drink invented for her. This televised bachelor party got weird when a munchkin-playing cast member from the *Wizard of Oz*, wearing only a diaper, urinated on Stewart. Other little people jumped out of silver serving dishes, and one former munchkin-portraying actor was enlisted to enthusiastically greet Stewart as "Daddy."[7]

Women, of course, deserve a chance to behave badly, too, and bachelorette parties bloomed in the late 1980s, their popularity growing just as the bridal industry as a whole mushroomed. Inflated expectations for big weddings demanded more dramatic rituals and more opportunities to spend money and plan particulars—a "warm-up" for the big day.[8] Researcher Diane Tye writes that the bachelorette party—called a hen party in England, or sometimes a stagette party—has "eclipsed" the shower for many brides.[9]

That some women may gleefully anticipate a night on the town and in fact value the hen party experience more than the shower, a ritual in which they could potentially receive dozens of gifts, is telling. A night on the town affords a bride two distinctive opportunities: She will have an evening (or weekend) of unbridled diversion, and she will also be the center of attention. Her friends will toast her, fawn over her, and recount stories about her—it's like a dress rehearsal for her wedding day.

It is easy to see how a shower could recede in the imagination of a bride who has lived on her own for years prior to her impending wedding. Employment has likely allowed her to purchase the household items she once coveted. Such a bride may choose a pleasurable night out with her friends over an afternoon of opening gifts.

FEEDING, AND HURTING, THE BRIDE?

Some cultures traditionally fatten a woman before marriage, a custom that contrasts with the American bride starving herself to fit into her wedding gown. In 1927 an anthropologist reported that in Sudan girls remained naked, their slender bodies seemingly unnoticeable, until they married, usually around age twenty. In preparation for their nuptials, they were fed "copious milk" until they were "bulging with fat all over."[10]

Mauritania in western North Africa also has a "force-feeding" tradition, with one source referring to ancient Berber verses glorifying stretch marks as comparable to "jewels."[11]

In the nineteenth and early twentieth centuries, Jewish Tunisian women were also intentionally overfed in preparation for married life. Beginning at the time of her engagement, a bride's family took charge of reshaping her body, restricting her physical activity and administering excessive feedings. A wife-to-be ate lamb fat, egg yolks, and starchy porridge. She was given oil to drink and kept in a dark room, isolated from her peers, while she endured a regime of routine feedings, even being woken in the night to eat.[12]

In addition, a bride was tutored on how to run a household and instructed in how to please her husband sexually. During this time of weight gain the future mother-in-law began to exert her authority over the bride, with one ritual being that she covered her son's fiancée with dough, buffing and bleaching the young woman's skin and then tearing off unwanted body hair in an early form of "waxing." Just before the wedding day, the bride's enlarged body was presented by degrees, beginning with the showing of her newly plumped hands, all in hopes that her rounded figure would please her intended husband.[13]

In parts of southern Nigeria, the practice of bride feeding continues, and the metropolitan city of Calabar houses special "fattening rooms" for wealthy clients. A 2015 health report confirms that the cultural ideal of large women prevails in parts of Nigeria and that the ability to send daughters to "fattening rooms" indicates status and attention to tradition and is instrumental in procuring a proper match.[14] This practice, of course, is under assault from Western influences, and many modern Nigerians eschew it, with Nigerian authorities concerned about public health and an exploding rate of diabetes.[15]

Comparing the stereotypical modern American bride, who has dieted her way into her gown and visited a tanning salon, and a Nigerian bride, with forcibly bleached skin and a staff to count her folds of fat, one can see that societal pressures and public scrutiny have driven both women. The hungry American bride, however, executes her prewedding beauty regimen alone, hoping for approval when she exhibits her desired figure in her wedding gown. The ancient tradition of "fattening" the bride, on the other hand, has always been a group act, paid for by the father, administered by mothers, with brides literally inert, their movements restricted to prevent burning of calories, and the success of the scheme a direct reflection of a family's standing in the community.

Buried in the literature about "fattening rooms" (much of it salacious and not used as reference) are mentions of female genital mutilation. In some cultures, this is part of the coming-of-age process, performed before the plumped bride is presented to her future husband or, in some cases, even prior to puberty.[16] Digging for information on the ritual feeding of brides brings varying and conflicting judgments from numerous sources. That profusion of viewpoints (about body weight) withers in comparison, however, to the explosive discourse concerning female circumcision, a topic one would not normally associate with the study of food. And yet inspection shows that there are comparisons between bridal practices in terms of how womanhood is defined, with some cultures directly linking genital mutilation with fattening, and both may be part of marriage preparations.

Restricting a young woman's movements, isolating her, and mutilating her body—such rituals are not exclusive to the African continent. One need only consider Chinese foot binding, a practice particularly prevalent among the wealthy intended to inhibit women's movement. Elizabeth Abbott writes that the "Chinese increased chances of large-scale chastity by crippling little girls' feet so that as nubile women they could barely hobble from room to room, much less past down the garden gate to indulge in sexual adventures."[17]

Consider rib-crushing American corsets or perilously high-heeled shoes, perhaps lesser examples of a willingness to sacrifice comfort in order to meet cultural ideals. All of these norms, however, work to control women, a fact brought to the fore in a public arena when a large bride meets her waiting groom or the skinny bride posts her wedding album on social media. Control and scrutiny bind these practices, whether voluntary or not.[18]

The United Nations declared female genital mutilation unlawful in 2012, and many African governments have outlawed the practice, with many political and celebrity detractors appealing to the public to discontinue it. Yet it is still prevalent, with one statistic stating that up to 32 percent of urban women on the continent have been circumcised. In many cases, the procedure is tied to premarriage rituals and even commercial "fattening rooms."[19] A conversation about male circumcision also leads into a tangled dispute, with yet another set of diverging arguments, all of which pit modern attitudes against cultural traditions.

ON A LIGHTER NOTE

Bachelor or bachelorette parties are the most famous of American prewedding rituals, and destinations such as Las Vegas are popular celebration sites for both sexes. The stripper industry is grateful for the existence of these parties, and the uninitiated need simply follow the "universal guidelines" published by the Suite Strippers of Las Vegas, whose site proclaims that all reputable party agencies in the United States observe these standards. This format includes distinct party phases, the first involving the introduction of the stripper, who is generally costumed according to a theme, such as cop, maid, nurse, or cowgirl. Another recommended stage is "trashing," where "the ladies will spank your bachelor, perform magic tricks on him, bash his face with their body parts and have lots of other fun with him."[20]

For a tamer evening, a person might want to know that in 2012, the Popemobile used in Pope John Paul II's visit to Ireland in 1979 got back on the road. Seating fifteen, it featured an open-air deck and a papal throne, and the owners stated they would market it as a "hopemobile" for select stag parties and hen nights.[21]

Anyone in need of advice may turn to *The Playboy Guide to Bachelor Parties* (2003), which suggests barbecues as a popular theme and gives tips to "make it a truly manly event." Apparently manly means enjoying a "hottest hot sauce competition," providing "exotic meats, such as ostrich, buffalo, maybe even snake," and hosting a hotdog-eating contest.[22] The guide helpfully describes how to plan a divorce party as well, in which the "lucky divorcé" is treated to "Break-Up Cake" and a "Bobbit Love Sundae."[23]

In December 2005, the Associated Press reported on the civil union of Elton John and David Furnish, who held a bachelor party at a former strip club in London, complete with rubber red chairs and glass walls. Bare-chested waiters in riding boots passed champagne. Former president Bill Clinton sent his best wishes in a video message, and guests included Ozzy and Sharon Osbourne, Kid Rock, and Bryan Adams.

The ritual plumping of a young woman with food and drink beyond what is necessary for survival indicates that her family can afford excess. And the desire to show "excess" links unlikely elements such as a retooled Popemobile and Jimmy Stewart's naked munchkins. Drinking all night, pawing at strippers, and making expensive forays to Las Vegas are all behaviors generally outside the realm of habit for many men and women. And yet this gaiety prior to the big day is tolerated, even glamorized, in current culture—especially if the "wildness" is part of a commercial exchange (for instance, at a nightclub or casino with hired personnel). It seems a certain amount of "naughtiness," in the context of celebrating an impending marriage, gets a cultural "pass," provided actual intercourse does not occur and the performer is never seen again.

This excessive merriment, a final send-off for the unmarried state, lies on the threshold of marriage, a condition that presumably demands self-control and prudence from both parties. In this context, prewedding rituals act as a bridge over a space of insecurity inhabited by nervous brides and grooms on the brink of a major life change. Prewedding rituals provide their own form of predictability and distraction as well as a link between two life stages. Navigation of this symbolic bridge in the company of the guest of honor's best friends is significant as the bride or groom take another step toward the finality of the approaching wedding.

❦ 4 ❦

Showers of Food, Showers of Gifts

DOWRIES AND BRIDE PRICE

A dowry included the goods or money a woman brought with her to marriage and in many ways determined her marriageability and thus her future. Beyond providing an income for the groom, dowries kept real estate within the bride's family, as property went not to the daughter who had wed but to her male children. Prenuptial agreements have always existed, with powerful families stipulating that dowry holdings stay with blood relatives of the bride.[1] Such provisions were the only resource available to women until the legal system evolved, and they aimed to protect the family line, not the bride herself. A large dowry, of course, increased a woman's pool of suitors.

Despite her possible wealth, a woman historically relinquished belongings to her husband upon marriage and effectively owned nothing by herself. Presumably her brothers would receive family inheritances, so some mindful families arranged for objects in a dowry to include jewelry or silver, items that a woman could stealthily "liquidate" should she need cash.[2]

Bridal showers—a public gift giving meant to increase a woman's appeal—may be construed as a replacement for dowries. Setting up a household was once very difficult, both in colonial America and in western settlements. Furniture, clothes, and linen could be fashioned at home, but cast-iron pans, tea kettles, and tools, for instance, required merchants and funds, neither of which was necessarily readily available. A woman who would enter marriage well equipped enjoyed increased desirability and faced an easier job of creating a comfortable home.

SHOWERS

The term "shower" may have come from the practice of placing gifts inside a lady's parasol, which then "showered" the bride upon being opened. Traditionally, women lived with their families until married and so depended on their relations and friends when setting up a new home. One way of spreading out the financial burden was to host a party to which each guest brought an item, usually something for the kitchen or dining table. Wedding gifts have traditionally been sent to the bride's home, and for this reason, the handling of showers intended for the bride and wedding gifts meant for both the bride and the groom are still generally considered part of the female sphere.

That gifts were sent directly to the bride may reflect that the bride's life was most altered by marriage, as presumably she would be taking the reins of a new household and learning new and unfamiliar management responsibilities. Silver and linen were generally monogrammed with the bride's maiden name or initials. At a time when a married woman was addressed as "Mrs." followed by her husband's full name, a bride's birth name may effectively have been lost to all except her intimates. Therefore, birth initials engraved on tea sets and tableware offered a wife recollection of her girlhood and reassurance that she had certain possessions exclusively her own.[3]

Researcher Barbara Penner reports that in the mid-1800s silver manufacturers worked double time to whip up a new audience for the silver market. Silver prices had decreased, and the invention of electroplating made silver goods accessible to an increased pool of consumers. The industry advertised intensely, capitalizing on and contributing to a progressively "specialized" way of eating. Salt, nuts, ice cream, mustard, coffee, eggs, and sugar now required special implements.[4] "Family-style" dining, with guests helping themselves to one or two entrees put in the center of the table, gave way to service à la Russe. Penner surmised that this new model, in which food was set on a sideboard after being served, left room for the decorative floral arrangements and centerpieces so favored in the later part of the nineteenth century. Meals came to feature discrete courses (soup, fish, meat, entrée, salad, dessert), with each requiring dedicated tableware.[5]

In September 1886, a home-decorating magazine, the *Decorator and Furnisher*, included the article "Fashionable Table-Ware," describing all manner of recommended items for the "young house keeper." The inventory included cracker jars, oatmeal bowls, sardine dishes, celery plates, ice-cream sets, scalloped oyster plates, and bone dishes, meant to "receive the bone and other debris that otherwise cumber the plate." The reader was discouraged, however, from purchasing a newfangled meat tray with a skewer to secure a roast, as it was "eminently destructive to carving knives and encourages indolence and carelessness on the part of the carver."[6]

In 1891 etiquette expert Amy Buchanan Longstreet wrote that it was "bad form" to send practical gifts to brides because items like linen and kitchenware insinuated that her family lacked financial resources. Unless one was very close to the bride, "bric-a-brac and embroideries" were preferred.[7] Of course, economics would have dictated the nature of any shower gifts or whether a bride had a shower at all.

A 1925 *Vogue* etiquette manual addressed the matter of bridal showers, commenting that despite its "foolish" name, the "friendly and hearty custom" could outfit the bride's kitchen. The tone was a tad condescending, and it was indicated that this information was intended for "country or small town people." The author warned off showers for those in "metropolitan smart circles." In response to a question about what kind of shower was appropriate to the elite, the article answered, "No kind. They are not given to *fashionable* persons at the present time of writing."[8]

Some showers were more like sewing bees, in which women together created aprons and dish towels, embroidering the bride's initials on new linen, with "needles flying with the tongues," as friends helped equip the future homemaker's kitchen.[9]

> Dolls and weddings—the two are inseparable this summer. The brilliant and successful career of the doll has been crowned by becoming the most fashionable souvenir gift associated with wedding ceremonies.
>
> —Mary J. Mount, *Good Housekeeping*, July 1911

Dolls were once weirdly popular in the bridal world, serving as a common cake topper prior to the standard bride-and-groom figure so recognizable today. Those with an incredible amount of free time in 1911 could heed *Good Housekeeping*'s advice to gather bridesmaids and create miniature replicas of their wedding dresses, then "mount the dressed dolls upon the tops of small boxes containing pieces of cake." The bride's milliner could assist by producing teeny hats for the dolls, which could even be mounted on mirrors with "white satin bags containing pieces of cake hung over their arms."[10]

A kitchen is a bride's work room.

—"Kitchen Wear," *Brides* 3, no. 2 (Winter 1936–1937): 88

Electric appliances began to flood American homes in the 1930s, and the sale of an array of toasters, mixers, and coffee pots coalesced within an opportunistic bridal industry. By this time, the modern shower, with themes, games, and party favors, had taken hold. In the 1930s the American literacy rate had climbed (to almost 96 percent for the population as a whole), and all socioeconomic groups were reading for entertainment.[11] New manufacturing processes enabled inexpensive mass printing, and an improved transportation system promised prompt delivery. Manufacturers created cookbooks crammed with advertisements, with recipes specifically designed to market their products, culminating in a glut of magazines and pamphlets distributed by producers of packaged food and electric devices.[12]

Between 1901 and 1930 food products represented 15 percent of advertising business, only being overtaken by automobile advertisements in 1930.[13] Food was big business, and advertisers knew that women were the head consumers in American households. They courted women as future customers through bridal publications; wedding gifts received might possibly translate into a lifetime of brand loyalty. Savvy advertisers assured women of the grave responsibilities of homemaking and adopted a professional tone, asserting housekeeping as a cherished occupation. In one of the many publications produced by manufacturers, Crisco assured its clientele that thriftiness in the kitchen was a virtue, stating, "A woman can throw out more with a teaspoon than a man can bring home in a wagon."[14]

No inexperienced housewife should attempt a French dessert alone.

—Eliza Leslie, *Miss Leslie's New Cookery Book*, 1857[15]

The wedding industry played on a new bride's anxiety about not being able to cook competently for her new husband, and advertisers positioned appliances and cookbooks to alleviate these fears. A bridal shower was an ideal marketing medium, and ads for kitchen supplies played heavily on brides' desire to please husbands through cooking made possible by the accumulation of products.

Nothing is quite so intimidating for a young bride as the thought of failing to feed her man with the same flourish as her mother-in-law did. Whether your kitchen will be a place of joy or a horror chamber depends primarily on your equipment.

—"For Your Kitchen," *Brides* 16, no. 1 (Autumn 1949): 153

"Will your husband be in love with another woman's cooking?" asks a 1978 Spice Islands cookbook ad. The other woman is the groom's mother, whom the bride must learn to emulate in a "quick course in the art of seasoning."[16]

In the past, females started preparing for their married life as girls, sewing and gathering goods in hope chests from a young age. After World War II, however, a newfound inclination to be modern rendered old items stowed in chests undesirable. Couples wanted new products, an attitude the wedding industry cultivated.[17] In a 1963 ad, a Libbey Glass "home stylist" told brides how to "choose a glass wardrobe," assuring them that breakage was no problem; they could "just pick up another set of Libbey. Happy Showers!"[18]

The trousseau became the object of intense advertisement, with bridal shops and department stores beseeching women to assemble a collection of clothes for the wedding night and honeymoon. They also entreated brides to create a "paper trousseau," stationery engraved with their new names. Princess Vicky, Queen Victoria's daughter, embarked on married life with twelve evening gowns and one hundred cases filled with artwork, furniture, books, and food from the luxury store Fortnum and Mason.[19]

The "boudoir shower"—in which the bride displayed the nightgowns and lingerie she received for her honeymoon—prevailed into the 1950s. As fewer brides began to live with their parents at the time of marriage, showers adapted, with one example being the "stock the bar" shower popular in the 1980s.

Men have occasionally been known to throw a "groom roast" or "bro bath," in which male friends give the groom tools or home-improvement items. One 1981 scholarly article gravely discussed the fad of so-called groomal showers. Time has shown that showers are still a female endeavor, although many couples opt for a Jack and Jill shower that fetes both together.

GIFTS

By the late 1800s it was customary for a wealthy bride to officially display her wedding gifts on a table in her parent's home; visitors were invited to peruse and presumably gossip about her loot. Some authorities recommended showing the name of each gift's giver; some did not. Even checks were propped up for show, and fashion dictated whether the name of the signatory was folded back. When the young American heiress Consuelo Vanderbilt famously wed the ninth Duke of Marlborough in 1895, the names of those who had sent displayed gifts were in full view, as were the detectives hired to guard them.[20]

At the turn of the twentieth century, manufacturers of fine silver, like Reed and Barton, even sent employees to homes to arrange the "exhibition" of gifts.[21] Fashion and geography governed whether to "display" or not. Some clearly denounced the practice, with heavy hitters like Reverend Henry Ward Beecher preaching that it encouraged ostentation. By the 1870s wedding invitations commonly included the phrase "no presents received"; yet it was also common to encounter ostentatious gift exhibits arranged by professional decorators.[22]

Etiquette experts continued to recommend displaying gifts, and because "people do love seeing them on parade," it was best to organize a "concentrated siege" rather than endure a slow trickle of requests to view the bridal swag. After a large wedding, with a "raft of presents, the bridesmaids should be invited to review the cache, after which a luncheon should be arranged."[23]

Spoons have always been traditional wedding souvenirs or gifts and long a source of much lore. For example, two spoons on a saucer indicate an impending wedding, and the gift of a spoon to a bride from her groom is a promise she will never go hungry. Love spoons, their handles carved in the shape of bells, anchors, or hearts, are a common gift in Wales, as noted by the press when Catherine Zeta-Jones's Welsh hometown sent a love spoon when she and Michael Douglas married in 2000.[24] In Jewish ritual, the bride and groom step over a spoon placed on the threshold of a room, leading with their right feet.[25] Researcher Margaret Visser writes that spoons "inspire affection," being associated with a baby's first foods and connoting nurturing.[26]

Knives are also the subject of much folklore and often associated with bad luck. Receipt of a knife as a gift is said to predict the end (cutting) of a friendship or romantic relationship. Some people say that if a woman drops a knife on the floor, she will happily soon be visited by a man, but knives allowed to overlap or cross on the table foretell an argument. And yet good knives can be expensive and are a desirable shower or wedding gift. Some knife companies package a penny in their gift sets, a nod to the belief that if a knife is bestowed as a present, the giver should receive a penny, transforming the exchange into a monetary transaction.

La borsa, the bag for wedding money, Domenic and Filomena Smargiassi, 1919. *Source*: Author's collection.

In 1886, when President Grover Cleveland was wed, his gift from the fish and game commissioner was a giant salmon, weighing in at close to thirty pounds.[27] That same year, inventor Thomas Edison's wedding gift to his bride, Mina, was a twenty-nine-room mansion in West Orange, New Jersey (he had tapped out his marriage proposal in Morse code).[28] Then as now, the range and extravagance of wedding gifts varies across ethnic and regional lines. Anyone who has been to an Italian American wedding on the East Coast will recognize what is known as the "boost," that little bag the bride carries to receive envelopes of cash as the newlyweds go from table to table, visiting their guests.

> The idea that a wedding invitation necessitates a present has, sensibly enough, gone out of fashion, and only those who are bound by ties of blood or close friendship have the privilege of sending a gift to the bride.[29]
>
> —Cora C. Klein, *Practical Etiquette*, 1899

The preceding quote serves as an example of how varied and contradictory wedding etiquette advice could be, depending on the source and the intended audience. All the while, retailers encouraged sales, tying consumerism to self-esteem and the notion that doing things correctly included purchasing the correct items. This philosophy would blossom fully by the twenty-first century.

୧   ᛡ   ୧

Table Manners Matter

DAINTY FOOD?

Victorians were enamored with the idea of "daintiness," and food, especially for women, was whipped and fluffed and gelled. The popular *Smiley's Cook Book and Universal Household Guide* (1901) warned readers, "It is not the age of heavy dinners," and the tables of "fashionable people are things of lightness and delicacy." Recipes included peach whip, flummery, pink cream, red currant snow, strawberry foam, molded snow, and snowed fruit.[1]

By the 1900s American sophisticates had turned to Europe for culinary inspiration, and Victorian menus featured multiple courses and numerous pieces of flatware for each place setting (making silver a standard wedding gift among the elite). While "creamy" may have sounded dainty, this fare was rich and calorie laden. In "Continental" dining, manipulated food suggested refinement, and food in its natural state, especially raw food, was vulgar.[2] And so vegetables were blanketed in cream sauces, and French chefs, a generation away from the stoves of the disbanded royal palaces of Europe, found a new audience to consume their culinary riches.

Victorian Methodist missionary wedding in Bareilly, India, ca. 1885.
Source: Author's collection.

NEW YORK FOUR HUNDRED

Etiquette practices are ingrained in most social interactions, especially in the case of wedding celebrations. The upper echelons have traditionally handed down the standards, with the lower classes eager to replicate the restrained behavior of their so-called betters.

The stories of luxury hotel dining rooms and East Coast society weddings are intertwined and form part of the bedrock of American culture. Society maven Caroline Astor legendarily presided over the New York Four Hundred, an inventory of true high society members said to equal the number of people who could fit into her ballroom. Regardless of the literal truth, Mrs. Astor guarded entry into society in her day, and it was her particular business to keep "new money" out of her established circle. Social events like balls and weddings were hunting grounds for prospective mates, so keeping the undesirables out helped keep the classes separated. Caroline, of stalwart Dutch stock (then considered the founders of elite society), embodied the sentiment of her fellow custodians, forever on guard against interlopers.

William Waldorf Astor, upon his father's death, supposed his wife was now in line to be called "*the* Mrs. Astor." His aunt Caroline disagreed. She won that round.

The Astor clan had earlier constructed their Fifth Avenue palaces next to one another, and in the ultimate bad-neighbor move, William Waldorf, Caroline's disgruntled nephew, tore down the family mansion and built a thirteen-story hotel, the Waldorf, condemning Caroline to live in a "commercial" neighborhood after 1891. Caroline's son, John Jacob Astor IV, probably more from shrewd business acumen than spite, leveled their family mansion and built a hotel three stories higher, dubbing his creation the Astoria. Thus began the saga of the famous Waldorf Astoria Hotel, originally sited where the Empire State Building now stands.[3]

Historian Molly W. Berger notes that with all the money poured into these great houses, meant to signal the exclusivity of their occupants, their occupants were dismayed to see their style of living served up for public consumption. These hotels were patterned on, and in some cases literally furnished with, the paraphernalia of Gilded Age mansions. Members of the public were given a look into, and even a chance to enjoy temporarily by renting a room, a lifestyle they had never before witnessed.

> Within less than a decade, being married in an Astor ballroom became a possibility for many New Yorkers, not just those few whose Fifth Avenue addresses and fortunes could accommodate hundreds, and even thousands of guests.
>
> —Molly W. Berger, "The Rich Man's City," 2005[4]

Before the hotel controversy unfurled, Caroline Astor tangled with the newly moneyed Alva Vanderbilt. Alva was planning a much ballyhooed ball to inaugurate her enormous spread at 660 Fifth Avenue and cunningly used this occasion to scramble into Caroline's society. The Vanderbilt ball was absolutely slated to be the party of the year, and Carrie Astor, Caroline's daughter, had long assumed an invitation would arrive. Carrie's synchronized quadrille dance routine, well rehearsed with friends, included costumes with electric stars that lit up their foreheads.[5] The upstart Alva purposely left the Astors off the invitation list, reacting to Caroline's snubs of the past. Legend says that Caroline relented and sent her calling card to Alva, surrendering so that her daughter could attend the celebrated ball.[6]

THE GILDED AGE

Boldness and innovation shaped the American character; yet the fledgling country was in social upheaval. The Union was quickly adding new states, incorporating people and expanding every day. The populace comprised wildly disparate peoples, with cultural patterns heavily dictated by social class and geography. Privileged diners in 1850s New York City could order goose liver with truffles from a menu printed on silk, or tuck in to larded grouse with Madeira sauce, or perhaps choose a drink from the Metropolitan Hotel's "breakfast wine" list.[7] On any day in the 1850s, for example, one American could be bumping along on a wagon train heading west, while another reclined in New York's Astor House Hotel, with its own press to print new menus for its restaurant every single day.[8]

The dining rooms of early luxury hotels distanced delicate Victorians from their coarse frontier cousins. Access to fine ingredients, expatriate French chefs, and cheap labor for service as butlers and maids encouraged a frenzy of hotel and restaurant construction. The wealthy had always furnished grand meals in their mansions, and those who lived in the country, even those of lesser means, hosted dances and outdoor celebrations. Yet the hotel building boom would give those living in urban areas their first taste of grand living.

Hoteliers competed for opulence, modeling their extravagant buildings' interiors on the residences of the affluent. Hotels did not just rent sleeping rooms; their dining rooms also offered a chance to rent time in a setting once unavailable to most citizens. All did not welcome this development, however, perceiving danger in the mixing of social classes and fraternizing of delicate women with strangers.[9] This innovation also soon transformed the hotels of Europe, as all these new American palaces had electric lights, telephones, and showers. Well-heeled Americans would now demand the same when traveling abroad.[10]

Meanwhile, back on the frontier, Billy the Kid was robbing banks (he was shot in 1881), and Jesse James was robbing trains (he was shot in 1882). In 1883 Buffalo Bill Cody started his traveling Wild West show, spreading the romantic myth of the cowboy at the very time that the Brooklyn Bridge opened to foot traffic. New York blue bloods were busy squabbling over who exactly qualified as high society, and the completion of the Waldorf Hotel caused more than a few society matrons to squirm at the notion that soon anyone could get married in an Astor ballroom.[11]

In fact, the bill of fare from dining establishments may act as an example of the split identity at play in this early era of American history. Menus from the mid-1880s were often written in French (as at the Astor House) and sometimes listed prices in British currency. Historian and past food critic for the *New York Times* William Grimes explains that British money was used for some time after the American Revolution,[12] evidence of the young country's slow transition to exclusive use of the dollar.

American promise of social mobility was layered onto a jumbled cultural identity of established citizens and constantly arriving immigrants. The land of opportunity, however, was very confusing, and etiquette books would help bring order. How-to guides helped motivated readers negotiate interactions with those above them in the social order, preventing "exposure" of those with murky or humble pasts who had risen in status. "Marrying up" was one limited path to social mobility, so the stakes were high, and it was imperative, especially for women, to exhibit respectability.[13] Etiquette manuals served as training guides, offering conditioning exercises to prepare readers for the big marriage game.

ETIQUETTE

Those born to wealth—already secure in their positions or able to hire wedding specialists to ensure the social correctness of their events—did not need these manuals.[14] The etiquette industry, which playacted that its readers were all wealthy, most likely targeted its advice to the working classes, which had no training ground for learning how the elite did things.

> At a large formal dinner it is rather dangerous to pay compliments to the food or table decoration. It is too personal a topic.
>
> —A Woman of Fashion, *Etiquette for Americans*, 1898[15]

Table manners consumed a large portion of these etiquette manuals; yet they generally referred to dining as an act to endure, rarely indicating that food was a source of pleasure. Eating could in fact be dangerous, with table manners a potential "dead giveaway of one's true social origin."[16] Conversation at the table was to be regulated, and to prevent willy-nilly banter, refined diners were encouraged to "choose from a small assortment" of topics, such as "the opera, the theater, music in general, horses, dogs, games, and other general themes."[17]

Etiquette for Americans, first printed in 1898 by an anonymous author (named Woman of Fashion), took a hard line, both in its staunch posture and in its assumed authority over the pupil. Readers were told "the etiquette of weddings is so formal and so important—for weddings would be so ridiculous if they were not done in order—that they are usually put in the hands of some experienced manager who gives all the suggestions and, indeed, does all the arranging."[18]

TIMING IS EVERYTHING

If married in Lent, you are sure to repent.

—Wedding superstition

The choice of the date and time for weddings has traditionally depended on one's social position. English law historically dictated that ceremonies could only occur between 8:00 a.m. and noon, unless special permission was granted (this was not changed until the 1930s, but even then nuptials were not allowed past 6:00 p.m.). In the United States, too, ceremonies needed to take place during daylight hours in order to be properly witnessed. Those of modest means could not spare a day's labor and would need to get to work. So they often exchanged vows early in the morning and then reported to their jobs.[19]

In June 1926, *Good Housekeeping* advised that "simple and definite rules govern the etiquette of the wedding in church or house." The magazine stated, "Although a few ultra-smart weddings take place at high noon, custom has established the hour of the ceremony for four or four thirty o'clock." The same article noted that a noon wedding should host "the breakfast at one o'clock," confirming that the term "breakfast" was in common American usage in the 1920s and presumably familiar to *Good Housekeeping*'s middle-class readers.

Monday for health,
Tuesday for wealth,
Wednesday the best day of all;
Thursday for losses,
Friday for crosses,
And Saturday no luck at all.

—English rhyme referring to choosing a wedding day[20]

Superstitions are rampant in wedding date selection, and trusting couples may choose to confer with an astrologer, consult tarot cards or numerologists, or even interpret animal entrails. According to lore, the hands of a clock should be "rising" between the six and the nine during the exchange of marriage vows, and the first celebration in a new home should not be a wedding. It was said that May was an unlucky month and that Fridays were bad luck.

In 1914's *Complete Etiquette*, Marion Harland wrote that most weddings took place on Wednesdays, and Sunday weddings were "not good form." Harland also remarked that a heavy wedding breakfast "was a tedious and unnecessary affair."[21]

In 1922, the pragmatic Emily Post reported that Friday weddings "were never encouraged" and said that the "superstition that Friday and the month of May are unlucky, is too stupid to discuss."[22] Queen Elizabeth II was married on a Thursday, as was her mother, the queen consort, known as Elizabeth the Queen Mother. In the United States, there has long been an unspoken tradition that the truly wealthy host weddings on weekdays as an indicator of status, demonstrating that neither they nor their guests have to show up for work.

The British author of *The Etiquette of Engagement and Marriage*, first released in 1903, reported that breakfasts were outdated, and it was fashionable to have a later wedding. Breakfast had been "a rather trying affair for all concerned," and now "the smarter section of society has spoken in favour of the reception."[23]

> The menu at a wedding breakfast is never elaborate. Consommé or bouillon, salads, birds, ices, jellies and bonbons are the usual order. Coffee and dainty cakes are served last. The wedding cake, if one is served at all, is set before the bride.
>
> —Lillian Eichler, *Book of Etiquette*, 1921[24]

According to *Good Housekeeping*'s May 1933 issue, a "smart wedding" took place at the conventional hours of either noon or 4:00 p.m., but in the West and South, during warm weather, weddings were often held at 8:00 p.m. In her 1939 homemaking guide, Enid Wells advised that "4:30 in the afternoon is the most fashionable hour at present."[25]

Emily Post had come on the scene in 1922 with her best-selling *Etiquette in Society, in Business, in Politics, and at Home*, cornering the etiquette market for years to come. Post warned that acceptance into the "Best Society is a long and slow road," and one must not "push or

presume." She recommended beginning the journey up the social ladder with joining the right church, the right civic activities, and the right
clubs.[26] Marrying the right sort of person would take planning.

A 1936 *Brides* article advised that, if possible, a wedding should be
held at home; otherwise, "you will have to hold your festivities in a hotel
or club." The inference is that a family unable to host a wedding had a
small or unsuitable house and lacked real estate as well as staff.

Country club wedding, 1950. *Source*: Author's collection.

*Amy Vanderbilt's Complete Book of Etiquette: A Guide to Gracious
Living* (1954) devoted its first twelve chapters to wedding procedure, a
symptom of the high marriage rate in postwar America. This exhaustive
book also showed that people felt their country was flush with possibility:
the text covered scenarios such as what to wear for an audience with the
pope, proper seating in the dining room aboard a ship, and how to dress
for a radio appearance and "if you appear on television." In deference to a
nation that had sacrificed its young to war, it gave much space to military

matters, with advice for the woman invited to a "hop" at West Point or Annapolis, a chapter on caring for the flag, and behavior pointers for the wife of a soldier.[27]

Culturally specific customs can indeed be fairly impossible to decode without guidance, as evidenced by a researcher who related the story of a Taiwanese student staying with an American family. At the conclusion of a meal of roast chicken, the student gravely announced to his hosts that he would move out as soon as possible. The hostess had placed the cavity of the chicken facing the student, which in his culture meant that a person was unwelcome.[28]

Cake cutting, Ray and Bonnie Nutkis, 1971. *Source*: Used with permission from Bonnie and Ray Nutkis.

In 1966 *Brides* related that by being a good hostess and "helpmate to her husband on his way up the ladder," a bride could earn prestige. By "acting as a social asset as he climbs upward," she could propel his career. A slovenly wife, on the other hand, could harm her husband's prospects for a company promotion.[29] Here we see a continuation of the need to keep up appearances in order to ascend upward, particularly if a bride had landed a husband higher in social rank than herself. Embedded in a conservative era, 1966 was also a period of intense antiwar protest on the brink of the summer of love. It would soon be slow going in the bridal business.

> My husband is in a mental institution for the rest of his life. My daughter is getting married soon. Should his name be on the wedding invitation?
>
> —Amy Vanderbilt's "Guide to Weddings: Questions the Etiquette Books Don't Answer," *McCall's* 91, no. 7 (April 1964): 70

Judith Martin, known as "Miss Manners," began her advice column in 1978, and *Miss Manners' Guide to Excruciatingly Correct Behavior* and *Miss Manners' Guide to Rearing Perfect Children* offered humorous yet astute advice. Miss Manners had in fact been in the vanguard, speaking out against the runaway indulgence and loss of decorum that began to loom large in the 1980s. She called out a mercenary bridal industry and a grasping public, bearing witness to a shift in etiquette that abandoned correctness and yielded to hedonism.

In the updated 2010 version of *Miss Manners' Guide to a Surprisingly Dignified Wedding*, she titled one chapter "Wedding as Fundraiser" in which she lambasted gift "extortion" and referred to overblown bridal showers as a form of "money laundering."[30] She filed "bridezillas" under "unprincipled notions" and classified other behaviors under "parent abuse," "bridesmaid abuse," and "guest abuse." She wrote that the practice of copious gift giving at engagement parties had "developed about the same time that adults started giving annual birthday parties for themselves."[31]

When queried about wedding favors, she replied, "Who told you that you had to give out wedding favors? Etiquette has never thought of weddings as comparable to children's birthday parties, where the guests might need consolation for not being the center of attention."[32] Ouch. Most important, Miss Manners was an early whistle-blower, but her commentary at the onset of modern wedding mania failed to slow an explosion of "the greed and exhibitionism encouraged by an engorged bridal industry."[33]

The "controlling" voice of etiquette experts had given way to the lenient spirit evident in 1997's *Weddings for Dummies*. Scholar Dennis Hall noted the irony that this book, for "dummies," was not at all a text for the uneducated; it was instead a choice for the smart and the practical. Busy brides no longer needed instruction on how to achieve social standing; they merely craved specific information on one particular topic unfamiliar to them, and they wanted it in "quickly accessed chunks."[34] On the very edge of an era in which the Internet would completely take the reins, these brides desired more substance than offered by the advertisement-stuffed bridal magazines.

During the Reagan era, etiquette turned away from its traditional role of allaying class insecurities and instead fanned an escalating trend toward shrewd shopping. It now addressed anxieties that stemmed from "mistakes that could be made in purchasing, as opposed to social errors."[35] The improper selection of goods and services could reflect poorly on a couple charged with their first big job in administration (planning their wedding). Rather than chancing errors in their treatment of guests' egos and feelings, brides and grooms now risked selecting passé food or hiring a lackluster band or bungling DJ—reckless decisions by which they would embarrass *themselves*.

> He just said July 6th and if you tell a guy July 6th they're going to think it's this year.
>
> —Wedding guest Dave Barclay, who in 2007 flew from Toronto to Wales to attend a friend's wedding and arrived exactly one year early[36]

❦ 6 ❦

Chicken or Beef?

Choice of Entrees

*R*eligion and ethnicity have long determined whom a person married, and religious traditions have always greatly decided how a wedding was celebrated. Whether held in a church, a temple, a mosque, or on the beach, a marriage ceremony still often depends on the couple's faith. That Catholic couple cannot get married at Disneyland, and that Mormon couple will not be having an open bar. Many contemporary brides and grooms only explore organized religion once they begin to plan their weddings, and many look for hybrids of traditions that can please them as well as family members. For this reason, it has become common for couples to dig up "nondenominational" vows.

NATIVE AMERICANS

Now you will feel no rain,
For each of you will be shelter to the other.
Now you will feel no cold,
For each of you will be warmth to the other.

—"Apache wedding prayer"

This famous wedding prayer, penned by the script writers of the 1950 film *Broken Arrow*, remarkably wriggled its way into the canon of meaningful, nondenominational wedding vows.[1] Few knew it was not a real Indian poem, and by the 1970s it had caught the imagination of couples eager for a spiritual anthem that eschewed the traditional and conservative. Wedding planning books and websites still present it as an option. One can only wonder how many earnest newlyweds have recited these words, believing they were connecting to the peaceable spirit of their Native American forebears.

Native Americans, who well knew the rigors of acquiring sustenance, endowed food with spiritual properties and integrated it into their wedding rituals. Corn, regarded as one of the Three Sisters (corn, beans, and squash), was high in protein and could be dried and preserved, like beans. Hot stones were dropped into cooking vessels to make stews of venison or buffalo, seasoned with mustard seeds, roots, and nuts. On the Great Lakes, wild rice was harvested, ground to make wild rice flour, and formed into flat breads or made into a porridge sweetened with maple syrup. Squash was simmered with dried blueberries and maple syrup to make a dessert.[2]

In a Hopi ritual, a woman wanting to marry prepares piki bread as a way to show her suitor that she will be able to cook for him. The female proposes marriage, leaving the bread at her intended's door. If he takes it, he has accepted her. The bread is made with blue cornmeal and patiently cooked in paper-thin layers, an art that takes years to learn and is in danger of disappearing. Other tribes may see the woman preparing a basket of food or grinding cornmeal for her intended. One custom in particular, mudslinging, has caught the media's eye. A Hopi woman to be married stays at home with her future mother-in-law, and all the women of the community throw mud at her house while hurling insults. Afterward the two women clean the house thoroughly. Next, all the women return with gifts, and everyone enjoys a meal.[3] This ritual may serve as a form of bridal shower, creating a bond between the bride and mother-in-law, with the act of cleaning symbolizing new beginnings and the insults hurled by the guests perhaps serving as an opportunity to clear the air and encourage a fresh beginning for the new family.

Native American cultures are diverse. Northwestern coastal tribes expect guests to drink before and after a meal, but to drink during a meal is considered rude. Customs such as this are specific to certain tribes, and many traditions have been lost through the passage of time and the adaptation of Indian culture to the mainstream. It is safe to say, however, that Native Americans put great stock in etiquette, and wedding customs are often quite formalized and include reverence for elders and the tribe as a whole.

RELIGION IN THE NEW WORLD

A religious movement that railed against the somber practices of Puritanism began in England in the early 1700s and soon spread to the colonies. Called the Great Awakening, it found a place for emotion in church practices and sought to ease the restrictions that dominated marital norms. By the early 1800s, a certain religious fever had erupted, led by Presbyterian, Baptist, and Methodist preachers with an eye on reform. From 1800 to 1820, church membership in the United States doubled.[4] Turmoil ruled in the antebellum South, the seeds of the Prohibition movement were sown, and conditions ripened to make room for a swarm of religious sects and cults. Many of these church groups and religious communities have vanished; nonetheless, their foundations often rested on the rejection of conventional marriage and family customs, and their existence led to an overall reform in attitudes toward marriage and family life.

Of course, there was lots of room for exploitation and for charlatans. John Humphrey Noyes advocated multiple and "complex marriages" and insisted, "There is no reason why sex should not be done in public as much as music or dancing."[5] Founding the Oneida Community as a home for his beliefs, he preached, "The new commandment is that we love one another, not by pairs, as in the world, but en masse."[6]

Isaac Bullard billed himself as the Second Christ and carried the message that God had instructed his followers to not bathe or to change their clothes. His flock fasted, drank milk through quills from a common bowl for nourishment, and eschewed any creature comforts. They did approve of free love, however, and practiced communal marriage.[7]

A more modern example of religious fervor occurred in the 1960s and 1970s, epitomized by the work of self-proclaimed messiah Reverend Sun Myung Moon of the Unification Church.[8] Moon preached that marriage was central to salvation and, as Jesus had died before taking a wife and having children, it was Moon's job to populate the earth with "sinless children" born of couples blessed by him. In 1982 he paired and married 2,075 couples (all dressed identically, men in blue suits, women in white gowns) at Madison Square Garden in New York City.

In 1997 Moon (fresh from a prison sentence for tax fraud) hosted "Blessing '97," another massive wedding, in which he hoped to marry or bless the existing vows of 35,000 couples at RFK Stadium in Washington, DC. Estimates of the number of attendees vary, and millions also "attended" via satellite hookups. Whitney Houston was reportedly paid $1 million to perform, and Reverend Louis Farrakhan, then leader of the Nation of Islam, spoke at the stadium event as well.[9]

The Amana Society (initially called the Community of True Inspiration) was one of the largest and most prosperous of the many utopian groups. Settlers in New York State with German origins moved to eastern Iowa. Reform societies like the Amanas tended to push west to spread their messages, to escape harassment, and to colonize inexpensive land. Especially after the Civil War, with improved travel conditions and the threat of Native Americans "removed," religious groups took to the road to proselytize.

The Amanas lived in large, orderly villages, and after initially discouraging marriage and childbearing, they soon saw the need to augment their numbers. Weddings were very simple, with lunch at one of the nearby communal "kitchen houses." There was no kissing at traditional Amana weddings, but celebrants did drink homemade beer and enjoy a large variety of cakes, with the feasts emphasizing dessert.

The Amana organization thrived intact until 1932, probably because it stayed flexible, adapting to changes in the economy and to the greater society. Although it remained a communal entity, members well understood capitalism and ran a successful mill, engaging in trade all over the country. Church members voted to discontinue communal living and disbanded in what they call "The Great Change," whereby they turned their many holdings into a joint, for-profit stock company. Amana craftspeople, led by George Foerstner, built the first commercial beverage cooler, launching the profitable Amana line of refrigerators, and in 1967 introduced the microwave oven (the company is now owned by Whirlpool).[10]

Older residents who live near the settlement recall delivery of "carloads of cake" to Amana weddings, which still take the display and variety of homemade cakes as a focal point. Locals report that guests are still expected to bring homemade cakes to receptions and that these are preferred to the conventional white cakes expected at modern celebrations.[11] Much of the Amana Society's network of butcheries, smokehouses, and breweries has been preserved and is overseen by the National Park Service. The seven Amana settlements are thriving tourist locations, with dining venues hosting contemporary weddings that feature hearty German food, served family style, along with local craft beers, wine made from berries and fruits, and meats from restored Amana smokehouses.

The Amish, who also have roots in Germany, are mostly known for their refusal to live with modern technology, not driving cars or using electricity. They are Christian and interpret the Bible literally. Mennonites are similar but not as strict in their rejection of modernity. The Amish are also known for their food and their craftsmanship. Weddings are usually held from late October to early December after the fall harvest, before harsh weather sets in. The ceremony and feast are held at the home of the bride's parents. Tuesdays and Thursdays are popular days for weddings, with Saturday not an option, as Sunday is their Sabbath and their wedding feasts require a lot of postwedding cleanup. The entire community is invited, and it is standard to host multiple seatings in order to feed as many as three hundred guests.

The newlyweds sit together at a corner table called the "eck," with the bride on the groom's left, as when they ride together in their horse and buggy. The Amish are known for their hearty cuisine, and because they shun technology, they have never cooked with preservatives and have always grown their crops and raised their livestock organically. The wedding meal is called "the roast," and in Pennsylvania it will nearly always include roast chicken with stuffing, creamed celery, mashed potatoes, gravy, and apple sauce.

The Rumspringa (meaning "running around") is one of the most interesting aspects of Amish society. At sixteen or so, youngsters are given the opportunity to experience all that their community forbids. They can drink alcohol, use computers, and mix with the "English" (the non-Amish). The hope is that, having tasted another life, youth will learn to value their family's ways (or else leave the fold). The harrowing 2002 documentary *Devil's Playground* traces a group of Amish youth on Rumspringa, detailing the dangers of "forbidden fruit" and the impetuousness of teenagers no matter their faith.

MORMONISM

Members of the Church of Jesus Christ of Latter-Day Saints (LDS) celebrate weddings according to the guidelines of their Doctrine and Covenants. They do not condone the use of tobacco or alcohol and disapprove of "hot drinks" (usually construed as caffeinated beverages; there are varying tolerances for herbal teas, decaffeinated coffee drinks, and alcohol burned off in cooking). Mormonism is known for its onetime endorsement of polygamy, and its marriage ceremonies are intimate and simple. Performed at the temple, the "sealing" is reserved for close family members and those of the same faith.

From 1852 to 1890, 20–30 percent of Mormons lived in plural marriages. Before 1852, polygamy was practiced in secret, and the system was banned in 1890. Church leaders were the most likely to have four or more wives, with two-thirds having two wives and 20 percent having three. The average progression was that a twenty-three-year-old man would marry a twenty-year-old woman and then, twelve years later, take another wife, who was in her early twenties, and so on, thereby populating the community and ensuring a high fertility rate.[12] Plural marriage was always controversial within the LDS community, and the tradition was always ammunition for critics.

SEVENTH DAY ADVENTISTS

Seventh Day Adventists do not consume meat or seafood, and their wedding receptions will not include alcohol or caffeinated drinks. Their doctrine espouses healthful living, and they believe the body is a temple for the spirit. The church was founded in Battle Creek, Michigan, as a sanatorium. The director in 1875 was John Harvey Kellogg, who invented corn flakes, grape nuts, and shredded wheat, all of which he deemed "moral foods."[13] Seventh Day Adventists are so named because their religious week starts on Sunday, with Saturday being the seventh, therefore holy, day. Their wedding celebrations will not include dancing and are often held on the site of the church.

ISLAMISTS

Islamic marriage celebrations follow the teachings of the prophet Mohammed, guided by the Quran and the Suma. Meat from carnivorous animals and swine should not be consumed and is considered *haram*, meaning forbidden. Halal meat must come from an animal slaughtered with a sharp knife and minimal suffering and drained of as much blood as possible. Many adherents also require that a Muslim perform the slaughter. The "Crescent M" is a packaging label used in the United States to indicate that food is halal, but its use is not universal, and halal labeling practices are not consistent across cultures.[14]

Marriage practices among the members of mosques in the United States reflect the affiliation of a particular community, so, as with other religions, interpretations of what is considered suitable vary. Birds of prey are always rejected as a food source, but opinions are shifting as to the acceptability of seafood. For some, the only acceptable food from the ocean comes from fish with scales that separate easily from the body. Shellfish may or may not be acceptable, as evident from a perusal of halal restaurant menus, some of which include a selection of seafood and some of which are devoid of any shellfish.

Afghan wedding welcome feast, 2015. *Source*: Used with permission from Kathy Allen.

An Islamic wedding may include a dividing wall separating men and women, or it may feature free mingling of the sexes. The Afghan American community in particular generally hosts large wedding feasts, and commercial banquet halls with halal food are abundant. Whole roasted goat (*sajji*) is a standard celebratory dish, and sweets are popular. At some services the groom's mother formally serves candies to the bride. The *nikkah*, the actual marriage ceremony, is usually brief and intimate, without a lot of observers. The *walima*, the wedding celebration and feast, may last for several days.

Both Muslim and Hindu women gather prior to a wedding to adorn the bridal party with temporary tattoos, the most elaborate being reserved for the bride's feet, hands, and ankles. The *mehndi* ceremony is usually held at least two days before the wedding (so the dye can set on the skin) and is a festive, anticipated event. Henna leaves (and/or turmeric) are dried and crushed into a paste, which is then used to make intricate designs. It is common for the bride's mother to apply the first dot of henna on the bride's palm, and there is a saying that the darker the *mehndi* on the skin, the deeper the love the husband will have for his wife. Modern *mehndi* designs can be ambitious creations, often featuring peacocks and flowers and reflecting the name and attributes of the groom. Professional bridal *mehndi* artists have design books from which to choose, although do-it-yourselfers can purchase stencils.

HINDUISM

Many adherents of Hinduism are vegetarian, although this is not a requirement of the religion, which has numerous versions and interpretations. For most Hindus, dairy-based foods are acceptable, but meat is not eaten, with chicken and pork considered especially unclean. Gifts of food—often nuts, fruits, and sweets—are offered to gods in prayer services and, once blessed, are fed to participants as a source of purification. Halvah is a favorite. Food meant for blessings (called *prasada* or *Prasad*) is a prominent element of Hindu marriage rites. Parents of the bride and groom exchange sweets as a symbol of connection, and marriage banquets begin with a rice dish and usually end with a sweet.[15] Coconuts are a symbol of prosperity, and cumin seeds and brown sugar may be crushed into a paste, put in a betel leaf, and placed on the heads of the bride and groom as a symbol of both the sweetness and the sourness of life.

Wealthy Indian grooms once rode on decorated elephants or horses to collect their brides on their wedding days, and this tradition continues in America—it is in fact gaining in popularity.[16] The grand entrance of the groom, called the *baraat*, is kept alive by companies such as Have Trunk Will Travel, which provide elephants and decorations all over the country.[17]

SIKHS

Sikhs, who have achieved particular success in Northern Californian agriculture, are a prosperous community known for large and joyful wedding ceremonies. Sikhism originated in northern India in the 1400s and became a large presence in the 1960s and 1970s in the American West.[18] Sikhism rejects superstitions, so there are no restricted dates or times to wed. Dowries or payments between families are forbidden, as marriage should not be viewed as a business arrangement. As the religion rejects social inequality and the caste system, most male Sikhs have the last name Singh (lion) and female Sikhs the last name Kaur (princess), so there can be no association between status and name.

On his wedding day, the groom is fed sweets by his mother, and, as in Hindu ceremonies, the groom and his wedding party collect the bride in a ritual called the *Braat* (or *Baraat*). They all travel to the *gurdwara* (the Sikh house of worship), where they have tea and sweet snacks before the service begins. Sikhs sit on the floor to show humility, and feet should never point toward the holy scriptures at the front of the room. It is forbidden to have the religious marriage rites performed in commercial establishments like restaurants or hotels, and most are done at the *gurdwara*, often with over one thousand people in attendance.[19]

A dessert pudding called *kara parshad* is sent around to guests at the end of the ceremony. The Sikh temple will have a *langer*, a communal kitchen, and it is a hallmark of all Sikh *gurdwaras* that a free meal is offered to everyone who enters.[20] Sikhs will not consume ritualistically prepared food, so they will not eat kosher or halal meat, and they do not drink alcohol in the *gurdwara*.

BUDDHISTS

Buddhists are primarily vegetarians, although some may consume fish or meat under certain circumstances. There are five requirements for a

Buddhist marriage: to harm no creatures, to take nothing that is not given, to refrain from sexual misconduct, to consume no alcohol or drugs, and to be truthful. These five ideals are known as the "right actions," or "precepts," and act as guides for behavior. Buddhists are not required to marry Buddhists, and their weddings may be small and informal.[21] Buddhism arose in the fifth century BC in what is now northern India and Nepal, when Siddhartha Gautama meditated in order to understand the cause of suffering. He fasted on six grains of rice a day while seeking enlightenment and eventually came to an "awakening." Buddhists eschew dogma, and their marriage rituals vary widely and can be interpreted liberally.

RESTRAINT

Bent on homogenizing the taste buds of immigrants, home economists of the early twentieth century had a particular contempt for strong flavors. They characterized bland food as healthy and robust and flavorful fare as somehow excessive.[22] Eastern Europeans, Greeks, and Italians had a fondness for aggressively flavored food, and garlic was a favorite. Victorians viewed this predilection with scorn, believing that strongly flavored food caused "disorderly and licentious behavior" and was associated with being "morally corrupt."[23]

The cookbook *Foods of the Foreign Born* (1922) deemed pickled food injurious. Its author opined that since "by nature the Jews are an emotional people," if they would merely adjust their diet, they would be cured.[24] Next came a listing of the many forms of pickled foods sold by Jewish shopkeepers:

> They have cabbages pickled whole, shredded, or chopped and rolled in leaves; peppers pickled; also string beans; cucumbers, sour, half sour, and salted; beets; and many kinds of meat and fish. This excessive use of pickled food destroys the taste for milder flavor, causes irritation, and renders assimilation more difficult.
>
> —Bertha M. Wood, *Foods of the Foreign Born*, 1922

Smiley's Cook Book of 1901 included a "Foreign Cookery" section, with recipes for French, German, Spanish, Russian, Turkish, and Italian items. All were fairly innocuous, many of them indistinguishable from nonethnic recipes. The book warned readers that the dangerous French used enough garlic to render their cuisine "unpalatable," a snag resolved by including no garlic at all in the volume's French recipes.[25] Tellingly, "Jewish" was listed as a category of "foreign" food, a commentary on the unease that the establishment felt at the influx of non-Christians.

JUDAISM

Immigrants poured into the United States, many Jewish, and clung to their native foods, setting up stores to sell familiar ingredients to their neighbors. Food was a way both to retain cultural ties with home and to assimilate, a notion not lost on commercial food companies, which marketed packaged food as a way to "eat like an American."

Prior to World War I, middle- and upper-middle-class families had enjoyed inexpensive household help. After the war they suffered a "servant problem."[26] Their former maids and cooks now ensconced in factories and office buildings, many middle-class women had to cook for the first time in their lives. And these women, who would have once learned to run a household from their mothers, lived in rented rooms in cities, far from their families. Someone needed to teach Americans how to cook. Manufacturers looking to sell their products often sponsored cooking classes, and colleges began to churn out trained home economists (one of the few respectable career options for ambitious women of the era).

Jewish philanthropic groups spurred Jewish women to break into cookbook publishing and insinuated that poorly prepared food inspired men to eat outside the home, which could make them leave their families altogether. Yiddish newspapers told of men who left home to eat at restaurants and "just never came back."[27] Wildly popular, *The Settlement Cook Book* (1901) strove to teach Jewish women to cook "like Americans." For years ads featured "the bride of today," gazing at the *Settlement Cook Book*, and reminded readers that good cooking was "the way to a man's heart."[28]

The first Jewish settlers in America, with roots in Spain and Portugal, arrived via Brazil in the 1600s. German Jews arrived in the 1840s and mostly came in large numbers just prior to World War I. They found their way to Cincinnati, soon opening shops along trade routes in the smaller towns of the Midwest.[29] The 1880s launched the arrival of more than 2 million Jews, most fleeing the ghettoes of eastern Europe.[30] Between 1880 and 1924, eastern European Jews flooded into America, settling in the poorer neighborhoods of large American cities, such as New York, Chicago, Boston, Baltimore, and Philadelphia. Jewish families, with a history of forced relocation, moved to the new world as a unit, and while they sent for relatives once they could, husbands and wives tended to immigrate together.[31] As far as publishing cookbooks and writing food columns in magazines, Italian and Chinese women were invisible for much of early American history, whereas Jewish women, with a robust tradition of education, wrote marriage advice columns, published recipes, and managed the assimilation of Jewish families.[32] Jews were practiced at dealing with persecution, and preserving Jewish food traditions was both a way to keep their culture alive and a tangible expression of respect for the struggles of their ancestors.

Challah blessing, Irving Gelber, bride's grandfather, 1971.
Source: Used with permission from Bonnie and Ray Nutkis.

Kashruth, the Jewish dietary laws, require that dairy and meat be kept separate from one another, with cooking vessels, utensils, and tableware sanitized and also kept separate. *Kosher* means "allowed," while *trefa* means "forbidden"; *pareve* means neutral. Animals to be consumed should have cloven (split) hooves and be ruminants (chew their own cud); swine is forbidden. Animals are slaughtered under rabbinical supervision, with a sharp knife, and their meat is soaked in cold water, treated with kosher salt, and drained. Fish must have scales and fins, and shellfish, as well as scavenging animals and birds, are also prohibited. Duck, goose, chicken, and turkey are generally considered acceptable, but any item not treated within guidelines can become nonkosher. Blood is considered the life force of animals; hence any consumption of blood is spurned.[33]

Due to Shabbat, which begins on Fridays at sundown, modern weddings are not held until after nightfall on Saturdays. Orthodox Jews follow the Torah literally, and both brides and grooms are encouraged to fast on their wedding day until the rites begin. A challah bread is blessed by a senior family member or honored guest and shared with invitees, signaling the beginning of the feast. Modern reformed Jews take honeymoons, but traditionally, during the week after marriage, friends and family of newlyweds host a stream of lunch and dinner parties, honoring the couple and easing them into married life.

GET ME TO THE ___ ON TIME

It is difficult to generalize the customs of any religion, and traditions vary widely among denominations, regions, and spiritual leaderships. Geography plays a large role, as does the prevalence of intermarriage between races and religions. The American diet has always been a patchwork of food traditions from multiple countries, and many of the food practices of immigrants have been adapted and now reside in the American mainstream.

ʊ 7 ʊ

Jumping the Broom

$\mathscr{M}$arriage traditions among African Americans, as for any group with origins outside the United States, evolved from the wedding customs of a home country adapted to life in a new land. Modern African Americans, however, live with the knowledge that their ancestors did not undertake the voyage to the New World voluntarily, and their history is rooted in suffering and deprivation.

EARLY DAYS

The desire for coffee, tea, and chocolate (for both the products and the profits from their sale) incited American colonists to build their own nation in which to produce and export items.[1] Starvation and sickness ravaged the first settlers of the New World; during what they called the "Starving Time," Jamestown colonists were even forced to eat "recently deceased neighbors" in order to stay alive.[2] Globalization is actually the story of food, and our world is significantly shaped by its pursuit. A quest for spices led to the exploration of the globe, and sugar production and greed provided the impetus for human slavery.

SLAVE MARRIAGES

The horrific practice of human slavery in the Americas is linked to food acquisition (particularly of sugar and rice), and the impact of the slave trade rightfully lingers on the American consciousness. Slaves married and reproduced, often at the behest of their "owners," and here the rituals of marriage and food are tied in with a topic as distasteful as slavery.

The food eaten by slaves included a mixture of New World ingredients, adapted to and fused with African traditions and carried on with each generation. Slaves, captured and imprisoned in a common locale, came from very different parts of Africa, each home to its own cooking rituals. These regional traditions blended, and a new cuisine formed, born of suffering yet grounded in memories of a life in Africa before capture.

The sustenance provided to slaves was meager, subject to geography and the varying temperaments of slave masters. Slaves in South Carolina generally labored in rice fields and had a modicum of control over their diets. Rice was a favored crop in the South, as it was particularly profitable and also a nutritious staple that could sustain the same slaves who harvested it.[3]

Many plantation owners in the South allowed slaves to grow their own crops, and the sheer ratio of Africans to Europeans in the South engendered a culture permeated by African food customs. In the North, however, the food available to slaves was more restricted, as land was scarcer. Also, a smaller population of Africans had a reduced impact on the larger society. Much of the existing information about what exactly slaves consumed is undependable, written by those who ate the cooking (slave owners and employers) and thus recording not so much what African Americans ate but what they cooked.[4]

It is often said that Southern cooking is unique in that the enslaved plantation cook prepared only one style of food. Slaves and their owners ate the same cuisine, "some low, and some high on the hog," albeit with slaves getting less desirable and smaller portions.

In the North, farming families typically owned one or two slaves, who were thus isolated from other slaves and had little chance of finding a mate. On the big plantations of the South, slave owners found that allowing slave marriages was profitable. They also used the threat of separating families as a method of control.[5]

Whether a slave couple could wed was the prerogative of the slave master, who generally officiated the wedding ceremonies and needed to approve the match. Some slave masters seemed to feel an inflated sense of generosity when they hosted a slave wedding in the "main house," perhaps congratulating themselves for benevolently providing clothes or food for the couple.

Most believe broom jumping, an African American wedding tradition, to be an old African ritual, one that slaves cherished as an expression of their history. Broom jumping, however, is probably Welsh in origin, and has a complicated and muddled position in African American history.

A NOTE ABOUT BROOMS

Patrick O'Neil's research, as well as the findings of others, reveals that slave masters introduced the practice of jumping the broom, inadvertently using it as a way to keep slave marriage ideologically separate from their own rituals. This stark practice was not religious and required little planning and expense. That an act as humble as jumping over a broom could seal a marriage indicated that owners considered slave marriages transitory and not endowed with the emotional or spiritual import of white unions.[6] In England, "marriage over the broomstick," or the "besom" (a historic word for a broom), referred to a hasty marriage or to a couple living together but not formally married. A "besom wedding" indicated a couple was "living tally," without a church blessing. This was common in England as late as 1850 among the poorer classes.[7] A couple would together jump over a broomstick in the company of friends and family; if, within the first year, they wished to dissolve their partnership, they would invite the witnesses back and jump backward over the besom. An estimated one-fifth of the population of rural England between 1750 and 1850 had at some point "lived tally."[8]

Jumping the Broom, a guide to planning an African American wedding published in 1993, gave the practice a positive character.[9] Plantation slaves often had secret weddings in their own quarters, free from the ministrations of masters; they generally did not jump the broom on those occasions. O'Neil wrote that after slavery, African Americans did not necessarily choose to jump the broom at their weddings, perhaps rejecting a practice that embodied the precariousness of slave marriages. At any moment, a husband or wife could be sent to the auction block or a child taken and never returned.[10]

The African American community has reappropriated the practice, however, perhaps viewing it in the same context as embracing soul food—turning something born of tragedy into a symbol of adversity overcome. Many modern African American weddings indeed include a broom-jumping ceremony, and companies sell various customized brooms for display in the couple's home.

WORLD WAR I AND THE MOVE NORTH

After the Civil War, sharecroppers, now free to marry at will, fared little better than when enslaved, and many families lingered on the threshold of starvation. Sharecroppers lived on a diet of canned food, rarely supplemented with fresh vegetables, because they rarely stayed in one place long enough to establish a garden.[11]

As World War I unfolded, suffragettes reined in their clamor for the vote, reckoning their patriotism would be rewarded once the war ended. These women used food to illustrate their nationalism, sponsoring enormous group canning and baking efforts and producing special "war" recipes with limited supplies.[12] Governmental food rationing gave way to a deep economic recession, fanning a migration that changed the country forever. By 1917 almost five hundred thousand southerners had moved to the North and Midwest, eager to fill newly created jobs.

In *Hog and Hominy*, Frederick Douglass Opie examines how eating outside one's community was particularly dangerous for people of color. Throngs of African Americans carefully packed sandwiches in empty shoeboxes and boarded trains east, their fares paid by their new employers. En route, they could not hope to eat at the same lunch counters as whites and instead stayed aboard during rest stops, hoping to avoid the ubiquitous lynchings and beatings.[13]

Green Book, 1952. *Source*: "Front cover," Schomburg Center for Research in Black Culture, Jean Blackwell Hutson Research and Reference Division, New York Public Library Digital Collections, http://digitalcollections.nypl.org/items/62cf40b2-d0fc-346b-e040-e00a18065229.

It was practical for those on the road to have a "mental roadmap" of where they could purchase food from black-owned establishments.[14] Later, Victor Hugo Green, a Harlem postal worker, began to publish the annual *Green Book*, detailing which gas stations, motels, and eateries were safe for blacks to frequent. Printed from 1936 to 1966, the *Green Book* grew to include tips for all forms of travel and was used to plan many honeymoons.

Green Book, 1954. *Source:* "The Negro Travelers' Green Book: 1954," Schomburg Center for Research in Black Culture, Jean Blackwell Hutson Research and Reference Division, New York Public Library Digital Collections, http://digitalcollections.nypl.org/items/3c85ba30-9374-0132-9292-58d385a7b928.

LOOKS LIKE YOU MAID IT?

Bridal magazines by nature have a limited subject matter, so in addition to dissecting weddings and honeymoons, they to this day often give advice for a happy marriage. Throughout most of the twentieth century, magazines devoted a lot of space to instructing women on how to run a home, working on the assumption that prospective brides lived with their parents until wed and were new to homemaking. *Brides* magazine, educating women about managing household help, ran a 1936 article titled "How to Capture and Train Your Maid." This article, which appeared in several variations (in an industry meant for a temporary audience, items were often recycled), warned how hard it was to get good domestic help: "There is some disagreement as to which nationality makes the best servants. Probably it is safe to generalize in the following order: Swedish, English, Scotch, German, and French—the latter are good cooks but not overly clean and prone to unreliability."[15]

This quote is an example of the prevailing attitude toward immigrants, and these types of writings often made shameless generalizations about ethnic groups. Readers were told that "brogues and accents, while amusing, aren't practical" and that a "trimmish figure is also a necessity despite there being a certain charm about a lumbering cook." Men are not spared, and when a gentlemen hired a butler, he should bear in mind that "Chinese boys are noted for their devotion, and the English are touchingly loyal."

It is easy to see that the preferred help was the palest, and the media reserved special scorn for African Americans. As for hiring them as maids, readers were told, "Harlem and Southern colored have been left out of the listing purposely, because it is impossible to generalize about them. Like the little girl with the curl, 'when they are good they are very, very good . . .'"[16]

CHANGING TIMES?

In 1958 the Virginia home of Mildred and Richard Loving was raided at 2:00 a.m. The couple was arrested and put in jail for violating the Racial Integrity Act of 1924. Newlywed Mildred was African American, and Richard was Caucasian. The judge who heard their case stated that God had placed the races on separate continents for a reason, and they were not meant to mix. He would suspend their felony convictions if they agreed to leave the state of Virginia, so the couple moved to Washington, DC, where they could live legally. They spent five years making secret trips to visit family members. In 1963 they looked to Attorney General Robert F. Kennedy for assistance, and the American Civil Liberties Union took on the case. Incredibly, interracial marriage was not rendered constitutional until 1967.

In 1947 *Ebony*, a magazine highlighting African American achievement, featured a black bride in a full, white formal gown. That the issue used the theme of marriage is indicative of the era. African Americans were becoming public figures, pushing into new jobs and positions in the community, and, like their white counterparts, they were eager for their fair share of postwar prosperity. Of course, this mentality would spread to the bridal business.[17]

A boycott in 1951 led to blacks being able to shop at department stores in Baltimore, but they were not allowed to try on clothes, and "not being allowed to try on wedding gowns was a frequent indignity."[18] Like any bridal industry, the black bridal industry has adapted, and black bridal expos and online magazines, such as *Black Bride*, work to sell to their demographic.

In 1975 La Deva Davis, an actress, debuted a cooking show on PBS called *What's Cooking?* There was an economic recession at the time, and her food was simple and inexpensive. Her cooking knowledge was limited to what her mother had taught her, but her mother was Southern, she said, which she joked qualified her as an apt tutor. Her show was called a "down-home" version of Julia Child, and little did the public know that many down-home versions would be coming soon once the Food Network arrived.[19]

SOUL FOOD

Soul food was not new, but the term mushroomed in the 1960s, albeit with divergent subtexts. Activists railed that the food of the South was merely that which slave masters had allowed their slaves to eat. In 1965, Black Panther Eldridge Cleaver exclaimed, "The people of the ghetto want steaks, not chitterlings," and admonished his culture for romanticizing a cuisine born in anguish and poverty.[20] And yet this food originated in Africa and may serve as a precious link to an old homeland. Soul food can offer a reminder of the ingenuity of ancestors surviving under the most horrific of circumstances. Gumbo, black-eyed peas, and greens (slaves being given only the "tops" of vegetables) are foods that slaves adapted to a new world with new ingredients.

Princess Pamela's Soul Food Cook Book, written when the civil rights movement had seen some successes, contains a trove of recipes that honor the slave roots of African Americans. At its publication in 1969, soul food was establishing its credentials with the mainstream public. Princess Pamela wrote that soul-food recipes make eating an act that is "still close enough to honest-to-God hunger" and that the cuisine should be enjoyed with the understanding that it was like a baby "rocked from a troubled birth in the cradle of the South."[21]

In the fall of 2006, researchers reviewed the advertisements inside *Brides*, *Modern Bride*, and *Elegant Bride* and found that less than 2 percent of the women depicted were of color. Current thought is for some to feel that separate magazines for African Americans is a version of segregation, while others suspect this is a smart marketing strategy targeting specific audiences.[22]

Certain features, such as libation ceremonies and the jumping of the broom, characterize African American weddings; yet, as in other communities, food rituals tend to be regional, religion based, and subject to economics. Average spending of African Americans on weddings aligns closely with that of other races, and *Jet* magazine continues a thriving wedding announcement section.

Studying the food habits surrounding wedding customs of African Americans is to study the food habits of a United States rife with contradictions. To study the wedding traditions of African Americans is to study a culture that yearns to embrace rituals that honor the past but must also adapt to be sustainable.

⚜ ♂ ⚜

What Are You?

Regional Cuisine and Weddings

BLAND IS GOOD

Wedding receptions of today almost always feature food that at some point in history was considered ethnic. Having pasta on a wedding menu now is hardly considered exotic, but there was a time when it would have been unusual or considered "Italian." Early cookbooks often included versions of multinational food with instructions for toning down recipes to fit American standards, thereby making such dishes palatable to the masses. *The Joy of Cooking* in 1936, for example, included a recipe for Italian spaghetti, which instructed readers to fold in butter with a can of tomato soup. Chile con Carne called for a can of tomato soup treated with garlic powder and canned kidney beans.[1]

YES, WE USED TO HAVE NO BANANAS

The use of packaged foods, like canned soup, enabled this dampening down of exotic foods, and industrialization changed all aspects of wedding culture, from the type of food served to the staff who cooked it to the mode of transport that took honeymooners away. Fast trains swiftly transformed life in America, most especially with regard to the food supply. Trains first shipped meat across the nation (a dodgy effort), and by the late 1890s capitalists were profiting mightily by transporting fresh produce. Once large-scale, reliable refrigeration was in place (the early 1900s), California was steadily shipping fruit across the country. Investors who fitted train cars with refrigeration quickly doubled their money. Bananas, in particular, as they required a long voyage and a controlled temperature to stave off ripening, exemplified an entirely new way of eating that "defied" the seasons and showed human mastery over the elements.[2]

Banana recipes starting showing up in cookbooks soon after the turn of the twentieth century, proof that those living on the American prairie were familiar with and could afford a food grown very far from their homes. While the moneyed in port cities had always had access to imported foods, this new accessibility to foreign foods allowed even the poor to partake in and exhibit modernity and American ingenuity.[3] Items like bananas demonstrated the country's corporate affluence, yet not individual wealth, so they were not considered luxury foods, despite the infrastructure needed to transport them to American tables. Bananas were part of a large industrial complex, albeit one so successful that their price dropped low enough to deprive them of "specialness."

GOING WEST

Food habits and wedding customs historically differed among those in cities and in rural surroundings, and variation in these customs on the East and West Coasts can serve as an exaggerated illustration of old versus new societies.

The West has a shorter history in the cultural consciousness, though an equally rich one. In the pioneer era, the remote mining camps of the West offered little opportunity to consume fresh food, and disease spread quickly, hastened by adulterated food and milk. The price of supplies was colossal, and canned food was cherished. Oysters, so prevalent on the coasts, were canned and provided a welcome source of protein.[4] Cities like San Francisco grew, and the rugged missions carved out by Spanish friars gave way to grand hotels, glossy restaurants, and country clubs—all locales for a variety of regional cuisines and wedding feasts.

The prairies and streams of Middle America had once boasted an abundance of food supplies; yet herds of zealous travelers, on their way to hunt gold, drained this bounty and tested resources once considered infinite. The year 1849 saw fifteen thousand people pass through the plains.[5] For those living on the trail, jerked meat supplemented beans cooked over campfires constructed with dried buffalo dung, and cooking pits were dug for baking bread. One legend holds that sourdough bread is a result of a starter dough, one piece of which was always kept warm under the cook's rocking saddle as the wagon trains headed west.

TV, LOTS OF WEDDINGS, LOTS OF BABIES, AND LOTS OF CASSEROLES

It is claimed that World War II soldiers returned stateside with an appreciation for foreign foods, their palates educated by their time in Europe. Food historian Linda Civitello, however, says this is a myth. She concludes that troops received canned American foodstuffs while at war, and food shortages were so severe in Europe that it is unlikely soldiers experienced much local cuisine.[6] Indeed, after Ettore Boiardi (renamed Hector at Ellis Island), a former chef of the Plaza Hotel in New York City, introduced canned spaghetti in 1928, his brand, Chef Boyardee, became an American staple, and his company became the largest U.S. importer of Parmesan cheese from Italy.[7] It also snagged the U.S. military contract to provide rations for soldiers, and its American factories ran around the clock to produce canned spaghetti to be sent abroad. The real Chef Boiardi was even awarded a Gold Star for his home-front efforts to feed the troops.[8] So American GIs were indeed eating "foreign" food, but it was canned and prepared in the United States by an Italian immigrant living the American dream.

Yet these soldiers did return home to a society basking in a new modernism. By the 1950s it had become the norm to work a forty-hour, five-day workweek (not possible in the agrarian society of the past), and memories of the deprivation of the Depression and wartime food rationing faded. Cocktail parties and backyard barbecues flourished. Americans took to the road in their new cars financed by rising salaries, and families packed groceries into new kitchens full of appliances bought on credit. The new "car culture" fueled the spread of supermarkets, which offered one-stop shopping in bulk, rather than individual trips to the butcher, the produce store, the bakery, and so forth.[9] Supermarkets especially blossomed in suburbs as a response to a housing explosion fueled by low-cost loans for veterans. Neighborhood ethnic grocery stores gave way to supermarkets, further homogenizing the food supply. Seasonal foodstuffs were now obtainable all year long, and retailers sold the same products and the same brands all over the country. By 1952 an average grocery store stocked more than four times the items it had in the late 1920s.[10]

This standardization amplified with the rise of television (due to advertising), reaching a peak in 1953, when food met technology in the debut of Swanson's TV dinner.[11]

Members of the numerous ethnic groups in the United States may be considered free from the cultural call for "restraint" in wedding fare, instead exercising a tradition of generous and lavish wedding feasts. Bountiful selections of food, prepared with intense care, act as an indicator of economic achievement in an adopted country, a culturally explicit expression of wealth not shared by the Protestant middle and upper classes, which had little tradition of using sumptuous wedding meals as a means of signaling affluence.

THE CHINESE IN AMERICA AND
HOW THEY STARTED RESTAURANTS

Chinese immigrants found work building the railroads, and by 1869, 25 percent of all workers in California were Chinese.[12] In addition to tolerating low wages, Chinese workers seemed to get sick less than their white counterparts. They had no taste for the food on offer in the makeshift camps and pooled what little money they had in order to send to San Francisco for fresh supplies, thereby avoiding the pathogens in so much of the camp food. The Chinese drank a lot of hot tea (which meant they boiled their water) and thereby skirted dysentery outbreaks as well. Their standards of personal hygiene were generally above those of white staff, and they also probably benefited from the herbs, often medicinal, found in their tea.[13] These Chinese, who seemed unnaturally healthy, became objects of suspicion, and accusations of "devilishness" degraded into mass lynchings. The eventual passage of the Chinese Exclusion Act in 1882 stopped Chinese immigration all together.

Many Chinese men, who had left their wives at home, worked as cooks once the railroad boom was over, and their restaurants became popular and remained inexpensive. La Choy introduced a line of factory-made Asian food, and canned bean sprouts joined canned chili on American pantry shelves. The Japanese, too, with their own strong culinary traditions, tended the rich farmland of California and laid the foundations for their economic achievement of the future.

A historic resentment of migrants was fanned by the fact that newly arrived families were willing to work for less money than those already established in the country, thereby decreasing wages and enraging the labor movement. Criticism of Asians was especially fierce, and labor organizers were key in the passing of legislation such as the Chinese Exclusion Acts of 1882 and 1902 and California's 1913 Alien Land Law. This land ruling, making it illegal for the foreign-born to buy property, took aim at the Japanese and attempted to curb their success as farmers and investors. Such laws were an affront to the Asian community and symptomatic of the racism of the day, but ultimately ineffectual, as the American-born children of the targeted could own property, and holdings were merely put in their names instead.[14]

Chinese wives tended to remain in China while husbands established a livelihood in America, just as Italian and Japanese men also generally chose to arrive alone and send later for loved ones. Remember, too, that in 1900 many Chinese women had bound feet. They were not accustomed to appearing in public and would not have traveled to a new and untested land.[15] Living as bachelors, Asian men grew accustomed to cooking their own meals, which in turn led many to open restaurants.

> All Chinamen can read, write and cipher with easy facility— pity but all our petted voters could. In California they rent little patches of ground and do a deal of gardening. They will raise surprising crops of vegetables on a sand pile. They waste nothing.
>
> —Mark Twain, *Roughing It*, 1872, commenting on the poor treatment of Chinese[16]

Mark Twain wrote that no true gentleman mistreated the Chinese and that the policemen and politicians who did so were "dust-licking pimps and slaves of the scum." Later, the Immigration Act of 1965 led to a particularly large stream of Chinese arrivals, and, unlike in the past, families arrived together as a unit, making employment an especially pressing concern. They found work in the garment industry, and employment in restaurants has always been a popular option for many ethnicities. There have been several waves of Chinese immigration over a long period, and because China is such a large, diverse country, few sweeping generalizations can be made about Chinese food customs.[17] And yet, as far back as the gold rush era, the Chinese in America established a reputation for taking food seriously, as modern Chinese American weddings still demonstrate.

CHINESE OLD SCHOOL

Back home in China, the Chinese calendar is often consulted to set a lucky wedding day, and fortune-tellers may be used to verify a good match by analyzing a couple's birthdates. Meals often end with fish, served after many other courses (usually at least nine); this final course symbolizes "surplus" and a hope that the couple will prosper. In one prewedding ritual the bride places a cooked fish on the stove with its head pointing toward the front, and its tail to the back, an indicator that she will go forward in the correct manner of a dutiful wife.[18] Fish may also be served in a similar fashion at the wedding banquet, which will always feature seafood as well as noodles, which symbolize long life. Abalone is a common wedding food, as is sea cucumber.

In some traditions, a roasted pig was sent to the bride's family if the groom was satisfied on his wedding night that his bride had come to him a virgin. If the bride's family received a roasted pig with its tail and ears cut off, the groom indicated the opposite.

"Four" in Chinese sounds like "death," so monetary gifts that end in four are never given. (Jewish wedding gifts are given in multiples of eighteen, and Hindu and Buddhist money gifts are given in amounts that end in one.) Red is always a lucky color; white and black are associated with funerals, so wedding gifts and their wrappings should not be in those colors.

Chinese American wedding banquets are known to be very generous feasts, and shark fin soup has gotten a lot of attention as a banquet item meant to signal prosperity. This dish, on New York City Chinatown menus as early as 1898, is not a new creation, but the controversy surrounding its consumption is.[19] Sharks, once their fins are removed, are discarded, left to sink to the ocean floor, where they die a slow death, unable to swim or protect themselves from other sea life. By definition, then, the eating of shark fin is a display of lavish excess, that one can afford to consume only a portion of an animal and waste the rest. In China, the groom's family traditionally pays for the wedding banquet, and luxury food suggests his ability to provide for his wife; therefore, skimping on the food budget causes a family to lose face.

Shark fin soup is not a universal wedding tradition in China, however, and was once only known in the south. It did not become a banquet standard until the flourishing Chinese economy of the 1990s.[20] Hong Kong luxury hotels began to remove shark fin soup from their banquet menus around 2010, and many young metropolitan couples find it unfashionable or a source of embarrassment. Their parents, however, often want it on the menu, so whether it is served may be a matter of who is paying and the extent of a couple's willingness to disagree with elders.[21]

In the United States, thus far nine states have banned the sale of shark fins, with legislation underway in other states. They appear on menus anyway, with some restaurants using other seafood but still calling the dish shark fin soup. Other chefs may in fact purchase the genuine item and not admit as much to outsiders.

PALESTINIAN AMERICANS AND IDENTITY

Palestinian American wedding receptions in the United States offer a good example of a common trajectory, one that traces weddings from their history as small and informal to their ripening into large, joyful exhibits of successful integration into a new home. These wedding celebrations also act as an affirmation that the country of origin has not been forgotten.

Weddings for Palestinian émigrés in the United States were once simple affairs, with the feast prepared by the women of the family and served at home. As first-generation families grew, weddings began to require more planning and to take on greater import. The once single-night event has come to include an engagement party for the couple and a large, orchestrated henna party for the bride, now usually hosted in a rented hall. Researcher Randa Serhan writes that there is a heightened nationalism apparent in the community's weddings, which have seemingly become more "Palestinian" than if they had been held in Palestine. Families return from homecoming vacations with patriotic trinkets, wristbands, and beads used in wedding celebrations, all serving as ways of consolidating a cultural identity.[22]

This desire to participate in the culture of forebears, evident in many ethnic groups, is especially exhibited by a renewed interest in traditional cooking and a new availability of ingredients once reserved for ethnic grocery stores. Italians arriving in the mid-twentieth century, for example, were apt to give their children "American" names and typically worked hard to ensure the assimilation of their young. Now the great grandchildren of these immigrants are likely to sport ethnic Italian first names and to wish they had been taught a second language at home.

ITALIAN AMERICANS LOVE WEDDINGS

Prohibition facilitated the ruin of many dining establishments, and families struggled to eat during the Depression. Ethnic food found a niche in this new order, and Italian pasta in particular provided a low-cost source of protein and carbohydrates. Ethnic food often had little meat, making it economical, and cooks and manufacturers could subdue its "foreignness" by replacing alien ingredients with recognizable ones.

Anyone accustomed to the rowdy and lavish Italian American weddings of the East Coast may feel they are visiting another planet when attending a staid Protestant wedding supper in Middle America. Ticket holders to the long-running Off-Broadway hit *Tony and Tina's Wedding* were literally guests at a loopy Italian American wedding, first going to the church and then walking to a catering hall for Chianti, pasta, and raucous family infighting. Send-ups such as *My Big Fat Gay Italian Wedding* have duly followed.

Italian American weddings are ripe for comment insomuch as they have a reputation for lavish spending and an abundance of food. This tradition is illustrated by a receipt from a 1949 wedding in New Jersey. In this case the Italian immigrant father of the bride spent what was then comparable to two years' wages in order to marry off his oldest daughter, who was one of eight children.

Over 4 million Italians flooded into the United States between 1880 and 1920. According to researcher Jennifer Jensen Wallach, they came literally in search of food, escaping poverty in the aftermath of unification and crushing taxes that made nutrition very expensive. According to one statistic, Italian families spent close to 85 percent of their total income just to feed themselves.[23] Typical Italians ate little meat, as it was pricey and reserved for festival days or special occasions. In 1880, the average Italian ate eight pounds of meat per year. Italians who arrived in America were thrilled with the comparatively low food prices, and, given a cultural tendency to invest in eating well, once in the United States they consumed 120 pounds of meat a year.[24]

Social workers and home economists considered themselves accountable for the welfare of newcomers and tasked themselves with bringing immigrants into the fold of proper American cuisine. These reformers were frustrated by Italians' unwillingness, for instance, to surrender their garlic and herbs and annoyed by their use of olive oil instead of butter. And, like the Chinese and Japanese, Italians pooled their money and

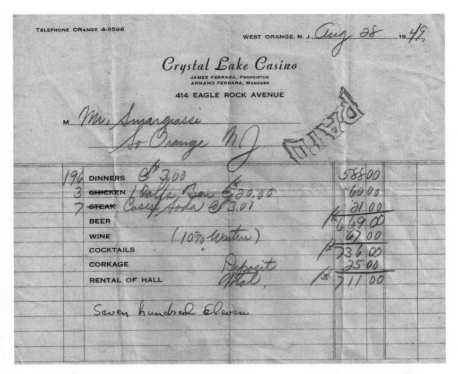

Bill from a 1949 New Jersey wedding reception. *Source*: Used with permission from Valarie Maffei Smith.

arranged to have favored ingredients shipped to America. They were also willing to use their hard-won money to provide the types of meals that social workers thought beyond their means.

A majority of the Italian immigrants were from southern Italy and, prior to their arrival, had not mixed with Italians from other parts of the country. The current Italian food identity—an amalgamation of regional foods—was formed in America, not Italy.[25]

BEEF CAKE?

Mexican Americans were also encouraged to make their diets blander, and it was recommended they "learn to eat the simpler foods of the American people, boiled and baked, with less spice and fat."[26] Hispanic cultural identity, however, has remained strong, reinforced by the consistent flow of Spanish-speaking immigrants, whose large numbers and bold food traditions have hugely defined the modern American diet.

In Argentina, marriage banquets climax with the presentation of the *pata de ternera casamiento*, a veal leg set alight and rolled out to the newly-weds on a cart. The couple ceremonially slices the meat. Wedding feasts are long, with pauses for dancing and tango exhibitions. Celebrations, held at banquet halls, go on all night and often end with a breakfast in the morning. Trinkets are tied to ribbons in the wedding cake, and, as in the New Orleans tradition, the single woman who gets the ring charm will be the next to marry.

Argentinean beef cutting. *Source*: Used with permission from Alejandro Cantagallo.

In 2000's *Kitchen Confidential*, celebrity author and chef Anthony Bourdain wrote that the reality of the fine-dining restaurant world is that the menu may be French or Italian, but the cooks are Spanish speaking, hailing from Ecuador, Cuba, Mexico, El Salvador, and the Dominican Republic—and they could "cook you under the table." In a 2015 interview on SiriusXM radio, Bourdain commented that the restaurants of America would shut down if they lost their immigrant labor, stating that never, in all his years as a chef, "not once, did anyone walk into my restaurant—any American-born kid, walk into my restaurant—and say, 'I'd like a job as a night porter or as a dishwasher.'" This willingness to bide their time, work their way up, and fill the jobs no one else will take is common among many immigrant groups. They can finalize their pursuit of the American dream by hosting a large, expensive wedding, perhaps orchestrated by an industry in which they once worked.

JAPANESE AMERICANS

Early in the 1900s, single Japanese men came to work the plantations of Hawaii, and with arranged marriages being a norm, they sent home for "picture brides" to join them.[27] The Japanese continued to arrive in the mainland United States as well, with their numbers increasing until enactment of the restrictive Immigration Act of 1924. The Japanese were skilled farmers and found success working and buying up California soil. Until they could afford more, they fished for eel from the rivers and ate thinned miso soup, pickles, and lots of rice. The Japanese brought with them a cultural belief that only the poor ate wheat, so they rarely supplemented their rice, rice cakes, and mochi with Western bread.[28]

The term "war bride" often referred to a woman who married an American soldier during the U.S. occupation of Japan after World War II up until 1960, when America completely withdrew. Many Japanese considered such women traitors, so the brides lost one culture, yet were not necessarily embraced by another. The American press, however, was enamored of these "exotic" women whose demeanor and imagined submissiveness squared with the 1950s ideal of exaggerated femininity and docility.[29]

During World War II, Japanese Americans, despite being born in the United States, were imprisoned in camps due to fear that they posed a threat to national security, with more than half of those interned being children. The repercussions of and manner in which victims overcame this episode have become the subject of recent examination, and the food prepared in these camps has been a rich source of scholarship. The current largest population of Japanese Americans resides in California, followed by Hawaii, New York, and Washington. Southern California is home to more Japanese Americans than anywhere in North America.[30]

In Japan, weddings have traditionally been Shinto ceremonies, but a move to Western-style chapels began in the early 1990s, and the wedding industry in Japan's largest cities has been quick to market weddings that straddle both cultures. Flashy entrances by the couple, complete with fog effects and synchronized music, have become widespread. "The wedding" has morphed into a performance for couples willing to shell out the money for a luxurious, American-style festivity. The cake cutting, previously a Western convention, is now commonly staged in banquet halls with a plastic or wax cake, specially slit for the knife—ideal for the photo op. A spotlight trained on the couple will fade as bride and groom are shrouded in a cloud of white smoke, or the cake may emit a puff of fog when the knife makes contact.[31]

With the popularity of television shows that highlight the master-pieces of pastry chefs, it's no surprise that the imitation cake phenom-enon is on its way to the United States. Fake the Cake in California and Ultimate Fake Cakes in Michigan are just two companies that provide ornate wedding cakes, custom-made for the cake-cutting moment. They are inedible and coated with sugared icing, although some offer the op-tion of inserting a matching edible top tier. A magnificent cake lives on in photos without the expense, and less expensive sheet cakes for the guests to enjoy are sliced back in the kitchen. Everyone is happy. Yes, they had their cake and ate it too.

CHESTNUTS AND DATES

Koreans, like the Japanese, came to Hawaii in search of work, and they, too, sent home for "picture brides." The first twenty years of the twen-tieth century were a peak time for this phenomenon, and World War I created an opportunity for Koreans to carve out a living providing services to American military.

Korean American weddings are known for their efficiency, and ban-quets are not the marathons common to other cultures. Noodle soup is usually served, and a tea ceremony may be performed as a way to honor the parents. Korean cuisine relies heavily on pickled and fermented food, and dessert will include sticky rice cakes with sesame seeds or bean paste. In one old tradition, the groom gives the mother of the bride a goose, as geese mate for life and are symbols of fidelity. Modern grooms may give their mothers-in-law a wooden goose, or a goose motif may be incorporated into table decorations. A groom traditionally gives the bride a piggyback ride as a show of his willingness to care for his new wife, and some families will also have him give rides to her siblings and other family members.

Korean wedding rites will see rice wine poured into cups (historically it was poured into a halved gourd grown by the bride's mother), and the bride and groom each sip from their cups. Then the contents are mixed together and drunk as a symbol of their combined lives.

At the reception, the bride will hold out her wedding gown, or the couple may stretch out a piece of fabric, and family members will toss chestnuts and dates at them. The bride will try to capture as much as she can. The amount she catches will equal the number of children she will bear (chestnuts will be boys, and dates will be girls).

In contemporary South Korea, it has become a trend to hire "role players" to attend wedding ceremonies. To maintain prestige, couples may hire actors to bulk up wedding attendance, and they may be employed secretly by either the bride or the groom. Fake family members, coworkers, or bosses may be asked to assume a certain role or to create a certain effect, all raising prestige in what has been labeled a "hypercompetitive society."[32] Companies perform a similar service in Japan.

OPA!

A demolished homeland, poor economy, and civil war led to Greeks' arrival in the United States in large numbers from the early 1950s into the 1970s.[33] In Greece, a bride smears honey in the shape of a cross on the door of her new home. She then throws a pomegranate at the door, and if seeds stick to the honey, her marriage will be sweet and blessed with children. The bride and groom sometimes eat walnuts, which break into four parts, as a symbol of the bride, the groom, and their two families. In some traditions the bride and her parents drink wine outside her family home before going to the church for the ceremony. The bride throws the glass as a symbol of the end to her life as a single woman.

Greek weddings always feature the breaking of plates. Greek clients may bring their own plates to break, or catering companies, with an eye on legalities and fear of guests being struck by shards, may have plates reserved just for that purpose and a plan in place for minimizing liability.

GERMAN AMERICANS

The first big wave of German immigrants began early in the eighteenth century, and a large percentage settled in Pennsylvania. Most came as family units, with over half already married upon entry. The Germans who arrived between 1720 and 1820 were primarily Christians, with over 60 percent Protestant and a little over 30 percent Catholic. They tended to intermarry and assimilate quickly, especially after World War I, when many worked hard to demonstrate their loyalty to the United States. German women often worked as domestic servants, and the men were traditionally bakers, brewers, and farmers. Germans were always known for their raucous parties and love of food, and Americans, understanding boiled meat and potatoes, found their cuisine less confusing or distasteful than that of other groups. A stream of Germans arrived after World War II; their numbers crested in the 1980s and increased again between 2000 and 2010. They are still concentrated in Pennsylvania, Missouri, Michigan, and Illinois.[34]

REGIONALISM IN THE UNITED STATES

In addition to race and ethnicity, geography looms large as a factor in what families eat and how they celebrate. Wedding venues situated in regions with a definite food identity are especially eager to provide banquet menus that reflect it. Weddings bring visitors from out of town, generate tourism dollars, and can reinforce cultural identity, and food can have much to do with this. Menu items like barbecued brisket in Texas, walleye in Minnesota, maple syrup in Vermont, and clam chowder in Maine often receive a twist either to modernize them or to raise them to a level considered appropriate for a lavish wedding. Wedding receptions in Louisiana, for instance, might include mini muffelattas, andouille sausage, alligator meat, or red-eye gravy. Gumbo or grits might be reworked into more elegant preparations or to incorporate luxury ingredients.

Weddings in the United States are as varied as American culture, and this diversity of traditions is evidenced by the food served. Many Americans were (and are) not pleased with changes wrought on their communities by the arrival of refugees, despite the likelihood that they themselves are descendants of immigrants. Racial and ethnic insults and slurs have often referenced native foods, as evidenced by the terms "krauts, frogs, limeys and fish heads: slurs aimed respectively at Germans, French, English, and Asians. And within the U.S., 'greaser' and 'beaner' are still invectives directed at Latinos."[35] Clearly, scorn for immigrants is not a thing of the past, and as the Muslim population swells and refugees arrive from all over the world, it is a sure bet that the demographics of neighborhoods and workplaces will shift, as they always have. And there will be those who repeat history and lament the lost past, as if change in the American landscape were a new phenomenon.

❦ 9 ❦

Dating and Dining

THE FOOD COURT

Tracing how couples have interacted prior to marriage is one way to understand history, and habits of food consumption indicate how lives were once led.

The current manner of courtship in American society is intertwined with dining. Restaurants are often the location for a first date, as well as common sites for marriage proposals. Dating is a recent phenomenon, however, and a quick review of patterns of courtship will illuminate the important role food plays in betrothal customs.

In the High Middle Ages, knighthood was an occupation for sons in line to inherit their families' estates, leading to a pattern in which men married later in life than women. A knight in Renaissance England could not marry until he was financially independent, meaning that he could not take a wife until after his father had died. This delayed marriage for men of that class and also made for trouble.

As young knights traveled about, they honed their horsemanship and battle skills, using tournaments and informal contests to win reputations for bravery and athleticism. The victor gained the horse and equipment of the loser, so competitions were a way for these young men to earn independent income.[1] This instant cash in a testosterone-fueled culture, however, led to wild behavior for those not reined in by minders hired by their families. Unable to wed, and perhaps flush with money, knights reveled, away from home, gambling, drinking, and womanizing their way across the countryside.

Concurrently, women married early; their parents were anxious to settle their fates, and some were presumably married off before they could become smitten with one of these dashing bachelor knights. Female virginity was staunchly protected, and women were wed young in order to ensure their fertility. So, while knights in the Middle Ages often did not marry until their late thirties or early forties, women married, on average, by age sixteen. Thus, in the 1300s and 1400s, young girls were wed to older men in matches not of romance but of family advancement. The dynamic of the young, frustrated bride, besotted with a dashing yet unattainable knight, and her "cuckolded" older husband is a common trope in stage plays and early literature.

Members of the royal court vied for the favor of the king, whose gifts for loyal service could include land, title, or award of a vocational position (sheriff, steward, constable, and so forth). In terms of moving up the social ranks, however, an arranged marriage, orchestrated by the king, to someone of higher status and wealth was a true achievement. This marriage could produce any of the other attractions, as well as include monetary settlements in the form of a dowry.[2]

The first recorded knighting ceremony may have been when Henry I of England bestowed knighthood on Geoffrey of Anjou, just before he was to wed Henry's daughter Maud (Matilda). Geoffrey, eleven years younger than his once widowed bride, received golden spurs and a special sword, and the week prior to the wedding featured tournaments and banquets celebrating the impending marriage. Thirty of Geoffrey's companions were also knighted, and in addition to horses and arms, they apparently also received unofficial license to carouse. There was much public drunkenness, and the newly entitled bucks also left a wake of "illegitimate" children.[3]

BABIES NEEDED

The bubonic plague decimated the population of Europe, and in the fourteenth century, farms lay barren, with few available hands to work the land. The population needed to replenish, and for this reason, it is believed, sexual mores loosened. Most of the population was illiterate, so few written records exist, but church and civic records indicate that the sexual life of those who were not aristocrats was lively.[4] For the peasantry, pregnancy before marriage was common, as it ensured a woman's fertility. Children were needed to fill farms again with workers.

Prostitution, like premarital sex, was understood to be a fact of life and even regulated by the authorities, who worked to curb venereal disease and keep order. In 1566, Pope Pius V expelled all prostitutes from Rome, but the lost tax income so depleted city coffers that within a month he was inclined to reverse his decree.[5] While women in the upper echelons of society may have been closely guarded, men were not so insulated, and prostitution was tolerated to mollify those who could not marry until later in life, when able to provide a home for a bride.

BIRTH CONTROL

In seventeenth- and eighteenth-century France and England, the population had rebounded, in part due to an explosion of illegitimate births. Many children were abandoned to workhouses and churches, and community resources were stretched to care for the young. Girls were turned over to work "in service" on estates, and many found themselves impregnated by the men of the house, often victims of opportunity and ill equipped to dodge the attentions of persuasive males.

Well into the nineteenth century, domestic service was the primary occupation for females, creating a pool of young women at risk of exploitation with little opportunity for economic resistance.[6] One report holds that in 1836 Paris, one-third of the prostitutes were former servants who had borne babies out of wedlock. Naïve, plagued by economic hardship, and inhabiting a society with increased mobility, they were easily seduced by promises of marriage to social betters.[7]

Soon industrialization spread both in Europe and in the United States, and with it came the availability of some measure of birth control, curbing the birth explosion as well as redefining marriage patterns. Male and female workers were thrown together in large cities; yet, simultaneously, pregnancy out of wedlock became less common and less socially acceptable.

Charles Goodyear's vulcanization process for rubber, patented in 1844, inadvertently revolutionized family planning. Doctors were first allowed to legally prescribe contraceptives (to prevent disease) in 1918; yet the condom industry thrived once new technology allowed for more durable and dependable products. The first rubber condom was produced in 1855, and an early form of a rubber diaphragm was marketed beginning in the 1860s.[8]

The middle class began to grow in numbers, and its members, as always, emulated the characteristics of those above them in the social order. Abandoning a pregnant housemaid was ungentlemanly, and while sexual activity was common, unwanted pregnancies began to taper. Reformers, too, worked to guard against the chaos of a country in flux, and a religious revival, coupled with a wave of immigrants possessing Old World ideals, led to decreased premarital conception.

COURTING

Prior to the turn of the twentieth century, there was no such thing as "dating" in American culture. Traditionally, a young woman may have invited a suitor to her home, but the couple was monitored, and the invitation would have been approved, or even initiated, by her family. "Calling" on a woman may have progressed to "keeping company"; yet even activities outside the family home, such as attending church functions or local dances, were by nature public affairs.[9]

Young people working in factories and living in apartments in cities, however, did not have parents nearby to approve or disapprove of their evening plans. They went to amusement parks, films, music halls, and arcades—with no chaperones to hinder romance or subdue impulses. By 1900, pleasure parks like Coney Island's Luna Park and Dreamland were examples of a thriving leisure industry designed not only to amuse young attendees but also to serve as a place for them to first encounter each other. A proper lady could now meet a man other than through family connections, and this was indeed a major development.[10]

Prohibition had a part to play in the evolution of dating as well. In the 1920s a vibrant youth culture glamorized drinking; formerly perceived as a substance imbibed only in sinister, men-only saloons, alcohol became associated with carefree cocktail parties for both sexes. Drinking became as much a recreation as the new amusement parks, and both legal restaurants and illegal speakeasies were quick to court the economic value of a consumer class that practiced this new custom of "dating." Venues were also quick to welcome unescorted females—unheard of in the past for reputable women. Contact between men and women increased with the advent of a drinking culture, as did contact between differing classes and races.[11]

By the 1930s, a couple could "go steady," meaning they were exclusive, and if they were of marriageable age, this would often lead to a formal engagement. Prior to this time, the teen years had entailed no special privileges or characteristics. The concept of the "teenager" began to brew in 1904 when psychologist Stanley Hall identified these years as a specific period in human development. His studies, which identified teens as a specific group, coincided with other factors, such as a move toward standardized compulsory education in the 1920s and a dramatic increase in high school attendance by 1930. Children could not be kept away from school in order to work on the farm, and school performance came to reflect on parents' respectability. Government-mandated schooling triggered a new dating arena as well. American high schools were being built in unparalleled numbers, strengthening an "adolescent peer culture" and creating a pool of dating candidates.[12]

The new importance of automobiles ushered in a novel form of privacy for people on dates, and the popularity of these "bedrooms on wheels" flourished with rising affluence after World War II. Researchers Cele C. Otnes and Elizabeth H. Pleck note that dates to public venues such as baseball games and amusement parks eventually came to seem unromantic. Dinner in a restaurant, preferably a fancy one, became a "dating ideal."[13]

WHAT DO YOU WANT TO EAT?

This brings us to what Martin King Whyte deemed a "marketplace learning viewpoint," wherein dining at various locations with assorted companions could be considered a form of spouse-specific consumerism, likened to the manner in which a shopper buys various breakfast cereals before deciding on a favorite brand.[14] Whyte ultimately concluded that this "marketplace" mentality did not necessarily lead to longer, happier marriages for the group members he polled. Shopping around does not make for better decision making, but it does delay marital age and add to a consumer culture. Whyte concluded that marital success is greatly determined by a couple's ability to share in decision making and by compatibility in their daily lives. Deciding what to eat, whether on a date or once married, is a reoccurring act that reveals a couple's ability to compromise.

ARRANGED MARRIAGES

American culture has never been enthusiastic about formalized, arranged marriages, but this convention has always existed in some form, and for many, arranged marriages have enabled a better life and ensured a continuity of family ties. Immigrants from South Asia are especially known for using arranged marriages as a tool for preserving cultural identity in America, and their prevalence is not necessarily an indicator of "old-fashionedness." Participants can often refuse a mate chosen by their family, and candidates are well vetted. Even as numerous immigrants embrace modernity, the desire for a traditional marriage and a match that will please family members is very strong.

Professional matchmakers can be hired, but the Internet has stepped in as well. On one popular matchmaking website, Shaadi.com, a consumer can choose from categories such as "Mother Tongue" (such as Bengali, Gujarati, and Hindi) or "Religion" (including Sikhism, Jainism, Islam, and Judaism). Shaadi.com (which translates to "Marriage.com") advertises itself as "the largest and most trusted matrimonial service for Indian communities." It was launched in the United States in 1996, and at the time, 70 percent of its profiles were posted by family members of the intended. By 2012, about 80 percent were being posted by the eligible singles themselves.[15] Shaadi Centre is an offshoot and includes the use of personal advisors, called "relationship managers," who can comb a network of marriage bureaus across India. Another service provided by Shaadi Centre is Swyamvar, a type of speed dating involving both children and their parents. At a Swyamvar function, participants receive profile booklets, introduce themselves, and speak of the qualities they are seeking in a mate. They break for dinner and then mingle, after which they make known whom they would like to meet formally.

Jews have a long tradition of matchmaking, and websites such as SawYouAtSinai.com offer Shabbat singles events advertising "great food, great company." Companies such as JRetroMatch and Chai Expectations also combine online dating technology with matchmaking "advisors" who review profiles and present clients only after they have been interviewed or approved.

DATING AND RESTAURANTS

No matter how a couple has met, they must get through their first date. The most popular place for a first date varies according to the source, but food venues, not leisure activities like the amusement parks and baseball games of the past, top the list. A poll of 200,000 people, according to the dating app Clover, suggests that women who have met someone online prefer to meet face to face for the first time at a coffee shop, whereas men prefer a restaurant.[16] This can probably be explained by "safety" issues for women, who prefer to meet a stranger in the most public of places. It may also be a way to escape quickly should things not go well. A meal can last a long time if participants are uncomfortable, and a bill for coffee is certainly a lot easier and quicker to settle than a dinner check.

DINNER ROLES

In 1943, renowned anthropologist Margaret Mead dissected how families develop patterns of eating, noting that certain foods become imbued with certain characteristics. In *Dinner Roles: American Women and Culinary Culture*, author Sherrie A. Inness also writes of foods that society considers "male" and "female." Red meat, particularly beef steaks, is valued above all other foods and is therefore "manly" food. The outdoor barbecue is the realm of the contented suburban male, who may grill his steaks with no fear of emasculation.[17] Game, like rabbit and duck, even if bought at the store, is also "masculine," as are hearty foods like chili and stew.

> In North American food patterns, the father presides over meat and fish, the mother over milk, vegetables, fruit juices and liver, while adolescents tend to demonstrate their independence by refusing to eat what is good for them.
>
> —Margaret Mead, "The Problem of Changing Food Habits," 1943[18]

I'LL JUST HAVE THE SALAD

Maggiano's Little Italy, a small restaurant chain, featured a "Venus Is for Women, Mars Is for Men Menu" at its Houston location in 2005. This menu illustrates common associations of certain foods with one gender or another. The "Venus" menu includes salad, chicken picatta, spinach, and tiramisu. The "Mars" menu has stuffed mushrooms, lasagna, beef medallions, and cheesecake.[19] Heavier foods and meat, like backyard barbecuing, are typically assigned masculine attributes.

The writer and celebrity epicure James Beard had a culinary career that spanned from the 1940s into the 1980s. His string of successful cookbooks, with titles such as *Treasures of Outdoor Cooking*, *Fowl and Game Cookery*, and *The Complete Book of Outdoor Cookery*, positioned certain foods as decidedly masculine. Red meat, game, and whole fish, especially if prepared on the grill, were presented like spoils brought back from the hunt rather than bought at the supermarket.

The dust jacket for *Cook It Outdoors* (1941) proclaimed the volume "a man's book written by a man who understands not only the healthy outdoor eating and cooking habits, but who is an expert at the subtle nuances of tricky flavoring as well. And it will be invaluable to the woman who aims to please the masculine members of the household."[20] In the same work, Beard wrote, "Let the husband control the fire, and the wife the kitchen."[21]

In 1955 Beard collaborated with Helen Evans Brown to produce *The Complete Book of Outdoor Cookery*, whose preface (altered in later versions) stated, "We believe that charcoal cookery is primarily a man's job, and that a woman, if she's smart, will keep it that way." The cover art for Beard's cookbooks is a parade of images of raw meat, flames, burlap bags, and wooden cutting boards, manly images meant to assure male readers that cooking could be masculine.

Beard, who was openly gay, peppered his works with hardy assurances that cooking well was economical and that common sense in the kitchen could make for happy, simple eating. This was a departure from the tone employed in competing publications, which so often tied cooking to pleasing others, entreating the cook to be a good host and to use cookery to earn family members' respect and love.

In 1946, James Beard hosted *I Love to Eat*, an early television cooking show with a telling name. Beard seemed to make food for himself to enjoy, not merely to nurture others. This model was unusual for the era, and it was surely no coincidence that a male took the stance of eater rather than provider.

It would be years before cooking shows became more than a source for serious people to learn serious cooking methods and instead broadly peddled the mentality that cooking was an interactive pleasure. When the Food Network exploded onto the scene in the 1990s, part of its evolution was the shift away from teaching viewers how to cook toward showing them people eating, traveling, and cooking for entertainment.

MARRIAGE PROPOSALS

Valentine's Day is widely considered the most popular day for popping the question; yet statistics on this topic vary according to source. Thanksgiving, surprisingly, comes in second nationally, according to *Nation's Restaurant News*.[22] The Internet reservation service Open Table reports that Valentine's Day is by far the most popular day for marriage proposals, with February 15 and New Year's Eve close behind. In some reports Christmas Eve nudges Valentine's Day out.

Eiffel Tower, a restaurant overlooking the Bellagio fountains in Las Vegas, reportedly hosted the most marriage proposals in the country for 2014: 138 hopefuls booked reservations with the intent of proposing, and surely the restaurant was not informed at the time of many more.[23] In 2015, $500 bought a complete "marriage proposal package," which included a set menu, champagne, roses, and a photographer poised to capture the occasion.[24]

In 2016, Eiffel Tower's website advertised the option to have the wedding ceremony at the restaurant, which, for $1,000, included a bouquet, a boutonniere (or a combination thereof), and an officiant to do the honors. The couple would be seated at a window table overlooking the Las Vegas strip and served a custom dinner comprising dishes from the *Eiffel Tower Restaurant Cook Book*, a bottle of champagne, a photo package, and a copy of the aforementioned cookbook. In a nod to technology, a live video-streaming option could be added.

The popularity of getting married in a luxury restaurant, with only the couple present, highlights the use of food to indicate a special occasion and to demarcate lavishness. Yet such indulgence is achieved with less expense than having a pared-down formal wedding attended by a crowd. Sharing the photos and videos via social media satisfies the desire to "show" peers that a wedding has been deluxe.

Open Table reported that the second most sought-after venue for betrothals is the River Café in Brooklyn, followed by The View, also in New York City. Clearly tourism and population density skew statistics, and most cities invariably have their own lists of "most romantic" restaurants. They all share commonalities, however, in terms of what is deemed "romantic."

A dramatic view lends itself to passion, particularly if it comes from a tower. Sky City Restaurant (at the top of the Space Needle in Seattle), Top of the Hub (on the fifty-second floor of Boston's Prudential Building), or Spindletop (on the thirty-fourth floor of the Hyatt in Houston) all make the list of the top twenty American engagement locales for 2015. A view of water helps: Bertrand at Mister A's (on the San Diego harbor) and Latitudes in Key West (overlooking the Gulf of Mexico) also top national proposal destinations. Other aesthetic effects that lend to a romantic mood in dining are the presence of fireplaces, candlelight, and soft music.

THAT OLD TRICK

Food is often incorporated into marriage proposals, and wedding guides are replete with suggestions such as tucking a "Will you marry me?" message into a fortune cookie or having the words written in chocolate sauce on the dessert tray. Substituting a ring for a wrapped chocolate in a box is common, and for the less glamorous, a lover may find a ring in the egg carton at home or inside a Cracker Jack box at the ball park.

Radius, a Boston restaurant, reported to *Restaurant Business* that it keeps congratulatory cards on hand, and, when made aware that a proposal has occurred, employees rush over with complimentary champagne and a card signed by the staff.[25] Probably millions of engagement rings have been dropped into wine glasses across the globe; yet not everyone is a fan. Hubert Keller, chef and owner of the now closed Fleur de Lys in San Francisco, led the charge to refuse this practice, wisely noting the potential for swallowed diamond rings and lawsuits.[26]

Clearly food consumption is intertwined with courtship, and special foods and locations may serve as indicators of romance. Marriage proposals are especially tied in with restaurant culture, and, as in the case of Eiffel Tower restaurant, wedding vows may even be exchanged at the table.

CHEFS NEED LOVE TOO

Musclebound chef Robert Irvine, of Food Network television show *Dinner: Impossible*, wed professional wrestler Gail Kim in 2012. His best man was fellow Food Network star chef Guy Fieri. The nuptials, held at Charles Krug Winery in Napa, were attended by a bevy of wrestlers, who probably made a big dent in the sushi station led by celebrity chef and restaurateur Masaharu Morimoto. Most restaurant employees who wed one another are not celebrities, of course, but many couples have met while preparing a nuptial feast for others.

KISS THE COOK

The pervasiveness of romance between restaurant employees is derived from several factors, the primary one being the young age of many workers, meaning that much of the staff working in the hospitality industry is unmarried or unattached. According to the Bureau of Labor Statistics, in 2014 over 23 percent of the restaurant workforce was between twenty-five and thirty-four years old, and another 24 percent was between twenty and twenty-four years old.[27] Census reports show the average age of a first marriage in this decade hovers at twenty-six for women and twenty-eight for men.[28]

Anecdotally, many "front of the house" restaurant staff (e.g., servers, hostesses, bartenders) are physically attractive, a politically incorrect and unfair actuality. This is especially apparent in New York City and Los Angeles, where personnel often include actors and models who find the flexible hours and fast cash of the hospitality industry appealing. Restaurant personnel often refer to themselves as "vampires," coming out to work their shifts at night. In tandem with long hours and easily accessible liquor, propriety is easily eroded. The prevalence of those involved in the arts is also conducive to a generally diverse and culturally accepting environment.

The professional chef's hero, Anthony Bourdain, writes that restaurants attract an "elevated level of tolerance for eccentricity."[29] He goes on to categorize cooking staff into three groups. There are the artists, who are a high-minded lot; the exiles, who are unable to function in traditional jobs; and the mercenaries, who merely work in restaurants to make a good living, recognizing the opportunity the business affords them while negotiating the idiosyncrasies of the former two categories.[30]

A busy night in a kitchen is frequently compared to a battle, and in fact the classic kitchen "brigade," the hierarchical system of command (chef, sous chef, chef de cuisine) was perfected by Auguste Escoffier, who modeled the structure on his recent military service. Restaurant staff work in close, hot quarters, under pressure, in what one writer calls a "war game mentality" that fosters intimacy.[31] One restaurateur even joked that everyone has a preferred location for workplace trysts—"usually it's in the dry storage or the wine cellar."[32]

One poll reports that one-third of couples in workplace romances eventually marry and, again, relate that their romance was bolstered by "repeated exposure" to one another, physical proximity, and shared experience.[33]

One Chicago-area chef has reported that he and his now wife first consummated their romance on a sack of potatoes in their restaurant's storage closet—an act now reenacted yearly on their wedding anniversary.[34]

NO BODY KNOWS THE TRUFFLES I'VE SEEN

Certain foods are thought to inspire love, such as soufflés, platters of oysters on the half shell, and racks of lamb sliced tableside, and restaurants known for romance often feature these items. Lobster reigns as the most romantic entrée item, but lavish foods like foie gras, caviar, figs, truffles, and dark chocolate connote romance and are staples on Valentine's Day menus. Chocolate fondue, chocolate-covered strawberries, and chocolate molten lava cake are ubiquitous. Chocolate truffles are named after the fungi truffles that grow underground in a symbiotic relationship with the roots of certain trees. Both chocolate and truffles are commonly served at luxury weddings, and examining them sharpens insight into contemporary wedding culture.

Truffles have long been known for their "sexiness." In 1825 the French writer and gourmand Jean Anthelme Brillat-Savarin mused about the mystery of truffles, noting that "none understand how it's born or how it develops," and recounted the tale of a friend so enflamed with truffle-induced ardor that she nearly lost control of herself.[35] The Vatican weighed in on the ingestion of truffles, as did Islamic imams, all agreeing that their use ignited desire and could only lead to sexual misadventures. Even the Marquis de Sade employed truffles to "soften up" his victims.[36]

Truffles are expensive, difficult to acquire, seasonal, and somewhat mysterious. They are found in northern Spain, northern Italy, and Croatia, but are not exclusive to Europe, growing from Botswana to New Zealand to Oregon, and they are an ancient delicacy in the Middle East.[37] Their specialness lies in the difficulty of producing them, as they cannot be "planted." They require specific underground conditions in which to grow, a complex ecosystem that is difficult to replicate.

TRUFFLE TRADITION

Once a ground area has been intentionally inoculated with the truffle spore, it takes six years to see results. Animals are needed to force dispersal of the spores, and this delicate cycle has made forced cultivation a contentious issue.[38] Mass production has been curtailed by traditional growers who want to keep their output low and thereby force high product prices. Efforts to grow the delicacy have also been confounding, especially for North American growers. Chefs prefer European truffles, and their customers are willing to pay exorbitant prices for them.

In 2014, Spanish black truffles were selling for a minimum wholesale price of approximately $16 an ounce, and Italian winter truffles fetch significantly more.[39] White truffles are particularly elusive, and in 2014, Sotheby's sold the largest recorded white truffle on record. Tipping the scales at over four pounds, it fetched $61,250, working out to nearly $1,000 an ounce.[40]

HOG VERSUS DOG

Growers know they have truffles from knowing the history of their land; yet humans cannot detect where exactly the pungent nuggets lie. We need help from the animal kingdom for that. Traditionally, pigs have been used to "hunt" for truffles, their astute noses rooting out the prize (more than one chef has called overweight customers "truffle hunters"). Female pigs do not need to be "trained" to root for truffles, as their odor mimics that of a male's sex pheromones. However, pigs are, well, pigs, so it is a challenge to get them to cease and desist once they locate their quarry.

Dogs can also be effective truffle hunters, although they do not crave the fungi with the passion of pigs. Driven to please their handlers, they will happily yield their catch. Like any working dog, they must possess a hunting drive. The very specific training required to master the task of truffle hunting is very expensive if done by a professional, so do-it-yourselfers have jumped in. One novice trainer lamented the hours put into training, recounting that his dog, after successfully locating a single truffle, considered his mission accomplished and immediately went to take a long dog nap.[41]

Truffles still remain a source of wonder. Horticulturalists do understand how they are grown now, but their production remains difficult to master and their production expensive, planting them firmly in the category of luxury and special-occasion foods. It is ironic, too, that their scent suggests love for at least some animals.

CHOCOLATE

Chocolate is, of course, closely associated with romance, and it, too, was historically a luxury item, expensive and unattainable for the masses. Making cacao beans palatable requires labor, and although chocolate has always been consumed, it has not long been accessible to most people. Aztecs are known for introducing it to the world; yet only the most prestigious Aztecs and other Mesoamericans had access. Only the most elite tables featured chocolate, likely served in liquid form, at the end of an Aztec meal, with tobacco—a sort of ancient form of brandy and cigars after dinner.[42]

In order to be sweet, chocolate requires the addition of sugar, another expensive item not historically available to the public, which further added to chocolate's exclusivity. Like the Aztecs, Americans traditionally considered "chocolate" more a beverage than a food, and usage of the word has shifted. *The White House Cook Book* of 1913, for example, includes a recipe for "chocolate" that calls for grating it into a pan and adding milk and sugar to make what we now call "hot chocolate." *Smiley's Cook Book and Universal Household Guide* (1901) and the *Hotel St. Francis Cook Book* (1919) have mirror recipes for making "chocolate," as do many other works of the era.

THAT'S A WRAP

Well past the turn of the twentieth century, shopkeepers were likely to keep a chunk of chocolate behind the counter, requiring a hammer to chisel out portions for waiting consumers. The advent and popularity of the chocolate bar is another example of how marketing can affect consumerism. The ceaseless efforts of entrepreneur Milton Hershey created the phenomenon of individually wrapped chocolate with a recognizable logo and a standard size and price.[43] Hershey had hustled to win the contract to supply "emergency ration" chocolate for the troops overseas in World War I, and this cemented America's love affair with chocolate. Men came home with a taste for it, as well as a penchant for a comfortingly predictable prewrapped product.[44] The inexpensive manufacturing processes of an industrializing era democratized chocolate, but it retained its "specialness," as it was still sweet and sugary and could not be "grown" at home. Obtaining chocolate required a commercial exchange.

LUXURY IS KEY

Expensive food such as truffles, chocolate, and champagne all connote the specialness of an occasion, and their purchase can illustrate affection, the willingness to pay for them signaling initial attraction or continued devotion. Serving them at a wedding celebration can connote luxury and indicate that the hosts have found economic success. If striving brides and grooms have not yet achieved this success, they may aspire to and hope to project their ambitions and attract the like-minded.

Proposing marriage in a luxury restaurant is a popular practice, and its emergence can be linked to a bridal industry, and an American culture as a whole, that increasingly requires participants to assume an amount of temporary celebrity. Being the center of attention requires that a betrothal be witnessed and documented, and indulgence foods are often included in setting the stage for these endeavors, lending a flavor of sumptuousness to an already special affair.

❦ *10* ❦

Champagne Anyone?

The Toast

*B*everages are important at wedding receptions, and how freely the drinks flow, in alcohol-drinking cultures, is a candid indicator of the wedding budget. Catering venues often offer a cocktail hour before opening the doors to the seating area, and drinks may include champagne flowing from fountains or vodka streaming down carved ice sculpture "runways." The wedding toast, a focal point of the reception, stems from a time when unions between members of warring factions could serve to forge peace. The father of the bride drank from a communal cup, proving the wine was not poisoned. The clinking glasses, wine spilling from one glass to another, may also have helped ensure that drinks were not contaminated. The term "toast" may date from a time when spirits were often rancid, and a piece of spiced bread was put into the cup to improve the flavor.

Toasting at celebrations is ancient and nearly universal, and its appeal may lie in that it includes all five senses: taste, sight, touch, and smell, complemented by inspirational words and the sound of the glasses clinking.[1] Toasting superstitions abound, one being that the clinking of glass scares away evil spirits or the Devil, said to be repelled by bell-like sounds.

The touching of glasses can be considered a form of contact and sharing, but it has the sanitary benefit of stopping short of drinking from a common vessel. The practice of smashing glasses, prevalent in Russia, among other places, is an extension of this concept, the breakage lending finality to an oath and establishing that no other toast from that same glass can diminish or compete with the last pledge.[2] Many Polish Americans present bread and salt to newlyweds arriving at a reception, with the bread representing a life with no hunger and salt acting as a reminder of life's struggles. Next the couple is given two glasses, one filled with vodka and one with water. The bride, not knowing which is which, chooses one and drinks it, while the groom gets the remaining glass. Whoever gets the vodka, it is said, will be the boss at home. After the toast, the glasses are smashed, and if they break, it brings good luck.[3]

Some regions in Italy also have the tradition of shattering the glass after toasting, with the fragments counted and meant to symbolize the number of years the couple will be together. Jewish weddings include the ceremonial drinking of wine or juice from Kiddush cups, and after the blessings, the groom breaks the cup with his right foot, as remembrance of either the destruction of the Temple in Jerusalem or the fragility of life. Anyone who has spent time working in the hospitality business knows that the glass, wrapped in a linen napkin and broken symbolically, is usually a lightbulb, which breaks easily, does not create sharp shards, and is inexpensive.

Contemporary culture has appropriated and revised traditions like toasting, with a noteworthy example being the modern practice of "pouring one out," in which alcohol is tipped out onto the ground in a salute to a lost loved one or friend. The deceased hip-hop artist Tupac Shakur rapped about this in 1994's "Pour Out a Little Liquor."[4] In Shakur's accompanying music video, the performers seem to be drinking "forties" (large forty-ounce bottles, usually containing malt liquor like Old English or Mickey's Big Mouth) out of paper bags.

A rap song in context with a wedding toast may at first seem a stretch, but libation rituals are traditional in African weddings and common in modern African American ceremonies. In all instances the beverage is poured out, and in fact wasted, so that the *lack* of drinking more than drinking carries significance and pays homage to those unable to be present.

DRUNK

Revolutionary-era weddings featured a punch made from Jamaican spirits, and once the punch bowl was emptied, it was common for the men to race one another; the winner, the fastest who displayed the least signs of drunkenness, received a bottle of wine as a prize.[5] Public drunkenness has had varying degrees of acceptability throughout the ages, and weddings are a well-known occasion for overimbibing.

SOME HISTORY

There is a story that in the eleventh century Princess Matilda of Flanders rebuffed William the Conqueror when he proposed to her, but after he angrily pitched her into the mud and beat her, she was so smitten with his manliness that she agreed to marry him. The festivities, circa 1051, included streets laid with ductwork in which wine flowed for all to share. Royals and the wealthy often provided free wine (and food) for the masses on their wedding days, sponsoring street parties and carnivals at which citizens toasted the health and future fertility of party sponsors.[6]

William the Conqueror, also known as William the Bastard, eventually became the king of England, despite never learning English and preferring life in Normandy. His ascent to the monarchy was clouded by his illegitimacy, which perhaps made him particularly eager to ply a suspicious public with spirits.

Linguist Dan Jurafsky writes that contemporary herb-infused liquors, ciders, and signature cocktails actually hale from a 9,000-year-old tradition of mixed drinks. Herb-infused wines and honeyed beers were made over 4,000 years ago. The wassails of the court of Henry VII and the spiced wine of the eighteenth century all derived from the ancient practice of distilling fermented drinks in order to increase alcohol content.[7]

Just as food was long considered medicinal, so was alcohol, and it was standard for midwives to prescribe spiced wine or rum for women in labor. One childbirth manual recommended sage ale every morning when a woman was first known to be pregnant to "strengthen the womb."[8]

Historian Margaret Visser notes that at varying times in history, women have not been included in the drinking of toasts, and English etiquette mandated that should a woman be the subject of a toast, she was merely to smile in response. Men would raise a glass to the thought of an absent woman, drinking to the beautiful "toast of the town." As etiquette rules got more rigorous in the late 1800s, it was deemed ungentlemanly to mention a woman in a toast at all, as toasting became regarded as unrefined.[9]

SPARKLING WINE

Remember gentlemen, it's not just France we are fighting for, it's champagne!

—Winston Churchill, 1918

Champagne is emblematic of celebrations of all kinds, and the pop of the cork is closely associated with weddings. Oxford University professor Charles Spence researched the relationship between sound and food and proved that the flavor is enhanced when a particular sound is heard during consumption. For example, bacon's flavor is intensified if it is heard sizzling in the pan, and potato chips taste better if they make a crunchy sound when chewed.[10]

In order to be true champagne, the wine must come from the Champagne region in northern France and comprise certain grapes (Pinot noir, Pinot Meunier, or Chardonnay), and specific bottling and manufacturing processes add to the cost of producing it. Products not meeting these criteria are considered "sparkling wine."

SIZE MATTERS

Champagne, like all commercial wine, is bottled in standard sizes. One bottle contains a little over twenty-five ounces (750 milliliters), equaling about five portions. It is also available in bigger sizes, which are used for special occasions. A Magnum is equivalent to two standard bottles, and the Jeroboam equals four. The biblical names continue on up to the Balthazar, which holds twelve bottles of bubbly. The Nebuchadnezzar (king of Babylon) holds the equivalent of a whopping twenty bottles and can fill one hundred glasses.[11]

BUBBLES

As for chilling the bottles in readiness for weddings, sparkling wine bottles are thicker than traditional wine bottles, so they need to get on ice sooner than those holding flat wine. Cold helps preserve bubbles, so champagne is served as cold as possible. One glass has 100 million bubbles, according to a French physic professor who conducts "bubble research."[12]

Speaking of bubbles, a glass with a smaller opening (not the stereotypical wide-rimmed coupe glass) lets bubbles escape. As for popping the cork, it should be released quietly. Caterers will perhaps sacrifice an inexpensive bottle for the "sound" of the pop and then have staff quietly open the bottles to be poured. Wine expert Karen MacNeil writes that more than one Frenchman has advised her that "a Champagne bottle, correctly opened, should make a sound no greater than that of a contented woman's sigh. French men are French men after all."[13]

HISTORY OF THE BUBBLY

Dom Pierre Pérignon, called the "father of sparkling wine," was a Benedictine monk and cellar master of the Hautvillers Abbey in the Champagne district. Throughout his tenure, which began in 1668, he worked to find ways to keep wine from oxidizing, experimenting with glass containers in place of barrels and with corking methods.

In 1728, the French king Louis XV standardized wine bottle sizes (the imaginative naming of them came later), issuing an edict that allowed for the sale of individual bottles, which required corks. Prior to that, wines from Champagne had only been sold in barrels, which could be easily counted and therefore taxed. Workers who handled these new bottles, with stoppers held in place with twine, well knew the danger of exploding corks. One wine tradesmen reported in the nineteenth century that workers wore wire masks and that he knew of "a cellar in which there are three men who have each lost an eye."[14]

Improved glass technology allowed France to ship champagne abroad, and the distinctive "pop" of the cork was met with amusement. It became especially popular in England and quickly became fashionable.

As early as 1881 the use of champagne at festive gatherings was "a charming fashion that is beginning to be more common."[15] Champagnes, such as "dry" and "extra dry," were especially created to appeal to the tastes of specific markets, and producers made conscious efforts to position champagne as an item suitable for respectable women.[16] Intentionally marketing their product as symbolic of leisure time, champagne salespeople associated the beverage with horse racing, boating, and hunting. The bridal business aggressively advertised it as ladylike and sophisticated.[17] Luxury products, which entail paying a premium for something unnecessary, undoubtedly rely heavily on advertising and maintaining the notion that a particular product commands status. Here the champagne industry has excelled.

Champagne houses, in what researcher Kolleen M. Guy calls the "monk myth," elevated the legend of the long-dead Dom Pérignon to market their wares. By the 1860s, industry pamphlets told the tale of Pérignon, now blind with heightened senses of smell and taste, which explained his supernatural wine-making abilities. This aggressive marketing campaign lent champagne a spiritual air, considering it had been "invented" by a sightless, toiling man of the cloth. In 1910, the Universal Exposition (the World's Fair), held in Brussels, featured an "authentic reproduction" of the abbey in which he toiled, with wine barrels and presses said to have been used by the monk himself.[18] Jay Z would be proud.

Manufacturers as early as the 1800s hired celebrities to endorse their products, and champagne bottles featured labels depicting any number of lords, earls, and viscounts, the stars of the time.[19] As evidenced by the "cash for title" phenomenon, money was running out for the gentry in Europe, so one can imagine they were happy to get paid for sipping champagne. Modern celebrities, "famous for doing nothing," are not a new invention. Like some contemporary socialites, titled aristocracy might become well known just for being born wealthy.

A recent report of the Association of Hispanic Advertising Agencies noted that large American corporations devoted only 3.2 percent of advertising dollars to targeting Hispanics, as opposed to 13.5 percent for the general public. One major exception has been the firm of Veuve Clicquot, the world's third best-selling champagne in America. In recent years, Veuve Clicquot has spent close to 6 percent of its annual budget targeting Hispanics.[20]

THE CHAMPAGNE WIDOWS

The champagne Veuve Clicquot is named for the widow Nicole Ponsardin Clicquot, whose young husband died and left her to run the family winery. Riddling, the process for removing yeast particles that make sparkling wine cloudy, was perfected in her cellars in 1816.[21] The ability to rid wine of murky sediment, combined with improved technology that allowed for the manufacture of clear, inexpensive glass (for use in both bottling and drinkware), gave rise to the model of effervescent wine we use for toasting today.

Clicquot was the first of a string of widows who took over some of the great champagne houses of France, with the list including such famous last names as Pommery, Olry-Roederer, and Bollinger. Odette Pol-Roger took on her duties after the death of her husband in 1956. Prior to this, she had worked with the French Resistance during World War II, running messages via twelve-hour bicycle rides to Paris.[22] There must be something in the water in Champagne.

PROHIBITION

On January 16, 1920, the United States went dry. Passage of the Eighteenth Amendment was commemorated with mock funerals at bars and restaurants. In *Appetite City*, William Grimes writes that the Park Avenue Hotel draped tables and walls in black fabric, with "mourners" filing past a coffin filled with liquor bottles.[23]

Prohibition was hard on fine-dining restaurants in particular, as they counted on liquor sales to make a profit, and their recipes often depended on wine or spirits to prepare classic French cuisine. Chefs were forced either to cook creatively or to find a supply of alcohol, and waitstaff who had made a living in fine dining rooms preparing flambéed items like cherries jubilee or crêpes suzette lost their jobs.[24] In his Prohibition-era cookbook, the chef of the Hotel St. Francis in San Francisco wrote, "The recipes in my book calling for wines and liqueurs for flavoring may be followed by those whose legitimate supplies are not yet used up."[25] This winking reference to inevitable alcohol use (it was not, after all, illegal to have alcohol—only to make, transport, or sell it) was typical. The Volstead Act, passed to clarify the amendment, allowed people to keep alcohol purchased prior to July 1, 1919, so imbibers had six months to do some earnest stockpiling! Surely many families stocked up for impending wedding celebrations. There is little reason to suppose that wedding parties were bereft of champagne toasts.

MARRIED AND DRINKING

The Anti-Saloon League warned that women who drank were tempting misadventure and cautioned that alcohol inflamed female "sex impulses." Alcohol use was tied to promiscuity, and it was considered women's work to monitor societal morality. Nineteenth-century author Lydia Maria Child serves as an early prototype of the sturdy American woman whose frugality could shepherd a virtuous family through hard times. Child's "hard-core" cooking employed nose-to-tail cookery long before it was fashionable. As one researcher noted when reviewing his subject's cooking prowess, "Child put readers on notice that should the eyes drop out of a roasting pig, it was surely one-half done."[26] Child's writings championed a healthy diet as a means to overall health and cemented the American ideal that a man would do well to procure a bride whose adroit cooking ensured the survival of his offspring.

Lydia Maria Child married for love, against the advice of her affluent parents, and embarked on a life that kept her on the fringes of poverty. *The American Frugal Housewife* indeed includes a chapter titled "How to Endure Poverty." Her treatises on slavery, feminism, and the rights of Native Americans were high-minded; yet Child's domestic advice did not exist in a vacuum. Her arguments for social reform did not reside in a realm wholly separate from the kitchen. Child's body of work, encompassing poetry, recipes, medical advice, and political essays, reflected an American psyche that considered bodies and minds as a unit in need of discipline to retain order. The theme of restraint, applied to staid wedding feasts for so long, is rooted in this mentality. Author Frederick Kaufman ingeniously calls Child "a cross between Susan Sontag and Suzanne Somers, an intelligent writer who was a celebrity, a hostess, a diet-book writer, and a cultural critic."[27]

IT SEEMS THAT BRIDES LIKE TO DRINK TOO

By the mid-1920s, respect for the "noble experiment" had begun to erode, especially among the middle classes, who had tired of ubiquitous organized crime (empires built on bootlegging) and the violent raids conducted by the "dry" police.[28] Instead of purifying the masses, temperance made contempt for the law an ordinary part of life. Drinking became "fun," a forbidden fruit whose pursuit promised adventure for individuals who ordinarily never flouted the rules.[29] Again, the call for restraint runs all through America's relationship with food, and we see this pattern of restraint versus excess played out repeatedly in dining habits, particularly in wedding food traditions.

Brides who tipped back cocktails and danced in speakeasies had reason to embrace the freedoms offered by a new and more open American sensibility. Historian (and longtime editor of *Harper's Magazine*) Frederick Allen Lewis attributed women's newfound boldness to the scars of World War I, suggesting that women were merely infected with the same feelings of urgency for gratification that propelled war-weary men. Rushed weddings borne of eleventh-hour alliances, fueled by the danger of the battlefield, made for a population interested in embracing new and exhilarating experiences.[30] The image of rabid women rampaging into taverns in a fury (à la Carrie Nation) has indeed been burned into the public consciousness, but they were not particularly effective. These women were a small, albeit vocal, faction of reformers, and females did not even have voting rights when the Eighteenth Amendment was ratified. Despite being cast as shrieking anti-alcohol pundits, prim, formidable ladies who decried the violent actions associated with temperance activism had founded organizations such as the Women's Organization for National Prohibition Reform.

Conflicts of race, gender, and class simmered in America, at odds with the ease and assumed sense of refinement for those ensconced in the dining rooms of luxury hotels. A national diet mania began in the 1920s; women wanted a slim figure for the fitted skirts of the flapper look. A desire for modernity promoted a rejection of "old-fashioned" farm food, and processed goods signaled that modernity. Regional food tastes continued to blur as fast trains carted processed items across the country. Manufacturers convinced citizens that store-bought items, prepared in sanitary workshops by modern professionals, were superior.[31]

PROHIBITION WAS A FAMILY AFFAIR

Clever wine producers sold grape juice and blocks of dried grapes with labels that warned purchasers not to add water or yeast or the grapes would ferment and turn to wine. Some statistics show that wine consumption in the United States almost doubled by 1930.[32] America kept right on drinking. Researcher Eric Burns writes that Americans who had not hoarded alcohol for either personal or commercial use began *their* adjustment to a dry country at 12:01 a.m. on the day the Volstead Act came into effect.[33] The making of homemade alcohol was a family affair, with bathtubs all over the country filled with experimental batches of everything from beer to gin, wine, and any manner of moonshine.

> Mother's in the kitchen
> Washing out the jugs;
> Sisters in the pantry
> Bottling the suds;
> Father's in the cellar
> Mixing up the hops;
> Johnny's on the front porch
> Watching for the cops.
>
> —A popular folksong in the 1920s[34]

Alcohol was everywhere during Prohibition; yet only the privileged were able to get their hands on quality liquor. The bootlegging business was thriving, and unscrupulous suppliers poisoned more than a few unwitting customers. It is often said that Americans drank more during Prohibition, which is untrue. The context of drinking did change, however, and ironically the middle class became more exposed in the 1920s to alcohol, which became less associated with vagrants. Americans as a whole were indeed drinking less, but a forceful and educated youth culture romanticized a carefree lifestyle and eroded stereotypes that associated alcohol with tramps and dingy saloons. Two out of three college students drank during Prohibition,[35] which thus had much to do with a new commingling of the sexes. The consumption of illegal alcohol fostered a sense of cohesion as rule-breaking hurried intimacy in public venues.

REPEAL

When passage of the Twenty-First Amendment repealed Prohibition in 1933, the glee expressed in the bridal industry was explosive. No call to hock alcohol went unanswered. Champagne producers Mumm and Moët & Chandon advertised relentlessly in bridal magazines, and the frequency of alcohol ads in these periodicals was astounding. An article on anniversaries advised the bride to reserve five boxes of cake servings and to eat one with her husband on their first, second, and third anniversaries. Then she should open the fourth box on her tenth anniversary, and the fifth box on her twenty-fifth anniversary. By then, the reader is told, "the cake is pretty hard and tastes, alas, a bit queer," but a "tiny morsel washed down by some good wine, supplied by the now prosperous bridegroom," could take care of that problem.[36] Saving wedding cake to symbolically eat later was not at all unusual, as evidenced by the popular *Smiley's Cook Book and Universal Household Guide*, which in 1901 noted that its wedding cake "would last for years."[37]

Less than a year after repeal, Julian Street wrote that it was ideal for newlyweds to have a rich uncle who could build their wine cellar for them as a wedding gift, but, in any case, the groom was told, "The cellar must be founded." Street lamented that there were "few fine old cellars left" and tasked readers with the "establishment of young and hopeful cellars."[38] Wine dealer Bellows and Company also felt uncles were responsible for outfitting bars; its 1935 advertisement read, "To Worried Uncles: We suggest a well-rounded wine cellar as a most appropriate wedding gift." (A ten-case assortment is next suggested for $250.)[39]

DRINKING WITH THE MOUSE

The Disney organization is heavily invested in the bridal industry, and in 2010 Florida's Disney World was home to more than 1,500 weddings per year (some sources report significantly more; there are numerous venues at the Florida location alone, including cruises and off-site events, not to mention Disney's California, Hawaii, and international locations). For toasting, Disney bottles its own Fairy Tale Cuvée. Mickey or Minnie Mouse can be booked to attend your celebration, but they cannot stay for the toast, as Disney characters are forbidden to be on site while alcohol is being consumed.[40] Disney characters must also "correspond" with one another so as to not ruin the fantasy (for instance, Buzz Lightyear should not mingle with Pocahontas). There is a cottage industry of books and websites dedicated to all things Disney, even some dedicated, amusingly, specifically to drinking at Disney resorts. Disney works hard to promote its ideal of clean living, which somehow lends itself to attempts to do otherwise. The Drinking at Disney website offers a "slightly blurry view of the mouse" and has a section on "stealth drinking" that any adventurous honeymooning couple will appreciate.[41]

Cake with champagne.
Source: Author's collection.

VESSELS

Drinking a particular beverage or from a certain vessel is a nuptial ritual common to many cultures, with the Christian rite of consuming symbolic bread and wine at a Mass as only one example. Pueblo wedding vases have two handles, with double spouts that join at the top, meant to represent the union of the new couple. The vases sold on the Internet and in gift shops in the Southwest are generally decorative, as authentic wedding vases are only given within the Native American tribal community. The vase is filled with holy water and drunk from during the wedding ceremony. Similarly, the French "coupe de marriage" is a two-handled cup, often handed down within families, out of which a bride and groom drink to one another at their service.

Slavic weddings may include a tray loaded with glasses of water and wine, into which guests drop coins, with the bride keeping the money left in the wine and the groomsmen getting the coins dropped in the water.[42] In Croatia, Slovenia, and Serbian countries, bridal parties are toasted with a fruit brandy called rakia, often made from fermented plum juice.[43]

Japanese ceremonies use three sake cups, with the bride and groom each taking three sips from the three cups, followed by their parents, who do the same. Koreans sip wine out of a gourd traditionally grown by the bride's mother, and libation ceremonies, in which schnapps is poured on the ground during prayers for departed relatives, are particularly popular with Nigerian Americans.

Wedding-specific websites (such as TheKnot.com) are full of other examples, and it can be assumed that every region and religion has its own toasting traditions. Cultures that eschew alcohol have equally as many traditions, often using blessed water. Holy water was sprinkled all over the linens of English royals in the Middle Ages as part of the "bedding" ceremony. Female guests escorted the bride to bed after sprucing her up and undressing her, and male guests did the same for the groom. After leaving the couple alone for a while, the guests returned with wine and food, seemingly to shore up the couple after their first encounter.[44]

BEYOND CHAMPAGNE

Classic thirst quenchers like iced tea and lemonade have made a comeback, and it is common now to rework them into the signature cocktails served at wedding receptions. A 2016 poll reveals that over 38 percent of newlyweds felt serving a "welcome" drink upon entry to the reception was worth an increase in wedding budget, and over 36 percent wanted a specific drink (not just house champagne) served for the formal toast.[45] Rosé wine is making a comeback on cocktail menus, and many hosts are offering craft beers, hard ciders, and mead (honey wine) as alternatives to the staple red and white wines.

Wedding planners may encourage couples to serve cocktails based on their personal story (a Hurricane for the couple who went to college in New Orleans) or ethnic drinks as a salute to a past family homeland (grappa for Italy, ouzo for Greece, tequila for Mexico, and so forth). These drinks may be "upsold," of course, to include premium brands and feature the flair of edible flowers or custom flavored ice cubes to make them wedding worthy. Special glassware is also a trend, with the copper cups of the Moscow Mule, a vodka drink made with ginger beer and lime, leading the charge. "Flights" of various brands of scotch or whisky are also popular. Drinks like this are another reason for the popularity of the carbohydrate heavy, hangover-battling snack food served at the after-party.

HISTORY

The consumption of alcohol in America is an especially interesting topic, especially as alcohol use originated prior to the establishment of Europeans in the New World.

Alcohol serves an important economic function, as its production and use employ many people, and its sale is a source of income for many institutions. In contemporary culture, as in the past, the purchase of luxury products indicates status, and buying certain brands of wine or food evinces purchasing power.[46] Sparkling wine has a particular cachet because, unlike wine and beer, which are sold in large vessels and kegs, it is sold only in individual bottles and not generally in volume.[47]

ETIQUETTE OF TOASTING

One never ever drinks oneself, but babies being toasted at their christenings are among the few people to know this.

—Judith Martin, *Miss Manners' Guide to*
Excruciatingly Correct Behavior, 1982[48]

Speeches by the best man and maid of honor inevitably occur at the wedding reception, and if these speeches are long-winded, guests hope to have a full glass of alcohol. At his 2014 wedding to Kim Kardashian, Kanye West disposed of the need for a best man and gave a forty-five-minute toast to himself.

THE MORAL COMPASS

Cultures have historically assigned men and women different relationships to drinking. Alcohol has served as a vehicle for a type of push-me, pull-me relationship that glamorizes drinking, yet also insinuates that women should maintain a reserve not demanded of men. Wedding ceremonies and receptions, however, are places where alcohol use is infused with meaning, glamorized, and used to signify the importance of the occasion.

Let Them Have Wedding Cake

> Wedding cakes are so packed with symbolism it is hard to
> know where to begin.
>
> —Michael Krondl, *Sweet Invention*

*W*edding cake rituals are bound up with symbols of fertility, with seeds and grains symbolically added to breads and cakes. Early European cakes were dense affairs, comprising dried fruit and nuts and often not baked, merely cooked over an open flame, like a flatbread. The white layered confection known today is a fairly modern invention.

EDIBLE ART

Medieval subtleties, those sculptures crafted for the tables of the aristocracy, were often broken into pieces at the end of a feast, with guests invited to crack off a section to take home as a sort of party favor. Sugar sculptures were especially prized, as sugar was thought to be particularly exotic, having come from the Caribbean or Africa.[1] Like many modern wedding cakes, they were made less for consumption than for the "theater" and as a type of entertainment if impressive enough.

The story of the modern wedding cake begins with the colossal cake made for Queen Victoria and Prince Albert in 1840. At the time of their marriage, London had recently weathered a politically volatile summer of

Cake with cookie tray, Mario and Ann Maffei, 1949. *Source*: Author's collection.

riots and violence, as well as controversy over Victoria marrying a German. It would not do to have a cake that could be construed as "German" while an already nervous Parliament wondered how it would control the mobs anxious to witness a royal wedding.[2]

The massive cake was festooned with a sugar sculpture of Britannia (the female figure who stands in as the physical embodiment of Britain). A dog at Britannia's feet represented faithfulness, with sculptures of the bride and groom, amid fluttering turtledoves, draped safely in classical Roman garb (lacking any modern ethnic context). The cake, carted outside the palace among clamoring crowds, was more than nine feet in circumference and became a public curiosity and center of attention.[3]

Throngs pressed to glimpse the royal couple, while uneasy authorities held their breath and waited to see if the crowd would turn unruly. Onlookers who failed to catch a peek of the royal couple were still assured an eyeful (and possibly a mouthful) of the huge patriotic cake. National pride, spurred by this enormous and most British of offerings, carried the day. That the confection was made of English plums with traditional British ingredients signaled that this couple would together be entirely "English." There was nothing German about this cake, and there would be nothing German about the way these monarchs ruled.[4] This cake, coated with very heavy white icing (it had to be sturdy to withstand the attentions of the multitudes), gave rise to the term "royal icing."

Victoria's very public cake served to heighten the role of wedding cakes ever after, an interest fanned by the eventual marriages of her nine children, each of whom married nobility. Their nuptial celebrations would also feature extravagant cakes. Queen Victoria's cake had been gigantic, though it consisted of merely a single layer. With nowhere to go but up, her oldest daughter, Vicky, who married Prince Frederick Wilhelm of Prussia, boasted a six-foot-high dessert tiered with pearls and multiple columns. The couple's respective coats of arms and profiles were accompanied by cupids sculpted of sugar, all housed under an enormous candy crown.[5]

Many consider a wedding without a cake almost illegal.

—*Good Housekeeping* 126, no. 6 (June 1948): 206

Fruit cakes were the norm for Western weddings until the end of the nineteenth century, but once manufacturers could provide inexpensive processed white flour and refined granulated sugar, cookbooks usually offered two versions: the "bride's cake" (light with white frosting) and the "wedding cake" (heavy fruit cake). The fruit cake became interchangeable with the groom's cake. The lighter, sweeter bride's cake developed into the wedding portrait opportunity now known so well.

Simon Charsley, a Scottish social anthropologist, has surmised that wedding cakes have become a visual cornerstone and an iconic symbol for marriage more than a food item. Their ritual slicing, more than their eating, defines them.[6] Charsley, among others, supposes that the whiteness of refined sugar in modern cakes symbolizes virginity, with the bride's purity ritually severed by the slicing of the cake by the newlyweds.

Yet, as noted food historian Michael Krondl states, cakes have not always been white, and the rituals concerning them have not always been particularly refined. In one tradition, the bride holds a ring out while the groom thrusts bits of cake through it, with the little pieces next eaten by the bridesmaids.[7] Instances of "cake breaking," in which bread or cake is broken or crumbled on a bride's head, is evident in numerous cultures. Charsley remarks that the ring ritual and the cake-cutting ceremony are significant in that the bride participates in them rather than having something done to her.[8] It is also notable that this cutting is witnessed by family members, the bride's virginity publicly negated in a ceremony presumably arranged or paid for by her father.

FOOD AS MEDICINE AND HOW DO I MAKE A CAKE WITH CORNMEAL?

The first English-speaking colonists were confounded by the curious foods of the New World and distressed by the lack of familiar ingredients. They especially yearned for wheat to make bread and cakes. Corn was considered a lowly "swine" crop, despite being hardy and easy to grow.[9] But the colonists did learn to value corn and soon produced cookbooks that helped ensure the welfare of the next batch of New World arrivals.

Recipes and first aid were intertwined, and early cookbooks acted as all-encompassing survival guides for running a home, particularly for a colonist lacking experienced family members nearby to act as tutors. A glance at the index of Lydia Maria Child's *The American Frugal Housewife* (a best seller in 1844) shows a recipe for Indian pudding just before an antidote for "inflamed wounds," and a lobster recipe resides next to a cure for lockjaw.[10] *The White House Cook Book* of 1913 included recipes to cure nosebleeds, constipation, fainting, and bad breath. It also offered methods to destroy ants, cure hiccups, and remove freckles.[11] And nestled in with lifesaving advice, there were always wedding cake recipes.

BETTY CROCKER BAKED SOMEONE HAPPY

The home economists working to standardize American cuisine were starchy and fussy, attributes perhaps terrifying to a new bride first learning to cook or to a recent immigrant already flummoxed by a new world. The folksy Betty Crocker was "born" in 1921 to sell Gold Medal Flour for the Washburn Crosby Company (later General Mills). The account manager regularly received letters asking for cooking advice, and, with an all-male advertising staff, he routinely turned to his female office and factory workers for solutions. He in turn responded anonymously, although he soon recognized the appeal of a personal approach—hence, the genesis of the *Betty Crocker Cooking School of the Air*. Consumers could now feel they were getting cooking advice from a real person, and the Betty Crocker character was accessible and a marvel of marketing finesse.

Betty's image for use in packaging was carefully fabricated, and her face made its first appearance in 1937 on Softasilk cake flour. Nothing about her was an accident. The name Betty was chosen to sound "cheery, wholesome, and folksy," and even the signature affixed to her letters and boxes, still used today, resulted from a company drive to find the most pleasing design.[12]

Dozens of home economists, hired to play Betty Crockers, answered mail and crisscrossed the country giving cooking shows. Entire town populations turned out just to see the elaborate kitchen stage setup.[13] It was a secret, of course, that no true Betty existed, and the character was regularly inundated with love letters and marriage proposals. Betty received valentines and gifts from bachelors enamored of this woman who could cook and sew and seemingly answer any question.[14]

Trouble brewed when the secrecy of the company fanned public speculation that Betty was hiding something, and a rumor erupted that she was quitting and getting married. Betty took out a full-page ad, proclaiming, "Instead of practicing making biscuits for a husband, I'm afraid I will have to be content doing my cooking in the Gold Medal Kitchen."[15] Betty would remain single and devote her life to America. She would be sorely needed as the country faced the Depression and then endured food rationing in another war.

1940s: IT'S COMPLICATED

Meta Given's 1949 *Modern Encyclopedia of Cooking* was a whopping volume that taught how to cook bear, antelope, beaver, and opossum, how best to remove feathers and fur, and how to eviscerate a deer. In many ways, this was still how the country actually lived, and industry would have to be careful to not tamper with the ideals of home cooking. As early as the 1940s, the market included cake mixes that required only adding water, but sales were flat. Betty Crocker's parents (General Mills) hired psychologists, who established that homemakers felt they had not "baked" if they only added water. The producers altered their formula so that cake mixes would also require eggs, and sales soon increased.[16]

GROOMS CAKE AND RIBBON PULLS

The groom's cake has retained its popularity in the South particularly, and it is often rich or chocolatey, a sort of antithesis to the white concoction sliced for the photographer. It is sometimes decorated to reflect hobbies or to pay homage to an alma mater or sports team. It is sliced after the wedding cake, with care usually taken to not compete with or deflect attention from the main attraction.

The South has preserved culinary traditions with enthusiasm, and ribbon pulls are a New Orleans specialty. As with the bouquet toss, unmarried females vie for the chance to divine their futures. Charms are embedded in or laid under the cake, and on cue bridesmaids or good friends pull out their charms. Typical charms include a ring for the next to marry, a button for an "old maid," an anchor for hope, and a horseshoe for luck. Companies produce individualized charms, including sterling ones to be kept on a charm bracelet. Although attributed to the French, the practice is, according to Simon Charsley, Scottish in origin, an offshoot of the ribbon "favors" given at weddings as keepsakes. These ribbons were once lightly attached to the bride's dress and pulled off by her friends.[17]

Many cultures are known to bake coins or trinkets into breads and cakes, and the French did inspire Mardi Gras king cakes, which contain a bean or a small plastic baby. The recipient of the slice with the trinket becomes king or queen for the day and is expected to provide the cake for the next year. Charsley supposes the ribbons in New Orleans bridal cakes are probably an amalgamation of several such traditions.[18]

In early America, weddings were celebrated with "stack cakes." Neighbors and friends all brought cakes, which were stacked on top of one another, "glued" together with a dollop of apple sauce.[19]

Wedding cakes do get a bad rap, not being known for their flavor, and research bears out that this is not a new phenomenon. In 1882 a *Harper's Bazaar* columnist referred to wedding cake as "the black cement in which fossilized fruits, spices and slabs of gum-shellac are imbedded, and the plaster of Paris with which the indigestible and deadly edifice is crowned."[20] While the writer referred to the fruit cakes of a bygone era, there is no shortage of criticism of the dry and sugary offerings of lesser contemporary bakeries.

Once confectioners began to "pipe" icing through tubes, their creations became more detailed, and by the mid-1800s manufacturers were selling small metal funnels (pastry tips) and canvas bags to fill with icing.[21] American candy maker Dewey McKinley Wilton started the Wilton School of Cake Decorating in 1929, and his business flourished. In 1948 his rosters swelled with veterans utilizing GI Bill benefits, and he began to market decorating tools now found in any pastry chef's arsenal.[22]

Traditional cake cutting. *Source*: Author's collection.

CAKE BOXES

The top tier of the wedding cake is often saved for other occasions, such as the couple's future child's christening or an anniversary. The small white boxes for housing the obligatory cake for guests to take home triggered an industry of their own. Cookbooks recommended wrapping slices in waxed paper and securing them with a ribbon, but monogrammed and specialized boxes were very fashionable, and some companies even supplied the fruit cake to include inside. A 1905 article in *Good Housekeeping* advised making homemade boxes and wrapping the cake in a small amount of fabric from the assembly of the wedding gown.

A 1949 ad beseeched brides to "preserve all the tradition" and reported that Emily Post had commented, "There are at all weddings of importance . . . little individual boxes of dark fruit cake." In a nod to an increasingly industrialized society, this company's boxes came prepacked with fruit cake inside, with an option to have them monogrammed.[23]

CAKE TOPS

The availability of artificial flowers had an impact on cake designs, making it possible to keep a permanent wedding souvenir, often under a glass dome, for years after the event. Decorative flourishes no longer needed a vase in which to hold water, and modern manufacturing offered many new possibilities for making a cake look distinctive. Faux flowers, doves, rings, bells, and horseshoes began to perch on cakes, and clasped hands were a particular best seller.[24]

Cake toppers got less expensive as new manufacturing methods were able to mass-produce them. The popular Sears, Roebuck & Co. catalog brought cake toppers into the mainstream, and during the 1940s the company did brisk business with figures in military uniform.[25]

Contemporary cake toppers are available in many configurations with the theme of sports, video games, ATVs, motorcycles, Dr. Who, firefighters, bicycles . . . the list goes on. Figures are often sold separately, so shoppers can mix and match, choosing two males or two females (there are brides in gowns or white pantsuits) or figures of the opposite sex, featuring a particular hair color or dress. Most companies offer a choice of skin tone, and there are bald grooms, sari-clad brides, and grooms in Nehru jackets. There are Jewish grooms wearing yarmulkes, Asian and Hispanic figures, "curvy" brides, "burly" grooms, and even pregnant brides. The "geek groom" surfaces a lot too, wearing glasses and pants a tad too short. Facial hair may be added for an additional $4. If that does not keep the couple busy, they can assemble their bridal party to march across their cake, and they may also be attended by a range of dog and cat breeds.

Numerous companies create custom figures using uploaded photos, and 3-D printers can make detailed replicas. Couples with great self-esteem may choose to commission cake figurines depicting themselves nude, as soccer star David Beckham and Spice Girl Victoria Adams did in 1999.

In 2005 African American wedding planner Rena Puebla cast around for an apropos topper for the cake at her wedding to a Japanese man. She could not find figures that actually resembled them and was put off by how the black figure looked like the white figure with dyed skin. She hired artists to create forms with accurate facial details, with attention to cheek bones, eyes, and nose. She formed a company, Renellie, which quickly sold out of figures.[26]

Much of the merchandise follows the theme of being "caught." Various Western figures depict a bride roping a groom or a bride with a fishing pole and a groom with a hook in his back. There appears to be a dearth of grooms casting the marriage net; yet plenty look at their watches, as the brides have left a "gone shopping" sign. Perhaps the cake-topper industry lags behind the move for female equality or actually serves as an unspoken reflection of the bridal business as a whole?

PHOTO OP

Brides of the early 1900s cut the first slice, doling out portions first to their husbands and then to guests, simulating their new role as the family cook. As hiring of a professional wedding photographer became the norm in the 1950s, grooms were brought into the shot of the "cutting of the cake" as the couple fed each other a slice in a gesture of unity.

In the 1950s the Betty Crocker Junior Baking Kit came to the fore, featuring a portable, child-friendly oven and tiny boxes of Betty Crocker cake mix. A perusal of the EZ Bake Oven opportunities available in 2016 reveals that Betty is keeping up with the times. EZ Bake Oven videos feature enthusiastic tweens (clearly old enough to use a "real" oven") and downloadable recipes for dishes that could be served at any contemporary wedding banquet: red velvet cupcakes, rockin' pizza, pretzel "dippers," and whoopee pies.[27] In line with the prevalent need for everyone to be famous, the oven is advertised with the tag line "Lets kids feel like baking stars."[28]

As weddings became more playful in the 1970s, the bride and groom began to smash the cake into each other's faces, providing a "cute," albeit now predictable, pose. This injection of whimsy into wedding culture is particularly apparent in modern wedding cake choices. Alternative cakes may be constructed of cake pops, pizza, wheels of cheese, or doughnuts. An Internet search will reveal more than one teetering cake made of waffles, bride and groom lovingly pouring on the maple syrup. Of course, bacon has found its way into every menu item possible, and *Modern Bride* recently featured a BLT cake offering with ranch-style frosting and tiny tomato slices.[29]

A lot can go wrong with cake productions such as this, and in 2013 a disgruntled bride tried to sell her wedding cake on eBay for $1.54, listing it as the "Ugliest Wedding Cake Ever." It did not sell. In a more positive cake story, a man in Washington State discovered the top layer of a wedding cake in his attic in 2015. The fossilized cake was his grandmother's, hailing from 1915.[30]

Both Papa John's and Pizza Hut have commissioned artists to create wedding portraits on the surface of their pizzas, and Pinterest will show more than one version of meat cakes, with steaks or burgers layered with mashed potatoes and white gravy.

"Naked" cakes, so named because they lack icing, have made inroads in popularity, as have "drip" cakes, which feature a drizzle of ganache or caramel cascading down the sides. One 2016 poll suggests that nontraditional cakes such as these live mostly on social media, the stars of Pinterest and Instagram, while the majority of couples still crave a traditional iced cake.[31]

COOKIES

In Pittsburgh, Pennsylvania, weddings are known for their cookie tables. Family members bake and freeze cookies for months in advance, all in anticipation of loading a banquet table with hundreds and hundreds of cookies. The cookie table is a unique Pittsburgh custom, with locals reporting that it is more important than the wedding cake. The cookies are always homemade, with families known for particular types; lady locks (small pastry tubes with cream filling, similar to cannolis) are a regional favorite.

The cookie table is thought to be derived from the area's early Greek or Italian settlers. As many households contributed, it reduced the cost of a wedding and served as an alternative to an expensive wedding cake. In any case, it is a communal custom, and modern wedding hosts routinely provide personalized to-go containers or custom bags for guests to take cookies home. Pittsburgh claims it as the city's exclusive wedding tradition; yet Youngstown, Ohio, makes the same claim. An Ohio museum launched an exhibit on the latter's cookie tables, and "Youngstown natives were more than a little miffed that the state on the east side of the Ohio line has been claiming that the tradition originated there."[32]

MAIDS OF HONOR

One dessert, at least in name tied to weddings, are Maids of Honor, small tarts long established in England and Canada. Apparently Henry VIII witnessed Anne Boleyn's ladies in waiting eating them. Fond of his food, the king demanded some and so liked them that he named them in the ladies' honor. The London Maids of Honour Bakery, in existence from early in the eighteenth century, recounts the legend that the king so liked the treats that he had the recipe locked away in a secret box at Richmond Palace. There are even reports that the king imprisoned the lady who created the recipe, forcing her to cook the tarts only for him (although the bakery stops short of claiming this to be literally true).[33]

QUEENS

Brides do hope to be queen for a day, a sentiment surely embodied by modern celebrity unions. Imagine the cake served at the infamous 2002 wedding of Liza Minnelli and David Gest. The twelve tiers that towered above their heads cost $40,000, making it one of the most expensive wedding cakes ever. It would seem that when Michael Jackson is the best man (and Elizabeth Taylor the matron of honor), no ordinary cake will do. Of course, Liz, with eight weddings under her belt, knew her way around the cake knife. In 1991, her six-tiered chocolate mousse cake comprised a large portion of the budget of her $2.5 million nuptials to construction worker Larry Fortensky.

PINEAPPLE REPUBLIC

The late 1800s saw the introduction of canned pineapples and, not coincidentally, America's swift appropriation of Hawaii. The United States overthrew Hawaii's Queen Liliuokalani and established the Republic of Hawaii. Soon it ensconced a president with the last name Dole (although only a cousin to the Dole Pineapple family), and the resources of the islands—all that fruit and all that sugar—came under total American control. Like bananas, pineapples, at least canned ones, became an American staple and did not join the eventual roster of luxury food items coveted for wedding feasts.

SUGAR AND LUXURY

Sydney W. Mintz's 1985 *Sweetness and Power: The Place of Sugar in Modern History* traces the historical progression of sugar, detailing its evolution from amenity exclusive to the privileged to item of mass consumption in commercial goods. Mintz wrote that access to sugar became more important than its actual consumption, tracing how power is derived from access and, more important, how maintaining that power depends on exploiting the desires of others who want access as well. Roland Barthes, as discussed in this book's introduction, positioned coffee as a luxury good that became an item imbued with meaning that could exemplify how a person desired to be perceived.

DISPLAY

Ambitious dessert buffets have become standard at receptions, as have ice-cream sundae and cupcake bars. Yet the wedding cake retains its status. Guests often hesitate to leave before it has been cut. The sharing of the wedding cake, laden with symbolism, celebrates a shared life. The cupcake, by contrast, evokes nostalgia for childhood and is a sign of individuality. As Michael Krondl has posited, perhaps cupcakes are the ultimate symbol of a "selfie" generation?

Ostentatious displays were (and are) an important aspect in the pursuit of status and power, and sugar sculptures and elaborate exhibits of food were forerunners of extravagant wedding cakes.[34] Elaborate wedding cakes, towering above our heads, bigger and sweeter than need be, are physical embodiments of conspicuous consumption that can literally be ingested.

❦ 12 ❦

Do Me a Favor and Get Me Some Rice

FAVORS

Candy coated anise, caraway, and fennel seeds arrived in Europe from the Middle East, and because sugar was expensive and candy preparation was time-consuming, the treats were an extravagance. Wealthy Europeans began presenting their wedding guests with a *bonbonniere* (favor), a small box containing five candied items representing five wishes: for wealth, fertility, longevity, happiness, and health. Like the seeds and grains traditionally added to breads and cakes to celebrate marriages, these candies indicated the shift in perception of sugar from obscure medicinal item to coveted luxury good that conveyed status. European aristocrats threw these "comfits" at crowds after weddings, and spectators scrambled after them.[1] Paper confetti and tickertape are contemporary offspring of these little candies.

Candy-coated almonds, also called Jordan almonds, reflect this tradition too, with the white sugar representing purity and the sweetness of life. Greeks give out sugared almonds, called *koufeta*, in odd numbers, signifying that the married couple must share everything now and, like the almonds, cannot be divided. Wedding almonds will always be white; yet Italian candy retailers sell them in pink for christenings, green for engagements, and red for graduations. They are also sold in colors signaling various other meanings, such as pink for a first wedding anniversary, yellow for the tenth, and gold for the fiftieth.

Jordan almonds, Marisa and Tommaso Morin, 1961. *Source:* Used with permission from Rosemary Picinic.

For favors, modern couples can go online to buy biscotti with their wedding date written in sugar, mini wine bottles with personalized labels, or customized fortune cookies. Some couples buy packets of wildflower seeds, as did actress Natalie Portman for her all-vegan 2012 wedding to choreographer Benjamin Millepied. Liza Minnelli gave out cookies emblazoned with a likeness of herself and her groom.

FERTILITY

Food is used in many ways in relation to weddings, and often the underlying themes that bind food rituals involve hope for fertility and good fortune. At Chinese wedding feasts, an apple may be hung from a string and dangled in front of the newlyweds as they lunge to take bites, with the apple pulled away and causing them to kiss as they meet.[2] Look closely and a Greek bride may have a sugar cube tucked in her hand, indicating her hope for a sweet marriage. In many Middle Eastern regions, the bride's and groom's bodies are rubbed with turmeric prior to the wedding in order to "heat" them in preparation for their wedding night.[3] Muslim weddings may include a *haldi* rite, in which the bride wears yellow and her friends smear turmeric paste on her prior to bathing and dressing her for the wedding.

RICE

By the fifteenth century, Indonesia and its surrounding regions shared languages with similar roots, all owing to a collective trade system, with rice production a major factor in this commonality. Tending to rice production was part of the female domain because males primarily fished and harvested shellfish. The watery landscape, with no expanse of grassland, did not support agriculture. Rice production and its accompanying economic power, however, provided women with a measure of reverence, and mothers passed the technique on to daughters. Unlike in other societies, the birth of a female child did not spell economic hardship for the family.[4]

The use of rice is ubiquitous in weddings across the globe. In one Indian custom, the groom does not eat rice prior to his wedding in order to keep its consumption sacred. At the wedding ceremony, a small fire, fueled by ghee, is fed puffed rice to represent fertility and continuity of the family. One superstition holds that it is bad luck to visit the home of newlyweds until the bride has cooked rice for her new husband. Another tradition includes the Indian bride throwing rice at the family home when she leaves for the wedding ceremony as a way of wishing her parents abundant nourishment.

At Hindu wedding parties the bride and groom may compete to see who can heap more rice on the other's head; the winner will be the boss of the household.[5] In one premarriage Hindu custom a meal is cooked for the groomsmen at the bride's house. The bride is seated behind a mound of rice, and the groom's father presents her with coconuts and sweets. In yet another Hindu wedding ritual, the officiating priest pours raw rice into a tray held by the bride. The groom reaches behind her and knocks the tray to the ground seven times. In another version the bride fills a cup with rice and holds it on the ground while the groom kicks it seven times. In this way the groom asserts his potency, indicating that he, of the pair, will determine the couple's fertility. A different version has the bride doing the kicking, five times, as she strikes the mounds of rice.

RICE IS NICE

A shower of rice was once thrown at the bride and groom as they left the wedding ceremony, but due to thoughts that the grain might pose a danger to birds, the practice has largely stopped. Mary Jo Cheesman of the USA Rice Federation remarks that migrating geese exist on a diet of rice as they work their way north, and ornithologists concur that rice is no threat to birds.[6] Leftover rice will attract vermin, however; it does create a mess, and it may make a sidewalk or steps slippery.

> Care must be taken not to overdo this ancient custom. It is bad form to give the occasion any appearance whatsoever of vulgarity. Today the custom is still in vogue.
>
> —*Vogue's Book of Etiquette*, 1925,[7] referring to the practice of throwing rice

Rice at the church steps in New York City, Wes and Marilyn White, 1976. *Source*: Used with permission from Wes and Marilyn White.

In the 1980s throwing birdseed at newlyweds became popular, as did blowing bubbles at them. Retailers were quick to drum up items to sell in place of rice since no one was going to make money off birdseed. Lavender buds can be purchased to throw at the departing couple, and when crushed under feet, they release a scent. Merchants will tell you they are biodegradable and won't harm birds. You can also purchase puffed rice shaped like hearts.

BREAD

Bread often assumes a role in marriage rites, with the challah in Jewish ceremonies and the wafer in Christian communions obvious examples. Macedonian weddings feature koluk, sweet egg bread baked in a round shape to represent an unbroken circle. The groom places the loaf above his head in his left hand, and once joined by the bride, he begins a wedding dance with his family, who pass the loaf from person to person.[8] After the dance, the bride and groom each hold an end of the bread and tug; the one who manages to tear off the largest piece will be "head" of the house.

French settlers brought the practice of "the shivaree" to the American frontier. Local men would assemble late at night outside the window of a just-married couple and bang pots and pans, refusing to leave until fed a meal. This is thought to be the precursor of tin cans tied to the back of newlyweds' car. The shivaree was common in Montana until at least the 1930s, with couples on their wedding night waiting for the cacophony of bells and horns only muzzled with free drinks.[9]

The act of giving favors as a thank-you for attending a wedding may meet an expectation that people have always had: to receive a little something in return when they have given (a wedding gift). It may also be a way to perpetuate memory of the wedding, as souvenirs with monograms and engraving are personalized records of the event.

In the Italian American culture (and those of other groups known for large weddings) there is a belief that when attending a wedding and deciding how much money to give as a gift, you should choose an amount that "covers your plate"—meaning that the wedding gift should be at least equal in value to what the host spent to feed you. As in the Native American potlach, this reciprocity preserves traditions and ensures large lively festivities. A family that knows it will recoup most of the money spent is more likely to indulge in an extravagant celebration.

Bride and groom Anthony and Telma Caporaso distributing almonds while wearing their going-away outfits, 1955. *Source*: Used with permission from Roseanne Caporaso.

☙ *13* ❧

Honeymoons and Food

It is not etiquette for any person to inquire where the honeymoon is to be spent and nobody but the two most interested
is supposed to know anything of their immediate plans.

—Abby Buchanan Longstreet,
Social Etiquette of New York, 1879[1]

*H*oneymoon origin stories abound, with one holding that when the man "swept a woman off her feet," he was symbolically kidnapping her, and her relatives could be expected to search for her for the length of one phase of the moon. Alternately, the term "honeymoon" may stem from the practice of the newlyweds drinking mead (honey wine) for a month, as a nod to the sweetness of life. Another conjecture is that early marriage was sweet like honey, but its appeal waned like the moon, or that honey, so agreeable, derived from something that stings, such as the honeybee, which provides honey.

TRADITIONS

In one marriage ritual in bygone rural France, newlyweds were served a mixture of chocolate and champagne from a chamber pot. The couple's friends also burst into the pair's room on their wedding night. The raucous event, called *la rôtie*, was meant to mimic bodily functions and

147

embarrass the bride while also alleviating her awkwardness at losing her virginity.[2] Another French tradition was to bring newlyweds soup made from tripe, with milk and torn-up pieces of bread carried in either a bowl or a chamber pot.[3]

In the nineteenth century, upper-class Europeans took extended vacations after marrying, and as the middle class grew and emulated their habits, the "wedding tour" became more commonplace; the custom soon spread to the United States. The advent of airplanes and swift train and auto travel put honeymoons within the reach of people other than the elite. Researchers Cele C. Otnes and Elizabeth H. Pleck add that the rise of the honeymoon coincided with the advent of paid vacations for the working classes.[4]

Etiquette whiz Amy Vanderbilt remarked in 1954 that honeymoons had been scaled down from the past and that in previous generations they "could encompass a whole summer and might include the entire wedding party at the bridegroom's expense."[5]

Family members once often accompanied newlyweds on their "tour" as they traveled to visit extended family relations. These holidays increased in popularity as more people came to live in cities, making a retreat to the countryside novel.

The honeymoon ideal shifted to a more private concept, and as more partnerships were founded in love, rather than strategic alliance, the appeal of a secluded location away from relations increased.[6] Withdrawal to a private spot was especially significant to couples during a time when they were not likely to have been physically intimate before their trip to the altar. Another view sees the honeymoon, this retreat from peers, as a geographical "displacement," engineered as a method for adjusting to a new and thoroughly disorienting endeavor—the journey from single to married.[7] The wedding night came to be loaded with psychological import, and sexual themes abound in the rituals surrounding the honeymoon.

ENGAGEMENT

In much of American history, unmarried women had restricted opportunities to socialize. Their social circles were kept tight to hinder exposure to men who could jeopardize their reputations. Those situations considered "safe" usually limited them to the companionship of other respectable women, church activities, and charity work.[8] In the Victorian era, when all behavior was so carefully tracked, women were on guard to protect their standing, and for a man not her fiancé or husband to call a woman by her first name would "cheapen" her.[9]

> The hallmark of so-called "vulgar people" is unrestricted display of uncontrolled emotions.
>
> —Emily Post, *Etiquette in Society, in Business, in Politics, and at Home,* 1922[10]

Once engaged, couples were granted latitude in their behavior. Although messages to practice restraint were everywhere, it was silently understood that it was a matter of time before the pair could unleash their passion. They were still expected to behave themselves in the interim, however. In the 1950s Amy Vanderbilt warned that although society may indulge the canoodling of engaged couples, "if this joy becomes too tactile, onlookers are visibly embarrassed."[11]

Etiquette experts calling for restraint competed with a bridal industry that relentlessly invoked sexuality to sell products. Bridal magazines advertised lingerie, weight-loss plans, perfume, and cosmetics. It portrayed food and its preparation as a medium for enticing and pleasing a new husband.

By the early 1960s, bridal magazines included advertisements for "marriage manuals" and scattered clinical advice on sex and family planning in with recipes for tuna imperial. Interviews with Planned Parenthood doctors shared space with ads for baby furniture. Such divergent messages were typical of an industry that had already learned to offer something to everyone. Just as suffragettes had softened their image by producing cookbooks and feeding the troops, the wedding business used food to make precarious topics, like sex, palatable, clearing the way for the sale of goods packaged in the hominess of recipes and menu suggestions.

A display of appetite by women, especially in the late 1800s, was considered an indication of loose sexuality, with food consumption linked to a lack of control. Food was also disparaged because it was connected to "work," as its preparation required labor.[12] With women's sphere so small, a honeymoon afforded a new and heady entry into a society as yet unseen by average brides. Until recent times, the honeymoon was also perhaps the first time a couple ate together regularly, establishing a new kind of intimacy and opening a window onto personal routines previously unknown.

In 1936's *Gone with the Wind*, Margaret Mitchell's chronicle of the Civil War–era South, Scarlett O'Hara is told by Mammy, not for the first time, that she should eat before going to a society barbecue, it being improper for a young lady to demonstrate an appetite in the company of men. When Scarlett reminds her that her mother eats in public, Mammy tells Scarlet that married women can eat because they have already captured husbands.[13]

CELEBRITY HONEYMOONS

When Arthur Tudor, Prince of Wales (and Henry VIII's big brother), wed Spanish princess Catherine of Aragon in 1501, the streets of London flowed with free wine and food for the crowds. Henry, aged ten (and Catherine's future husband), escorted her to the ceremony. The bride was sixteen and the groom fifteen. Her vows included a promise to be "bonair" (amiable in bed) and "buxom at board" (at the table).[14] In keeping with custom, the couple was ceremonially led to the marital bed after the wedding dinner, a rite attended to by an entourage. Later in the evening, the same group returned with food and drinks to refresh the newlyweds. Catherine claimed their marriage was never consummated, and of course the disputed truth of this statement was the root of Henry's famous divorce claim.

TITANIC

At the turn of the twentieth century, luxury ocean liners, with their sumptuous dining rooms, were top honeymoon venues. At a time when honeymoons of the elite lasted for months, a lazy sea voyage was a stylish way to travel to and from a European tour. The *Titanic* hosted at least thirteen honeymooning couples on its fateful journey. The first-class dining room hosted four sets of honeymooners on its final evening, with the most famous being John Jacob Astor IV (who had built the Waldorf Hotel) and his bride, Madeleine. Dinner in the first-class dining room consisted of ten courses; yet grand food may have been no solace to the Astors, who had taken to the seas as refuge from gossipmongers. John

Astor had married a woman close to thirty years his junior, a year younger than his own son, scandalizing society with both his divorce and his new marriage. His ex-wife had friends onboard the liner, and despite being one of the wealthiest men in the world, he found his company shunned by the old guard, who requested a new table when seated near the newly-weds. Astor died on board the sinking vessel, although his newly pregnant wife survived.

The *Titanic's* captain, Edward Smith, was paid an exorbitant salary in comparison to other Cunard employees, and his ease and joviality with the elite were evidenced by his nickname: the "millionaire's captain." He favored the Widener family of Philadelphia, dining with them on what would be the last day of life for the captain as well as for George Widener and his twenty-seven-year-old son. Mrs. Widener, Nellie, survived. She was returning from a mission for her improbably nicknamed daughter Dimples, having taken her wedding dress to Paris to be trimmed with old family lace in preparation for her impending marriage.[15]

Sales of stale slices of wedding cake were outdone in October 2015 when a Greek investor purchased an official *Titanic* cracker for $23,000. The relic was from a survival kit installed on one of the lifeboats so famously underused on the night of the tragedy.[16] This particular cracker had been squirreled away by James and Mabel Fenwick, a couple honeymooning on the *Carpathia*, a luxury liner that arrived in time to rescue some *Titanic* passengers.

BED IN

One famous honeymoon was taken by John Lennon and Yoko Ono in 1969. From the honeymoon suite of the Amsterdam Hilton, they staged their first "bed in," allowing the press unlimited access as they sprawled on their mattress and appealed for world peace. They followed this with a "bagism" display in Vienna: concealed inside a bag meant to erase all reference to their physical selves, the couple nibbled Sacher torte and spoke to journalists. The Beatles song "The Ballad of John and Yoko" includes the lyric "eating chocolate cake in a bag," referring to this event. From their bed in Montreal, Lennon and Ono recorded "Give Peace a Chance"; the backup singers included a rabbi, a priest, Tommy Smothers, Timothy Leary, and a bevy of Hindu priests.[17]

WHAT HAPPENS ON YOUR HONEYMOON
STAYS WHERE?

Las Vegas is an obvious destination for quickie weddings, honeymoons, and bachelor and bachelorette parties before the big day. The streets of this city, once known primarily for its business conventions, now teem with wedding chapels. Las Vegas's prominence as a marriage destination arose from its loose divorce laws, with no waiting period between a divorce and a marriage. Vows can be exchanged at the Tunnel of Love Drive-Thru, on a gondola, or underwater at the Silverton Hotel Aquarium.

Gatlinburg, Tennessee, in the Smoky Mountains, is another prevalent American wedding site; it also has no waiting period or residency requirements and seeks no blood test. The "Honeymoon Capital of the South" is a few miles from Dolly Parton's hometown of Pigeon Forge, and tour companies have carved out an economy based on quickie weddings and southern hospitality. The Hillbilly Wedding Company advertises "simple basic weddings," and an ordained Christian minister promises to wear bib overalls while administering vows. The town's official vacation guide advertises Hillbilly Golf and tells of the Christ in the Smokies Museum and Gardens, home to a giant Christ sculpture with eyes that "seem to follow your every movement." The community, which has vied to break records with its "marry-thons," was largely founded by Reverend Ed of Gatlinburg Industries (subject of a lawsuit for violation of labor practices when it was revealed that every employee received a Bible upon hire).[18]

Niagara Falls became a popular destination in the 1880s and was especially fashionable in the 1950s as more honeymooners took to the roads in private cars rather than traveling by trains. By the late 1960s, its reputation had become somewhat threadbare. The location has come to be considered more kitschy than modern, but the Falls still court the bridal industry and provide an affordable destination for families.

Atlantic City was once a stylish honeymoon location, peaking in popularity in the 1920s. Strolling newlyweds paraded on the boardwalk and crammed the hotels and restaurants of the New Jersey shore. African Americans, who filled the bulk of the many service jobs in this seaside resort, experienced a lower measure of racism there compared to other regions, although Jim Crow laws were rampant all across the United States. In 1953, after Reverend Martin Luther King Jr. wed Coretta Scott at her parents' home in Alabama, the pair could not find a hotel to give them a room. They spent the night at a funeral parlor owned by a family friend.

Honeymooners on the Atlantic City boardwalk, Harvey and Gertrude Roscoe, 1923. *Source*: Author's collection.

SAME SEX

The legalization of same-sex marriage has opened a new revenue stream for tourism professionals, and gay-specific wedding expos, guidebooks, and websites can ensure couples that vendors welcome their business. Operators offer guidelines for choosing gay-friendly honeymoon destinations, and some of the trendiest are New Hope, Pennsylvania; Asbury Park, New Jersey; and Eureka Springs, Arkansas (the "gay capital of Ozarks"). Cape Town, South Africa; Sydney, Australia; Provincetown, Massachusetts; and Costa Rica are also known to be hospitable locales. Marriot, with its "Love Travels with Me" program, is one of many mainstream companies that work to sell honeymoon packages to the LGBT community. For years, the big tour companies have included information as to whether a locale is "gay-friendly," but there is current debate as to whether tourist dollars should support the economies of some countries or towns. Same-sex couples are courted because the local economy depends on tourism; yet this hospitality may only serve as a veneer that hides discrimination. Some organizations have a "just say I don't" category warning against certain businesses or locations.

HONEYMOONS OF COLOR

Highland Beach, on the shores of Chesapeake Bay, was founded by Charles Douglass, the war-hero son of abolitionist Frederick Douglass. Humiliated when barred from eating at a water-side resort, he bought as much property as was available in the area and sold parcels to his friends and family, soon creating the first African American vacation resort.[19]

Idlewild, in Michigan, was a bustling African American resort whose popularity crested in the 1950s. Once called a "black Eden," the region

A young couple, warned to carry their *Green Book*, on the way to their honeymoon: 1948. *Source*: "The Negro Motorist Green Book: 1948," Schomburg Center for Research in Black Culture, Jean Blackwell Hutson Research and Reference Division, New York Public Library Digital Collections, http://digitalcollections.nypl.org/items/6fa574f0-893f-0132-1035-58d385a7bbd0.

now hosts retirees and a diminished population, although community members hope to attract tourism by exploiting its historic significance. Like the shuttered Jewish resorts of the Catskills, Idlewild lost its allure when the 1964 Civil Rights Act integrated the hospitality business.

Oak Bluffs is a popular community on Martha's Vineyard and a current favored vacation spot for prosperous blacks. It is a celebrated honeymoon destination and recommended by wedding planners as an Afrocentric getaway. It is home to the Martha's Vineyard African American Film Festival, art galleries, and expensive restaurants.

THE NICHE MARKET

Muslim-specific tourism is a burgeoning business, with resorts now offering honeymoon packages that include halal foods and a variety of non-alcoholic beverages. Some promise that the women will have their own beaches and swimming pools, and almost all promise a culture of modesty.

A couple in 2016 may seek a honeymoon on which they take cooking classes or go wine tasting, cheese tasting, or foraging; they may also choose a vegan-only bed and breakfast in Mendocino, California; a raw-food hotel in Bali; or a gluten-free, all-inclusive getaway in the Caribbean. Virtual honeymoon registries allow couples to register for their dream vacation, giving guests the option to contribute to honeymoon expenses. These sites have thrived, as various niche wedding sites hyperlink to them, driving traffic from an audience already interested in a certain hobby or lifestyle.

POCONOS AND CATSKILLS

Jews, restricted from most resorts, went to the Catskills for their vacations, and the so-called borscht belt offered gourmet kosher food and live entertainment. Its many large banquet venues catered countless weddings and hosted innumerable honeymoons until the region's demise in the 1990s.

Once the most famous of the "honeymoon hideaways," Mount Airy Lodge in the Poconos, folded in 2001. Its longtime owner, Emil Wagner, shot himself the night before the bank was slated to repossess the property. In its prime in the 1960s, Mount Airy had been an outrageously successful, all-inclusive pioneer, shuttling guests from one activity to another nourished by all-you-can-eat buffets.

Early in the 1960s, heart-shaped bathtubs began to appear in the romantic resorts of Pennsylvania's Poconos Mountains. Hotelier Morris Wilkins laid claim to creating the first "sweetheart tub," yet was unable to patent his design (he did, however, succeed in patenting his champagne glass bathtub, which rises seven feet in the air and is still the star of innumerable publicity photos).[20]

The all-inclusive packages of the Poconos, the self-proclaimed "honeymoon capital of the world," included poolside pizza parties (in a heart-shaped swimming pool), breakfast in bed, wienie roasts, and a "Sleepyheads Coffee Bar." Cold War newlyweds were seated at communal tables for meals, and cocktails were served en masse at dances and live shows. In *Cinderella Dreams*, authors Otnes and Pleck surmise that the flurry of group activities reflected a postwar society that put great value on conformity. They write that shared honeymoon meals served as "rehearsals" for impending lives in the suburbs, surrounded by peers of similar race and class (these resorts did not admit blacks or Jews), and hotel staff indeed booked guests in clusters with similar backgrounds. Most of the lodgers were working-class, with an average age of nineteen for the brides, so the vacation often provided these young people with "their first hotel stay, their first restaurant meal, and their first glass of wine."[21]

A caustic 1933 article in the *North American Review* criticized the idea of honeymooning, suggesting it was engineered to keep couples away from each other more than together. Travis Hoke wrote that the practice was new because in the past there had been nowhere to go, and travel had been historically unpleasant anyway. He joked that during what he called the "Coy Age," it bordered on scandalous for brides visiting Niagara Falls to witness the indecently named Devil's Gorge, Cave of the Winds, and Maid of the Mist, their very monikers meant to "stir the nuptial pulse."[22]

Hoke's sarcastic essay of 1933 did hit on a topic contemplated now as then: that honeymoons, featuring attractions and entertainment, are instruments of distraction, driving attention away from an embarrassed bride and staggering the forced intimacy of new marriage. Hoke wrote that honeymoons actually served to "keep newlyweds from knowing each other for as long as possible."[23] If elaborate buffets and hay rides were intentional diversions in the Poconos, then the falls at Niagara served the same purpose, providing visual spectacles and topics of conversation, as did the nightclubs of Idlewild and the comedy shows of the Catskills. The sumptuous buffets, room service breakfasts, and candlelit dinners would also fill that function, but with the addition of a certain indulgence and sensuousness.

As time marched on and the likelihood declined that the wedding night was the first time a couple had slept together, a new mentality in the Poconos embraced bawdiness, winking at the sexual revolution and promoting a sense of freedom fueled by a fancy-free vacation. The comedian Mickey Freeman, a frequent performer in Mount Airy's Crystal Room, commented on the open sexual romping of the adults-only resorts, joking that the "food was lousy, but it was a legalized orgy." Referencing the bawdy décor, he kidded that he used to tell the newlyweds that if they broke their mirrored headboard, they would have "seven years of bad sex."[24]

As of 2016, Cove Haven (home of the first heart-shaped bathtub) offers a "Sinfully Sweet Package," which includes chocolate-covered strawberries and champagne, the specialty tubs still going strong. The Garden of Eden Apple Suite has mirrored headboards and a fireplace and promises no windows for the "utmost in privacy."

GOING AWAY

Princess Vicky (daughter of Queen Victoria) had a notable "going away," which involved cannon fire and fireworks, with one hundred Eton schoolboys unhitching horses and pulling the bridal carriage up to Windsor Castle, where the newlyweds would honeymoon.[25] A modern interpretation is the 2015 creation of a special police force intended to address raucous wedding celebrants in southern Russia. A custom of wild motorcades complete with gunfire has seemingly gotten out of hand; gleeful exhibitions originally meant to mark the joy of a new marriage have become threatening.[26] While Americans do not generally shoot guns in honor of weddings, they do make a lot of noise and are not above making a scene in order to mark occasions.

Couples of the 1940s and 1950s could be counted on to don smart "going-away" outfits, and before the reception was over, the bride and groom would ceremoniously say their good-byes before leaving for their wedding night. In many instances, the vows were timed to correspond with the departure of a ship or a train, as it was then not common for couples to stay until the end of their reception. The "going away" was often when newlyweds formally thanked their guests, perhaps parceling out little candies or favors and saying their farewells.

BREAKFAST AND HANGOVER

It has become a customary nicety to host a meal in the late morning following a wedding, especially if out-of-town guests are staying at a common location. This gives the family and wedding party a chance to rehash the previous evening and to relax and eat without the stress of the day prior. There may be hangovers for some, and a heavy meal, hot coffee, and a little hair of the dog may be in order.

For those honeymooning at a Disney property, a glass slipper and tiara could be waiting on a hotel pillow, or mouse ears and rose petals might be spread on the king-sized bed. For the morning after, newlyweds might choose to host a brunch at Tony's Town Square, a replica of the site where Lady (a cocker spaniel) and her sweetheart, Tramp (mixed breed), so affectionately shared spaghetti in Disney's *Lady and the Tramp* (1955).

Disney promotes engagement packages timed to coincide with the nightly firework show, with perhaps a ring presented by an English butler, followed by a dessert buffet or hot-air balloon ride. Themed venues—such as a sit-down wedding reception with a view of Cinderella's Castle—can feature everything from "shabby chic" or beachside casual to California, Moroccan, or Japanese cuisine, or even tea on a British-inspired croquette lawn. In *Cinderella Dreams*, Otnes and Pleck note that when people choose all-inclusive resorts for their honeymoons, they are expressing a desire to be somewhere exotic or new, yet safe, without contending with "lost luggage, rude cab drivers, or strange food." It is a sure bet you can drink the water at Disney World.[27]

APHRODISIACS?

> Whosoever pronounces the word truffle gives voice to one which awakens erotic and gastronomical drams equally in the sex that wears skirts and the one that sprouts a beard.
>
> —Jean Anthelme Brillat-Savarin,
> *The Physiology of Taste*, 1825[28]

Purported aphrodisiacs include truffles, oysters, figs, beets, chocolate, artichokes, strawberries, asparagus, and honey. In actuality, health is the greatest factor in libido; thus fresh vegetables, fruits, and exercise are the true aphrodisiacs. Science does not support the existence of aphrodisiacs;

yet there is undoubtedly a link to sexuality and luxurious indulgence. That an item is expensive or difficult to obtain lends to its romance, signaling that a lover worked hard to provide it and wants to share in its consumption.

An ancient Islamic recipe meant to promote male stamina prescribed a three-day regimen of twenty almonds and one hundred pine nuts with a cup of honey.[29] Hippocrates prescribed honey for virility, and still another folk legend holds that Attila the Hun died after gorging himself on honey on his too-boisterous wedding night.

Chocolate holds a special place in romance, and legend has it that Aztec rulers ingested dozens of cups of a cocoa bean liqueur to service their harems and perform at orgies. In *The True Story of Chocolate*, researchers Sophie D. Coe and Michael D. Coe debunk the notion that Aztec banquets were home to chocolate-induced orgies. Eyewitness accounts recorded by Bernal Diaz del Castillo seem less than reliable, and his tales of banquets featuring three hundred courses were surely exaggerated. Diaz wrote that he witnessed the Aztec elite drink fifty cups of chocolate at a banquet so as to ensure "success with women." The Coes surmise that the introduction of sex as a factor in feasting owed to a Spanish obsession with aphrodisiacs. They also note that equal to Spaniards' hunt for aphrodisiacs was their quest for laxatives. The conquistadors ate a diet heavy with meat and lard, with few vegetables and fruit, and they suffered for it.[30]

Chocolate has long been associated with sin and a sign of indulgence. Food historian Michael Krondl discussed the propriety of giving chocolate during courtship in the 1870s, as detailed by an etiquette expert at the time. A gentleman was instructed to give a woman a box of chocolate only if well acquainted, and a woman should never give a box of chocolate to a man, as offering something so sweet and decadent would surely appear wonton and promiscuous. She could, however, parcel out a few ladylike pieces of candy at a time.[31]

An ancient belief holds that food has attributes that affect one's "humors," thought to rule the senses, guided by the earth's four elements. Meat was considered "hot" and lusty, and fish was considered "cool" and purifying.[32] Chinese tradition also calls for a balance of energies, with certain foods considered either hot or cold. One Chinese aphrodisiac recipe called for ground peanuts, walnuts, almonds, and dates.[33] Dr. John Kellogg treated nymphomaniacs by advising against "hot," "overstimulating" foods like peppers.[34]

Pomegranates, strawberries, and nuts have long been lauded as fertility symbols, and fish have represented "plenty" and been featured in

Jewish and Chinese weddings.[35] The ocean is an obvious source of life, and during Lent, when fish were increasingly consumed, couples were thought to be especially amorous.[36]

Fertilized duck eggs, called *balut*, are eaten in the Philippines as a common street food and customary snack. The duck embryos are boiled in their shells at sixteen to twenty days old, at which point they have already developed beaks and feathers (the ducks would normally hatch at about twenty-seven days).[37] When men consume them, they are thought to gain increased vigor, and *balut* is considered a powerful aphrodisiac. Particularly in the countryside, it is eaten at male gatherings prior to a wedding and often consumed with lots of alcohol.

Enhanced manhood and a magical cure for impotency have often been pursued to the detriment of animals. Bear bile extracted from gallbladders, powdered rhino horns, and tiger penises are examples of products marketed to increase masculinity, often illegally, with many untested or unlabeled. Supplements with names like Rock Hard, Mojo Nights, and Lighting Rod are sold to the hopeful. In 1995 the Centers for Disease Control and Prevention reported findings in connection to four deaths attributed to the consumption of purported aphrodisiacs, all from a substance sold under the names Stone, Love Stone, or Black Stone. Supposedly made from the dried skin secretions of toads, the product was subsequently outlawed in the United States.[38]

THE HONEYMOON'S OVER

Honeymoons were especially significant during a time when newlyweds, prior to their wedding, may not have experienced any form of intimacy. Many couples may never have even been alone together unchaperoned. Dining acted as a form of distraction and an amusement with which to ease a potentially awkward situation. Honeymoons have long reflected how Americans choose to spend their leisure time. Couples committed to an expensive vacation in an exotic locale because the occasion was the inimitable honeymoon.

❦ *14* ❦

The Business of Love

POTLATCH TO POTLUCKS

American school children grow up learning about Native American potlatches, a supposed gift-giving extravaganza between tribes that conjures visions of banquets with piled-up blankets and outrageous gifts. At these festivals chiefs tried to outdo one another, upping the ante with each successive gift until one participant said "uncle" and admitted that there remained nothing else to give. Potlatch rituals, primarily practiced by natives of the Pacific Northwest, were indeed a method for displaying abundance, and the number of items given away was astonishing. Yet the practice, mirroring wedding culture in several ways, was far from irrational. Potlatches were good business.

Potlaches were very much a reciprocal endeavor and also meant to provide entertainment for the entire community. They were visual shows of wealth, a way to demonstrate the ability to give away valuable resources. Margaret Visser discusses potlatches in the context of a universal human system of "gift and return," in which participants expect the exchange of gifts to move parties up a perceived social ladder. With every gift came one in return, and each ensuing gift increased reverence for the giver.[1]

A potlatch would be called for important life events, especially those to do with reproduction, such as to celebrate the naming of a child, the onset of puberty, and, of course, a marriage. An enormous bounty of natural resources surrounded those living in the coastal Northwest and required careful management for the larger population to thrive. Strategic alliances curtailed the deadly raids that would have naturally occurred if one group routinely restricted access to a food resource (a fishing location, for instance).

Communities were primarily organized into kinship groups rather than formal "tribes," so gifting was a way to maintain cordial ties among groups as well as to reallocate goods.[2] Goods then could move *between* groups, ensuring a varied diet for individuals who did not use "money" and had no tradition of bartering. The potlatch system, seemingly bizarre to European eyes, relied on the expectation that every gift would be reciprocated and that the most prosperous would give the most gifts, thereby maintaining their status as well as sharing their resources.

Variety was a necessity in marital matches as well, and potlach feasts were social occasions that brought participants from far away to arrange, as well as to celebrate, marriages between members of discrete communities. Access, for instance, to a shellfish bed or a patch of land replete with certain foods (e.g., berries or nuts) was a common wedding gift that sealed marital alliances.

Europeans would have viewed the potlach as a blithe divestment of goods. Yet the very giving away of items elevated this ritual into a means of economic control. Prestige came from an ability to share resources—a concept opposite to the European practice of selling rather than giving away excess goods.[3]

CASH FOR TITLES: DOLLAR PRINCESSES

> There was a notable absence of jewels among the guests, as there should be for a morning wedding.
>
> —*New York Times*, reporting on the wedding of heiress
> Consuelo Vanderbilt, November 7, 1895

American tycoons of the nineteenth century may have been incredibly wealthy, but many still yearned for social status at a time when money could not open doors to the closed environs of the elite. "Old money" mattered in high society, particularly in New York. The heirs of "self-made men" like Andrew Carnegie and Cornelius Vanderbilt wanted to legitimize their standing by adding British titles to their names. The "land rich, cash poor" British aristocrats, who considered holding a job ungentlemanly, were being strangled by high taxes and plummeting agricultural prices. Needing funds to keep their crumbling estates intact, they awaited the American mothers and daughters who came to husband-hunt during the London social season. "Cash for title" unions gave rise to a special bridal industry that included high-end matchmakers and a quarterly magazine, the *Titled American*, which helpfully categorized bachelors by title and income.[4]

One such union brought Winston Churchill into the world. His father was Lord Randolph Churchill, son of the seventh Duke of Marlborough, and his mother was Jennie Jerome, a Brooklyn-born heiress. Jerome brought to the marriage in 1874 almost $300,000, in the neighborhood of $6 million today, and a yearly stipend of over $5,000.[5]

In 1895, 4,000 invitations were sent out for the wedding of Consuelo Vanderbilt to Charles Spencer-Churchill, ninth Duke of Marlborough (Princess Diana was one of these Spencers). Newspaper coverage of the event devoted paragraph after paragraph to the clothes, music, and church decorations and threw in a genealogical table of the Churchill family and sketches of the bridesmaids. The wedding breakfast at the bride's mother's townhouse catered to 115 people, with the meal declared "as dainty and inviting as any ever prepared," a mention of food eclipsed by a list of the attendees, what they wore, and precisely where they were seated in relation to Mrs. Vanderbilt. The press described two tables set up in the hall, one holding small white boxes containing wedding cake to take home and the other bearing orange blossom favors: corsages for the women and boutonnieres for the men.

The newspaper did not disclose, however, that the eighteen-year-old Consuelo had been forced to marry the duke, bullied by a mercenary mother who locked the crying bride in a guarded room to prevent her escape. The groom reportedly told Consuelo on their wedding day that he loved someone else and had no plans to be faithful and that theirs was to be purely a business arrangement.[6] The duke (known as Sunny) did not attend his own wedding rehearsal, telling a reporter, "That sort of thing is good enough for women," and went shopping instead, presumably to spend the money he had just received in exchange for his title.[7]

Many "cash for title" brides were mortified, on arriving at their grooms' sprawling estates, to find an expanse of unheated rooms, emptied of furniture sold to raise capital, and (in Consuelo's case) no indoor plumbing. The Vanderbilt wedding was a zenith in the dollar princess trend; yet it also deepened public resentment of the export of American wealth, which smacked of "gilded prostitution."

And that mercenary mother? She was none other Alva Vanderbilt, who had a few years earlier schooled Mrs. Caroline Astor by withholding invitations to her famous costume ball.

THERE HAS ALWAYS BEEN WEIRD

Productions called "Tom Thumb Weddings," a fad in the South of the 1920s and 1930s, were once common fund-raisers for churches and schools. Children in costumes performed mock wedding ceremonies, often with detailed scripts and plots.

Another once common practice, also reaching its height in the 1920s, was the "womanless wedding." These, too, were held to raise money, often for clubs like the Elks or Masons. The roles of bride, mother of the bride, and bridesmaids all were played by men in women's clothing. One could expect the bride to have chest hair comically popping out of "her" gown.

The most famous wedding of its time was that of the real General Tom Thumb, a man named Charles Stratton, who stood just thirty-six inches tall. Discovered and promoted by P. T. Barnum (of Barnum & Bailey circus fame), he became a wealthy and beloved celebrity. Charles fell in love with the wonderfully named Mercy Lavinia Warren Bump, who also worked for Barnum. Standing only thirty-two inches high, Lavinia was a schoolteacher and a descendant of a respectable *Mayflower* family.[8] Their nuptials were one of the most celebrated events of the decade, as their story gave the press an irresistible distraction from disheartening news of the Civil War.

On February 11, 1863, the *New York Times* fondly described the wedding of the "loving Lilliputians." Delighted journalists sought ever-new descriptors for their "microscopic hosts." Following the church service, a reception was held at the Metropolitan Hotel, where the couple perched on a grand piano to greet their 2,000, mostly paying guests (this was a Barnum event, after all). Their elaborate wedding cake featured an Egyptian temple decorated with cupids, angels, and harps and weighed more than both Charles and Lavinia put together. As was customary at the time, departing guests received favor boxes with a slice of cake.

The newlyweds left New York City for another reception two days later, this one at the White House, hosted by President Abraham Lincoln, a fan. Lavinia was again bedecked in her wedding gown, sporting two yards of lace train. High-ranking Union officers greeted these "thimblefuls of humanity," after which Washington notables extended a warm welcome. The six-foot-four Lincoln, Lavinia recounted later, lifted Charles up and placed him on the sofa next to him, while Mrs. Lincoln did the same with the bride. Together they shared wine and cake, the refreshments thoughtfully placed on a chair so the little people could reach.[9]

Charles had an appetite for the good life, supposedly insisting on wine with his meals from the age of five and smoking cigars from the age of seven. Lavinia's maid of honor, her sister Minnie, was even smaller than she, and newspapers ventured that she was even more beautiful than her sister. Minnie also had her own celebrity marriage of sorts, but she later died in childbirth, a fate Lavinia carefully avoided. On Charles and Lavinia's lucrative extended honeymoon tour, they hired a baby in every new town, pretending it was theirs, in order to exhibit their little family to a rapt public.

COMMERCIALISM

Even back in the days of Native American potlatches, the marriage industry could no doubt be a profitable enterprise for many—for those receiving wedding gifts and for those selling them. Consider Minnesota's enormous Mall of America, the self-proclaimed "Hollywood of the Midwest," home to over 7,500 weddings since its opening in 1995. Its Chapel of Love (on the third floor, next to Sears) offers package deals that can include a reception in the attached banquet hall. A bride may choose the "dream" option instead, which lasts a mere thirty minutes, officiant and background music

Mini elopement cake for two. *Source*: Used with permission from Dorothy Kyle.

included. The Chapel of Love also offers vow renewal, a "petite" vow renewal, and even a $99 special for couples married the first time at the chapel. At the mall, a time-pressed twosome in need of wedding favors may pick up mini gumball machines or chocolate bars embossed with their wedding date. For those truly in a hurry, the Chapel of Love hosted its first drive-through wedding in 1999.

In 2011 *Good Morning America* called Kim Kardashian's wedding to professional basketball player Kris Humphries "America's royal wedding." This horrifying statement may sound naïve in light of Kardashian's next wedding (to Kanye West). The Humphries wedding was broadcast as a two-day reality TV special and thought to cost $6 million (although much was donated in exchange for advertisement). When divorce papers were filed seventy-two days later, the pair had raked in close to $18 million in the sale of media rights.

ROYAL BLOOD

One genuine royal wedding was that of Catherine Middleton to Prince William in 2011. Although it created a media frenzy, a *New York Times/CBS News* poll found that wedding mania had not really blossomed this time, at least not as much as programmers had hoped. Many statistics as to how many people actually watched (23 million in the United States alone) were contested, leading Karen M. Dunak to observe that it seemed the "media supply exceeded demand."[10]

One might wonder what it says about American culture that the royal wedding did not capture the public imagination to the degree expected, whereas the Kardashian-Humphries wedding did. Is it that the Kardashian clan is American, and Americans reserve their zeal for their own kind? Americans were certainly smitten with Princess Diana. That Lady Diana Spencer was of royal blood was unassailable, but perhaps her appeal rested in flashes of her ordinariness—that she had not gone to college, seemed shy, and worked as a teacher's aide in a kindergarten.[11]

Did Americans gobble up the Kardashian event because it was merely purchased, something attainable through means as accessible as a basketball, whereas probably no amount of hard work could facilitate a royal wedding? Clearly a career in professional sports is out of reach for most, but such a fantasy resides easily in the American psyche and perhaps seems more possible than being, or marrying, royalty. Consider the intimacy offered by the TV exposure of the Humphries wedding. No matter how staged, cameras took audiences into the homes of this TV family. Television viewers watched catfights, family meals, shopping trips, and kitchen chatter. William and Kate, however, were beautiful mannequins, polished and well behaved, yet distant and inhabiting a life that one can only be born to.

ON THE LAM

In 2015 the FBI nabbed a drug dealer in Juneau, Alaska, who was eventually convicted of smuggling heroin and methamphetamine. This particular convict owned a bridal business and had funneled drug profits into her shop. The FBI's first big "bridal asset seizure" yielded three thousand pieces of inventory, including veils, bolts of taffeta, and tiny cummerbunds for ring boys. The U.S. Marshals Service generally auctions off confiscated items, using proceeds to compensate victims of crime. So, for this haul, it hosted a unique bridal fair. Federal agents, wearing tulle wedding dresses and mother-of-the-bride frocks, walked the catwalk in their government building, deftly decorated for the day. They sold nearly $500,000 worth of this surrendered merchandise.[12]

RSVP TO THE LGBT

By the 1990s, websites and guidebooks routinely featured gay-friendly venues, and kitschy same-sex cake toppers are no longer novel. In 2002 the *New York Times* made history with its decision to include gay weddings in its "Style" section. In 2015 the Supreme Court made same-sex marriages legal in all states.

Vendors such as EnGAYgedWeddings.com and *Gaycation Magazine* sponsored the enormous 2015 LBGT Expo in New York City. Met Life, too, was a sponsor, promising to "bring different points of view to your financial plan," as were Uber and Delta Airlines. Delta featured a website for planning a gay-friendly vacation or honeymoon, proclaiming, "If you see us waving our wings at one of the Pride Events, make sure to wave back." Exhibitors at the 2016 LBGT Expo in Sacramento, California, featured stalwart Sacramento regulars such as the Crocker Art Museum, Residence Inn, and Macy's.

In 2013, the refusal of bakers in Oregon to bake a wedding cake for a lesbian couple made headlines. Court systems across the country are handling cases involving business owners who, citing religious beliefs, resist the increasing tide of acceptance of gay marriage.

"Gay Days," held on the first Saturday in June since the early 1990s at Walt Disney World in Florida, is not officially sanctioned by the company. And yet the popular honeymoon and vacation locale is embroiled in controversy. Soundly criticized by fundamentalist religious groups, it is also the object of internal disagreement among the LGBT community.

> How would you feel if you entered the Magic Kingdom anticipating a normal day of fun with your family only to witness thousands of same-sex couples holding hands, hugging, kissing and wearing tee-shirts that promoted their lifestyle?
>
> —Florida Family Association,
> referring to Disney Gay Days[13]

The wedding industry delights in the prospect of ever more consumers, acknowledging that same-sex couples want ice sculptures and sumptuous buffets too. And the Gay Chapel of Las Vegas is unconventional not in its commitment to same-sex marriages but in offering a Grim Reaper ceremony in a graveyard. Like any religious, ethnic, or other group, the LGBT community may have special challenges and concerns to consider when planning weddings and honeymoons. And LGBT couples may or may not elect to have their weddings defined by their membership in that particular demographic group. A same-sex couple may wish to have an entirely traditional wedding, undistinguishable from a heterosexual wedding, perhaps particularly because this right was denied them for so long.

George Takei, of *Star Trek* television fame, married Brad Altman in 2008, and one could argue the least noteworthy feature of his wedding was that it was a union of two men. A Buddhist priest presided, sharing attention with a Scottish bagpiper, and cards were affixed to the favors (black bean paste candies), which read, "May Sweet Equality Live Long and Prosper." Nichelle Nichols, who portrayed Lieutenant Uhura on the original show, and Walter Koenig, who played Ensign Chekov, acted as maid of honor and best man. The couple's wedding bands were made by a Navajo silversmith, and the pair compared their wedding to a moon landing, "taking two giant steps for gaykind."[14]

In 2003 the venerable *Brides* magazine made its first foray into the topic of same-sex marriage in a short piece answering a query about how to behave as a guest at a same-sex wedding.[15] Just as the periodical did not take sides during the Vietnam era, here, too, readers' involvement was credited as that of an onlooker, so as to not scandalize some readers by seeming to endorse untoward behavior. The magazine was not assuming its readers were gay but was admitting that they may have friends who were. Some might even say that the LGBT marriage market is not all that groundbreaking.[16] The wedding industry has always courted the newest group willing to lay down its cash, adapting and pulling the etiquette experts along with it.

What's Cooking Now?

HOMEWORK

In the 1980s Martha Stewart began an empire espousing a better life through food, telling her audience how to decorate their own wedding cakes, make favors, and create centerpieces. She also showed them how to decorate their homes, tend their gardens, and prepare gourmet meals once married. If her audience did not care to do those things, they could just buy her products to partake of her excellence. Stewart's *Weddings* helped ensure that the ambitious bride no longer deemed acceptable fruit cups and plastic tablecloths in the church basement.

By the 1990s chefs had become architects, devising new ways of plating and designing ever-taller towers of food. If a dish could be stacked, molded into a ring, and drizzled with a sauce from a squeeze bottle (roasted pepper coulis, anyone?), it was on the menu. Mesclun greens, radicchio, and baby lettuces had long since banished their ma-ligned cousin, iceberg lettuce, and truffle oil began its assault on the populace. Thanks to demanding foodie marriages, weddings were start-ing to feature good food.

The boundaries defining "gourmet" continued to blur. When sun-dried tomatoes and fresh pasta became available in grocery stores, chefs looked to science to help them distinguish their field. Harold McGee's seminal *On Food and Cooking* was a harbinger of the imminent marriage of food and science, and by the 1990s, this book had found itself in the hands of any self-respecting culinary student or curious gourmand. McGee ex-plained *how* cooking worked, debunking urban legends about the kitchen and giving clear scientific explanations for the wonderland of techniques that chefs already employed. The molecular gastronomy movement was germinating; meanwhile, Americans were also rediscovering comfort food.

Comfort food was becoming increasingly common on menus in a new kind of fusion cooking that mixed "high" and "low" foods: mashed potatoes pureed with Roquefort cheese, macaroni and cheese made with lobster, and foie gras perched along with a burger on a bun.

Chefs disassembled "serious" food in their laboratories and used chemistry and technology to redefine the very atoms that comprised ingredients. The molecular gastronomy movement toyed with distilling the core of a food's flavor and then reconstructing it in a new form. Frozen chocolate air, foamed hollandaise sauce, olive oil powder, and mozzarella balloons arrived, challenging diners' senses and setting chefs to work on ever more experimentation.

WHAT'S UP NOW?

The new millennium has seen menus continue to reimagine childhood and comfort food favorites. Hamburger sliders and mini grilled-cheese sandwiches lead the "bite-size" craze, followed by cake pops, mini cupcakes, and even microgreens and microherbs. Minifood has reached a bizarre apex with the advent of "tiny food" demonstrations. A quick tour of YouTube will reveal an outbreak of displays of tiny omelets made in doll-house kitchens and minuscule shrimp tempura fried on miniature stoves heated by candles.

Bacon has reached new heights of celebrity, and "whole-animal" technicians have made butchery cool. The rise of vegan and gluten-free food has transformed grocery store inventories. Urban foragers and "freegans" (who employ a form of disciplined dumpster diving) exemplify the ultimate in sustainable food practice. Raw food and low-carb meals enjoy notoriety, exalting vegetables and grains in a society that has legislated salt and fat content in fast-food fare. Food trucks are a medium for hordes of entrepreneurs to offer eclectic offerings at low prices, and social media and blogging make everyone a food critic with a platform.

The molecular gastronomy movement continues; yet detractors have tired of "shock-value food." Or perhaps the public has just become fatigued now that the chemicals and tools needed to work magic are sold at Williams-Sonoma and available via the Internet. Some techniques, however, like *sous-vide* cookery (in which a machine creates a vacuum and food maintains moisture and gains intensified flavor), seem destined to hold a permanent place in every cook's repertoire. Vegan thickeners like agar-agar, hardly employed in experimental cooking, have joined the mainstream. Mastermind Ferran Adria closed his renowned Spanish molecular gastronomy temple, elBulli, in 2012, but his mixtures, tools, and recipes live on online.

And so the engine that drives America's eating habits is a direct reflection of its history, as is the way Americans celebrate their weddings. So now let us see how these two come together within the rituals of marriage-related celebrations.

WEDDING FACTORIES

The decision to have a sit-down versus a buffet meal depends on the venue and the host's budget. How do restaurants and hotels manage these events? "Wedding factories" crank happy couples through their doors. Valet parking, coat check, and bathrooms are arranged to ensure no bride comes across another woman in a wedding gown, despite large operations orchestrating multiple weddings simultaneously. Catering halls stack preset tables one on top of another, complete with silverware arrangements and swan-folded napkins. The tables are lifted into the desired room so no time is wasted in the hurried turnover between clients. Or a look under the current tablecloth may expose the linen chosen for the next event scheduled in that room. Wedding guests are often mailed menu-selection cards to be sent back with their RSVPs. This allows catering companies to purchase only as much food as needed, saving them money and explaining why banquets are often more profitable than á la carte restaurants.

SOMEWHERE OVER THE RAINBOW ROOM

The famous Rainbow Room in New York City, reopened in 2014 after its closure in 2009, exemplifies several trends now at work in contemporary wedding food culture. The main room of the luxury space, with its spectacular restored rotating dance floor, is now open to the public only for Sunday brunch and select evenings. The venue seems to have exchanged fine dining for banquet events. The company's ambitious website has a special section just for weddings (as do most large banquet venues).

Any chef can tell you that banquet events, which feature a set menu for a specific number of guests, have higher profit margins than á la carte occasions. Banquets allow a chef to order specific amounts of food in bulk, eliminating unnecessary purchases. Staff can be scheduled efficiently, and rental of the room and equipment generate money as well.

The suggested sample wedding menu at Rainbow Room is a savvy mixture of old and new, featuring continental warhorses like filet mignon, béarnaise sauce, and baked Alaska. And yet even Rainbow Room, having served its time-honored fare to presidents and kings since 1932, provides the high/low mix of food. The "mini" vogue is represented, with hors d'oeuvres such as beef Wellington bites, miniature spicy tuna tacos, and small salmon tartare cones with crème fraîche and caviar. Sliders make the usual appearance, served at this tony institution with truffled Gruyère cheese.[1] The revenue from weddings will surely keep Rainbow Room's lacquered doors open, and menus such as these will serve as a model to which caterers of lesser pedigree will aspire.

While wedding planners push ice carvings and edible arrangements, upwardly mobile couples seek to use the wedding reception as a way to reinforce, or reinvent, their social standing. Second marriages, known as "encore weddings," give couples a chance to throw a party free

Gluten-free vegan cake for second marriage between Jewish bride and Protestant groom in Italian restaurant in New York City, Ken Franconero and Stacey Stolman, 2015. *Source*: Author's collection.

of the familial or cultural expectations that accompany a first marriage. Destination and theme weddings, paired with a heightened disposable income, also make for nontraditional choices. Couples who identify as "foodies" may cram their reception menus with adjectives like "cage-free," "organic," "heirloom," "local," and "artisan."

WHAT'S OLD IS GREEN AGAIN

Vegetarianism, during World Wars I and II, was a way of exhibiting patriotism, allowing a majority of available meat to go to troops, as well as conserving the natural resources needed to prepare it. During the Depression, pamphlets and inexpensive cookbooks shared creative ways to cook with little or no meat. A typical 1929 cookbook featured nut loaves, croquettes, and bean roasts, all bound with bread crumbs, as well as lettuce and peanut butter sandwiches and mock sausage made with lima beans. Conversely, the limited supply of meat led to an increased use of offal meats, and there was a flurry of imaginative recipes for stuffed hearts, breaded kidneys, and boiled tongue.

"Green," or sustainable, wedding receptions are growing in popularity, and couples may look for caterers that practice "zero waste," recycle trash, compost their scraps, and eschew products with a large carbon footprint. Choices might include free-trade coffee and chocolate, linens and dishes washed with minimal water use, and organic flower arrangements.[2]

As of 2012, the average American wedding produced four to five hundred pounds of garbage, and one year of weddings in the United States produced greenhouse gases equivalent to 8 million cars on the road.[3] Thriftiness and seasonal living were the norm until industrialization and conspicuous consumption took over. Being "green" helped ensure survival. Early colonists scraped together a mean existence when they arrived in the New World, and stubborn pioneers raised crops in forbidding conditions. Native Americans had long seen the practicality of managing their resources, and the urban poor have always been resourceful and squeezed out uses for any materials available.

The White House Cook Book of 1913, for instance, listed not just the vegetables but also the meats, fish, and game in season for every month. We now call those who only use what is naturally available "locavores." Herbal remedies were standard in vintage cookbooks, and recipes for flax seed tea and flax seed lemonade from the same 1913 cookbook could easily correspond to products on display these days at Whole Foods.

Ironically, it now can be more expensive to host a wedding that uses sustainable practices than a traditional one. The wealthy can afford to be high-minded.

The do-it-yourself (DIY) movement manifests in the resurgence of the potluck wedding supper, and hipster couples rush to bottle their own barbecue sauce for party favors (in personalized mini mason jars found online). A writer for the *New York Times,* discussing elaborate homemade party favors, christened Pinterest the "mothership of DIY projects" and noted that if you have to ask how much time it takes to make something like biodegradable confetti, then you probably don't have enough time to make it.[4]

A 2014 survey of 15,000 couples by The Knot found that 87 percent of weddings incorporated DIY items in some form.[5] This may seem significant—then again, the fact that we actually have a special term for making things ourselves is telling. Just as people compete to outspend others when producing a lavish wedding, they compete for "authenticity." Wielding a glue gun can be a modern way of achieving that.

NERD CULTURE

Singles looking for a mate online might visit ParanormalDate.com, which advertises itself as a way to meet someone with similar interests, such as "ghost stories, Bigfoot, and life after death." ConspiracyDate.com promises to help members find others who share a common interest in "what really happened."

A couple who met on these online sites might choose to wed at the Viva Las Vegas Wedding Chapel in Nevada. Those who choose the "Intergalactic Wedding" can be married by Captain Quirk, who beams in via transporter. Or couples may opt for the Godfather as their officiant, as part of the "Gangster Wedding" package, which includes exactly one Italian waiter as witness. The "Wassup Pussycat Wedding" gets you a Tom Jones impersonator as your officiant. He shares office space with Count Dracula, James Bond, and Alice Cooper, all eager to preside over nuptials. Elvis, of course, has his own category, with fifteen Elvis themes from which to choose (e.g., "Blue Hawaii," "Hound Dog"). While in Las Vegas, marrying at Denny's is also possible; $95 can buy a trip down the Denny's aisle, a Pancake Puppies® wedding cake, and matching "Just Married" Denny's T-shirts.

A quickie wedding in Vegas no longer connotes an elopement, and the number of reception halls attached to chapels offer proof that couples hope to celebrate with friends and family. At the Viva Las Vegas chapel, the "Doo Wop Diner" package includes root beer floats and White Castle burgers, and a "Kansas City BBQ" wedding package includes pork and beans.

In other parts of the country you can have a Harry Potter–themed wedding or exchange vows while queuing up for the next *Star Wars* film. In Minnesota, the Igloo Bar, housed on a frozen lake, can host wedding receptions during which guests ice-fish via holes in the floor and the kitchen staff cooks the catch.

ON THE MENU

High-quality whimsical items and comfort food have taken their place at the reception table. Tiny meatloaves (made with grass-fed beef), cheeseburger sliders (made with artisan bread), and macaroni and cheese (made with imported cheeses) have supplanted shrimp cocktail and Caesar salad. Sweet/salty flavors are trending now, as with the chocolate-chipotle-dipped potato chips at Pier Sixty, a high-end catering venue in New York City. This locale also offers "Hawker's Trays" for the cocktail hour, with "assorted snacks in whimsical bags and cups butlered on oversized stadium-style tray with ribbon straps that go around servers' necks."[6] Pier Sixty also employs another popular option: interactive stations, which in this case includes "Dunk, Drizzle and Dust." These buffets feature items like salted caramel and mocha kronuts (a croissant-donut hybrid) acting as "dunks." There is an option to add "drizzles," such as white chocolate pistachio and port balsamic, and "dusts," which include dried strawberries, candied bacon, coconut, and cookie crumbs.

PRECIOUS CARGO

Childlike food is trendy, and popcorn with a gourmet twist (for instance, with truffle oil or grated parmesan and basil) is a favorite for late-night or after-party menus. Pizza bars, taco bars, and milk-and-cookie stations offer midnight snacks, providing a new revenue stream for caterers and indulgence for partiers who don't want the evening to end.

Recently food trucks have started to cater weddings. Companies like Roaming Hunger connect customers to a network of food trucks, which can be booked to arrive on location with a prearranged menu.

FOOD TRUCKS ARE NOT NEW

As early as 1800, American cities swelled, and their residents wrestled with the effects of rapid and unplanned urban growth. Cities lacked sanitation systems, fresh drinking water was not available, and raw sewage and garbage lined the streets. Scholar Laura Schenone contends that, for the urban poor, cooking was a grueling activity and not feasible every day. A lack of indoor plumbing necessitated lugging water, fuel, and groceries up flights of stairs and down narrow hallways.[7]

Food hucksters, with their impromptu carts moving through the streets, sold everything from milk to oysters to sausages, and some even delivered door to door. Not particularly hygienic, this "street food" was more questionable than the fare sold by reputable vendors in storefronts. But it was inexpensive and easy to attain. In the mid-1800s there was little understanding of how diseases spread, and life expectancy hovered at forty years (and even lower for African Americans).[8] In later years, food vendors played a part in the Harlem Renaissance. "Harlem menus" listed inexpensive southern specialties sold from the cart that week and were a source of comfort. Residents called these menus—a reminder of a shared identity—"letters from home."[9]

Flash and pop-up weddings are another trend. Businesses like Pop! Wed Co. will arrange elopements, file paperwork at city hall, or orchestrate last-minute destination vows at impromptu sites like pizza parlors, amusement parks, and thrift shops. These companies organize conventional wedding services like photography, ministry, and champagne toasts but specialize in last-minute requests and can tailor weddings to host just a handful of guests.

In Japan, Cerca Travel specializes in "solo weddings," designed for the bride who wants high-production photos of herself in a wedding gown but is not getting married. The lucky nonbride can pore over bouquet choices, try on gowns, and spend the night in a hotel being pampered. After her makeup and hair have been done, her wedding coordinator takes her to the "ceremony," where she poses for her wedding portraits. Korean companies also provide these services, with some women reporting that they merely want to have their portraits taken when "in their prime," while others never plan to wed and use the opportunity to throw a party. The desire to enjoy the trappings of a modern wedding, while keeping the event unique, drives the wedding industry of today. In current culture, living together is socially acceptable, children born out of wedlock are not slighted, and marrying across racial and religious lines is barely noteworthy in many communities. And yet, even bohemians seem to want white weddings. Like Deadheads who panhandle in the street and then go for a bubble bath and a game of tennis at their mom and dad's house, many faddish couples are looking to force a form of grittiness into their wedding day, despite their economic entitlement. They want to show "rustic" ideals while simultaneously expecting comfort and good, hot food. They might want to be original or to challenge convention, but at heart they still want to exchange vows, carry flowers, have a best man, or cut the cake. The desire to participate in traditional wedding rituals is strong, despite the siren song of nonconformity. Food is a way to answer that call.

The children of baby boomers, called echo boomers or Generation Z, are the demographic currently in the wedding industry's crosshairs. According Antonia Van Der Meer, editor in chief of *Modern Bride*, this cohort presents a special marketing opportunity. Most young couples right now are not really antiestablishment; they want the trimmings of traditional weddings and expect help with the planning. Van Der Meer notes that this generation, sheltered unlike any previous one, is accustomed to coddling; they were the first kids strapped into car seats behind "baby on board signs."[10]

NO TWO WEDDINGS ARE THE SAME

It is true that the couples marrying today are used to having their movements managed. They have "never ridden a bicycle without a helmet" and always been told they are "above average."[11] Members of this group are sometimes called "snowflakes," a reference to their supposed uniqueness and fragility. This ethos is manifesting itself in their weddings, as these people interpret their special day as a big show, a production in which they are the stars, guests are the audience, and someone has made snacks.

Conclusion

You May Kiss the Cook

In "The Nourishing Arts," Michel de Certeau and Luce Giard write of the cultural implications of preparing food, calling its preparation and service "doing-cooking."[1] They speak of how food preparation is a form of reenactment, a way of reliving the past and recreating moments in time in tribute to those who worked before to feed their young. This is in homage to the hands that cooked in the past in order for the present to come to bear. De Certeau and Giard write that food has become ritualized in order for humans to live more fully in the present. This work in the past (preparing food) ensures life in the present (eating food). It is this "way of being in the world and making it one's home" that distinguishes food as an intense experience, unique to humans.[2] This harkens to Jean Anthelme Brillat-Savarin's idea that food provides a structure in which we may converse with one another, a means to communicate even across the constraints of time.

Food then, in relation to how weddings are celebrated, serves as more than an indicator of social status. It offers a way to measure one's level of security in a social grouping. These rituals also create an opportunity to increase traction in a community outside that in which one was raised.

In *A History of the Wife*, Marilyn Yalom writes of how social status differentiated wives' roles in Victorian life. Marriage was often a "sudden transition from carefree girlhood to dutiful wifehood."[3] Even a wealthy wife would have the duty of properly managing her domestic staff, and decisions about meals and the hiring of cooks and maids rested on her shoulders. So even if not preparing food, wives were perceived as responsible for it, and it still reflected on their wisdom and decision-making prowess.

Marriage was long a way for families to make alliances, and young women were a conduit through which to "transmit inheritances" from one generation to the next through proper unions. In medieval England, female virginity before marriage was an absolute necessity, and women were closely guarded to ensure their purity. For the wedding celebration, the bride wore white; yet after marriage she was expected to wear more restrained colors and, after giving birth, to wear a lace cap.[4] This was a means of broadcasting status to those who did not know the family and perhaps also of reinforcing that status to the very woman in question: Don't forget you are married.

Carole M. Counihan, in *The Anthropology of Women and Food*, discusses the relationship between poverty and family cooking habits. She writes, "In stratified societies, hunger, like poverty, is far more likely to strike people in disadvantaged or devalued social categories."[5] The poor are obviously more likely to go hungry, intensifying divisions already in existence.[6] This norm is amplified when it comes time to celebrate publicly and host banquets. A population, perhaps already marginalized, is often eager to snatch up and exhibit food items and customs that represent mainstream taste symbolic of success not yet achieved. Hence, hosting a wedding banquet far out of line with one's economic station is one way "to overcome feelings of deprivation."[7]

FOR EXAMPLE

The groom, wearing around his neck a garland constructed of folded paper money, received a Bell 429 helicopter as a wedding present. There were over one hundred foods to choose from, including Chinese, Thai, and Indian dishes. One popular feature was the Domino's Pizza stand. An elaborate tent was adorned with Roman pillars. Chinese furniture competed with Venetian sculpture.

All this was built on a sugarcane field outside New Delhi in 2011 for the wedding reception for Lalit Tanwar and his bride, Yogita Jaunapuriais, whose politician father spent anywhere between $22 million and $55 million (estimates differed wildly) for the festivities. The display of wastefulness and wealth enraged the Indian public, especially considering the pervasiveness of malnutrition in India.[8]

In 2016 Russian tycoon Mikhail Gutseriev hosted his son's wedding at a believed cost of approximately $1 billion. The twenty-eight-year-old

Oxford-educated Said Gutseriev and his nineteen-year-old bride, Khadija Uzhakhova, were treated to custom performances by Sting and Enrique Iglesias. Jennifer Lopez performed with a squad of dancers in front of the six hundred wedding guests, who were also entertained by a fireworks display. The nine-tier wedding cake was topped with a Muslim star and crescent moon.

The bridal party hailed from Ingushetia, a poverty-stricken republic with the highest unemployment rate of any area in Russia. Some reports state that the wedding cost more than the regions' budget for health care and education for an entire year.[9] Another report from Russia valued the tiara worn by the bride at "about half the cost of the budget for all the schools in the tiny fiefdom."[10]

Humans universally celebrate social milestones and rites of passage, and the consumption of food is an important part of those celebrations. A given cuisine often serves to reinforce the social importance of these festivities as it validates and cements ceremonial acts. Food acts as an indicator of status as well, and the extensive display of various food items at weddings defines and bolsters the social ranking of the hosts.

Modern weddings retain many of their traditions from a time when a bride's virtue was a necessity. A pregnant woman's social standing depended on her community knowing for a fact that she was indeed married. And so marital celebrations became public affairs, featuring witnesses and memorable banquets so that all would recall the marriage as an official one, condoned by the bride's family. These sanctioned nuptials, then, could never be refuted. Future heirs could not be renounced.

Expensive and unforgettable cakes exemplify how food can illustrate a couple's new social status. Historically, the cutting of the cake signified that the wedding had been duly performed and that the bride's family, particularly her father, approved of the match.

Maybe Yogita Jaunapuriais's father was not thinking about all of this when he allegedly paid over $30 million for his daughter's wedding. Then again, when treated to a buffet with over one hundred types of food, guests certainly cannot deny that a wedding indeed took place. No one can know what Russian tycoon Mikhail Gutseriev was thinking when he carpeted a Moscow restaurant with $200,000 worth of flowers for his son's wedding.

We do know that both moneyed fathers were following an age-old tradition of using weddings to establish and maintain social position. The names of the moguls blanketed international newspapers and social media, in categories other than the financial section. These "public interest"

Cake smash, Daniela and Matthias Raabe, New York City. *Source*: Used with permission from Matthias Raabe.

stories and entertainment pieces perhaps exposed many readers to their names for the first time. The vast wealth of these families was declared far and wide (no matter that the news incensed a public rightfully embittered by such inappropriate extravagance).

Lest anyone believe that spending outrageously for weddings while peers starve is a foreign phenomenon, consider that the average cost of an American wedding, as of 2015, was $32,641. The average cost in Chicago was $61,265; in New York City, it was $82,299.[11] The famous hotels and restaurants of New York City are less than twelve miles from the massive housing projects of Newark, New Jersey, where one in four people live far below the poverty line.[12]

I have examined foodways and the manner in which cuisine reflects the social and economic status of those preparing, selling, and consuming food. Wedding feasts and related meals serve as a solid template for studying such categorization of individuals and their communities. The bridal industry is a particularly interesting arena to consider.

Champagne and various luxury goods reflect the specialness of a wedding. A generous wedding feast broadcasts the newly created family unit's freshly defined social status. In addition, older family members probably paid for the celebration, demonstrating that they have sanctioned the match. In current wedding culture, couples want to parade their uniqueness and use their wedding feasts to demonstrate, and share food that symbolizes, their personalities.

Food preserves familial feelings, triggering memories of childhood and forging a link to ancestors who strove to feed their young and perpetuate their lineage. Import lurks behind those mini cheeseburgers at the buffet. In addition, rituals such as bachelor parties, bridal showers, and extravagant marriage proposals all work to reinforce societal standing. The messages inherent in these practices rest under the surface; yet they effectively bolster the importance of community.

In summary, numerous media enable an investigation into the many connections between food and culture. Each offers and enriches insight and occasions further investigation into the complex roles of individuals and communities as a whole. And the food rituals connected to weddings are a particularly rich source in which to delve.

MAKING WISHES

It is my hope that there will be a coming wave of newlyweds whose desire to perpetuate the importance of their communities and families trumps their yearning to display their perceived individuality.

It is my hope that a longing to trumpet individuality is accompanied by recognition that this perceived distinctiveness stems from opportunities carved out by a greater culture whose affirmation of identity kept its membership intact and afforded endurance. Those at leisure to flaunt tradition are heirs to and guardians of the cultural, regional, and ethnic identities that fostered their entitlement.

It is my hope that there may be a turn toward civility and decorum, with blatant greed eschewed rather than encouraged or laughed off. I also hope that all those who sit at a wedding feast will find a balance between frantic consumerism and a desire to enjoy and celebrate a truly happy day, mindful of the hands that brought the food to their lips. May all the hands that grew, paid for, cooked, and presented that food serve as both tangible and transcendent representations of the importance of a memorable meal. I have worked for over thirty years as a pair of those hands, cooking, and do I find a profound respect for cuisine and tradition alive and thriving in the wonderful kitchens of America? I do.

Notes

INTRODUCTION TO THE MENU

1. Roland Barthes, "Toward a Psychology of Contemporary Food Consumption," in *Food and Culture: A Reader*, ed. Carole Counihan and Penny Van Esterik, 2nd ed. (New York: Routledge, 1997), 34.
2. Kolleen M. Guy, "'Oiling the Wheels of Social Life': Myths and Marketing in Champagne during the Belle Époque," *French Historical Studies* 22, no. 2 (Spring 1999): 237.
3. "Identity," LVMH, https://www.lvmh.com/houses/wines-spirits/mercier.
4. Zach O'Malley Greenburg, "The Real Story behind Jay Z's Champagne Deal," *Forbes*, November 6, 2014, 3, http://www.forbes.com/sites/zackomalleygreenburg/2014/11/06/why-jay-zs-champagne-news-isnt-so-new/#4ad55e4d45d6 (accessed July 8, 2016).
5. Abby Phillip, "Jay Z's Gold Champagne and the Murky Story behind His Latest Business Deal," *Washington Post*, November 6, 2014, 1.
6. Greenburg, "The Real Story behind Jay Z's Champagne Deal," 4.

CHAPTER 1: A BRIEF HISTORY OF WEDDING FEASTS

1. Nichola Fletcher, *Charlemagne's Tablecloth: A Piquant History of Feasting* (New York: St. Martin's Press, 2005), 33–34.
2. "The Edible Monument: The Art of Food for Festivals," Getty Research Institute, October 6, 2015, http://news.getty.edu/images/9036/ediblemonument pressrelease2.pdf, 3 (accessed July 11, 2016).
3. "The Edible Monument," 2.

4. George P. Monger, "Orange Blossom," in *Marriage Customs of the World: An Encyclopedia of Dating Customs and Wedding Traditions*, 2nd ed. (Santa Barbara, CA: ABC-CLIO, 2013), 2:502.

5. Alexandra Shepard, "Family and Household," in *The Elizabethan World*, ed. Susan Doran and Norman Jones (London: Routledge, 2010), 360, https://www.routledgehandbooks.com/doi/10.4324/9781315736044 (accessed on November 27, 2015).

6. Shepard, "Family and Household," 364.

7. Lawrence Stone, *Family, Sex, and Marriage in England, 1500–1800* (New York: Penguin, 1977), 271.

8. Stone, *Family, Sex, and Marriage in England, 1500–1800*, 272.

9. George P. Monger, "Divorce," in *Marriage Customs of the World: An Encyclopedia of Dating Customs and Wedding Traditions*, 2nd ed. (Santa Barbara, CA: ABC-CLIO, 2013), 233.

10. Carroll Camden, *The Elizabethan Woman* (Houston, TX: Elsevier Press, 1951), 102.

11. Camden, *The Elizabethan Woman*, 146.

12. Camden, *The Elizabethan Woman*, 149.

13. Marilyn Yalom, *A History of the Wife* (New York: HarperCollins, 2001), 137.

14. Alice Morse Earle, "Old Time Marriage Customs in New England," *Journal of American Folklore* 6, no. 21 (April–June 1893): 100.

15. Jaclyn Geller, *Here Comes the Bride* (New York: Four Walls Eight Windows, 2001), 257.

16. Brian Murphy, *The World of Weddings: An Illustrated Celebration* (New York: Paddington Press, 1978), 64.

17. R. A. Houston, *Bride Ales and Penny Weddings* (New York: Oxford University Press, 2014).

18. Murphy, *The World of Weddings*, 53.

19. Geller, *Here Comes the Bride*, 315–16.

20. Richard Cavendish, "Tom Thumb's Wedding," *History Today* 63, no. 2 (February 2013): 9.

21. "Fashionable Weddings," *New York Times*, November 23, 1881, 5.

22. Barbara Penner, "A Vision of Love and Luxury: The Commercialization of Nineteenth-Century American Weddings," *Winterthur Portfolio* 39, no. 1 (Spring 2004): 5.

23. Mary Ronald, *The Century Cook Book* (New York: The Century Company, 1899), 1.

24. Gabrielle Rosiere, "A Kitchen Soldier Wedding," *Good Housekeeping* 66, no. 6 (June 1918): 65.

25. "Society-Mardi Gras Celebration," *New York Times*, February 10, 1918, 45.

26. Enid Wells, *Living for Two: A Guide to Homemaking* (New York: David Kemp and Co., 1939), 231.

27. "I'm Going to Be Married in June," *Brides* 3, no. 3 (Spring 1937): 38.

28. Yalom, *A History of the Wife*, 205.

29. Carolyn Kott Washburne, *America in the Twentieth Century, 1920–1929* (North Bellmore, NY: Marshall Cavendish, 1995), 750.

30. Laura Schenone, *A Thousand Years over a Hot Stove* (New York: W. W. Norton, 2003), 274.

31. "The Price of Freedom," National Museum of American History, http://amhistory.si.edu/militaryhistory/printable/index.asp.

32. Vicki Howard, "The Bridal Business," *OAH Magazine of History* 24, no. 1 (January 2010): 53.

33. Vicki Howard, *Brides, Inc.: American Weddings and the Business of Tradition* (Philadelphia: University of Pennsylvania Press, 2006), 207.

34. "Entertaining Wives," *Brides* 33, no. 6 (June/July 1967): 98.

35. Karen M. Dunak, *As Long as We Both Shall Love: The White Wedding in Postwar America* (New York: New York University Press, 2013), 70.

36. Cele C. Otnes and Elizabeth H. Pleck, *Cinderella Dreams: The Allure of the Lavish Wedding* (Berkeley: University of California Press, 2003), 49.

37. "Menus for a Newlywed Couple's First Get Together," *Brides* 34 (June/July 1968): 171.

38. "Freezer Wise," *Good Housekeeping* 130, no. 5 (May 1950): 98.

39. *Vogue's Book of Etiquette* (Ithaca, NY: Conde Nast, 1925), 458.

40. Howard, *Brides, Inc.*, 207.

41. "Style," *Brides* 35 no. 3 (May 1969): 48.

42. Letitia Baldridge, "Here Comes the Bride Again," *Saturday Evening Post* (May–June 1981): 56.

43. Howard, *Brides, Inc.*, 220.

44. Howard, *Brides, Inc.*, 228.

CHAPTER 2: FAMOUS AND INFAMOUS FEASTS

1. "Nancy Miller Weds Former Maharajah," Associated Press, *New York Times*, March 18, 1928, 1.

2. Ian Copeland, *The Princes of India in the Endgame of Empire, 1917–1947* (New York Cambridge University Press, 1997), 53.

3. Art Buchwald, "Buchwald Attends Wedding at Kelly Family's Invitation," *New York Times*, April 20, 1956.

4. Janet Theophano, *Eat My Words: Reading Women's Lives through the Cookbooks They Wrote* (New York: Palgrave, 2002), 33.

5. Nichola Fletcher, *Charlemagne's Tablecloth: A Piquant History of Feasting* (New York: St. Martin's Press, 2005), 4.

6. Ken W. Purdy, "Prince Philip: England's Most Misunderstood Man," *Look*, April 7, 1964, 35.

7. Harry Mount, "Philip at a Nazi Funeral and the Day His Sister Had Lunch with Hitler: TV Documentary Reopens Painful Chapter of Duke's Family Past," *Daily Mail*, July 19, 2015, http://www.dailymail.co.uk/news/article-3167585/Philip-Nazi-funeral-day-sister-lunch-Hitler-TV-documentary-reopens-painful-chapter-duke-s-family-past.html.

8. Sarah Helm, "Duke Will Tiptoe to His Mother's Grave," *Independent*, September 17, 1994.

9. "Prince Andrew of Greece," *Gay Influence*, August 30, 2011, http://gayinfluence.blogspot.com/2011/08/prince-andrew-of-greece.html.

10. John Burnnett, *Useful Toil: Autobiographies of Working People from the 1820s to the 1930s* (New York: Routledge, 1994), 198.

11. Gabriel Tschumi, *Royal Chef: Recollections of Life in Royal Households from Queen Victoria to Queen Mary* (London: W. Kimber, 1954), 193.

12. Freiderike Melchior and Julia Haedecke, *Royal Weddings* (London: Gardners Books, 2011), 111.

13. Cora C. Klein, *Practical Etiquette* (Chicago: A. Flanagan, 1899), 44.

14. Wilbur Cross and Ann Novotny, *White House Weddings* (New York: David McKay Company, 1967), 131–32.

15. "Longworth, Alice Lee Roosevelt," Theodore Roosevelt Digital Library, Dickinson State University, http://www.theodorerooseveltcenter.org/Learn-About-TR/TR-Encyclopedia/Family-and-Friends/Alice-Lee-Roosevelt-Longworth.aspx (accessed May 24, 2016).

16. Cross and Novotny, *White House Weddings*, 158.

17. Cele C. Otnes and Elizabeth H. Pleck, *Cinderella Dreams: The Allure of the Lavish Wedding* (Berkeley: University of California Press, 2003), 121; Ben Cosgrove, "Photos: JFK and Jackie's Wedding, 1953," *Time*, August 7, 2013, http://time.com/3494367/photos-jfk-and-jackies-wedding-1953; search results for "Kennedy wedding," Library of Congress, http://www.loc.gov/pictures/search/?q=kennedy%20wedding.

18. Jan Pottker, *Janet and Jackie: The Story of a Mother and Her Daughter, Jacqueline Kennedy Onassis* (New York: St. Martin's Press, 2001), 139–42.

19. "The Talk of the Town: Food Beat," *New Yorker*, August 21, 1971, 20-23.

20. "Heinz H. Bender, 83, Presidents' Pastry Chef," *New York Times*, February 7, 1993.

21. Karen M. Dunak, *As Long as We Both Shall Love: The White Wedding in Postwar America* (New York: New York University Press, 2013), 57.

22. John Lane, *A Taste of the Past: Menus from Lavish Luncheons, Royal Weddings, Indulgent Dinners and History's Greatest Banquets* (Cincinnati, OH: F&W, 2004), 29.

23. Lane, *A Taste of the Past*, 27.

24. Lane, *A Taste of the Past*, 30.

25. Lisa Anderson, "Happily Ever After? It Never Happened, Says a Bridesmaid of Princess Grace," *Chicago Tribune*, June 15, 1989.

26. "How Much Is a Scrap of Royal Wedding Toast Worth?" *Morning Edition*, July 23, 2012, http://www.npr.org/2012/07/23/157219617/how-much-is -a-scrap-of-royal-wedding-toast-worth (accessed January 24, 2016).

27. "Auction Results," Julien's Auctions, http://www.juliensauctions.com/ auctions/2014/icons-and-idols-hollywood/results.html.

28. Emily Jane Fox, "A $7,500 Slice of Fruit Cake," *CNN Money*, February 2, 2015, http://money.cnn.com/2014/12/06/luxury/royal-family-auction-sold.

29. "Auction Results."

30. Andy Weisbecker, "Wedding Bell Blues," *Food Safety News*, August 9, 2010, 3.

31. "Wedding Cake Culprit in 1000 Illnesses," UPI, August 26, 1982, http://www.upi.com/Archives/1982/08/26/Wedding-cake-culprit-in-1000 -illnesses/3223399182400.

32. D. S. Friedman et al., "An Outbreak of Norovirus Gastroenteritis Associated with Wedding Cakes," *Epidemiology and Infection* 133, no. 6 (December 2005): 1060.

33. "Food Poisoning Kills Twenty at Nepal Wedding," UPI, November 3, 1994, http://www.upi.com/Archives/1994/11/03/Food-poisoning-kills-20-at -Nepal-wedding/9160783838800.

34. Weisbecker, "Wedding Bell Blues," 1.

35. Weisbecker, "Wedding Bell Blues," 2.

36. Mercedes Laura Jimenez et al., "Multinational Cholera Outbreak after Wedding in Dominican Republic," *Emerging Infectious Diseases* 17, no. 11 (November 2011): 2172.

37. Jimenez et al., "Multinational Cholera Outbreak after Wedding in Dominican Republic," 2173.

38. Ellen M. Ireland, "Food Safety," in *Sage Encyclopedia of Food Issues*, ed. Ken Albala (Thousand Oaks, CA: Sage, 2015), 2:604.

CHAPTER 3: THE LAST HOORAY

1. Diane Ackerman, *A Natural History of Love* (New York: Random House, 1994), 270.

2. Lucius Beebe, "The Awful Seeley Dinner," *New Yorker*, January 16, 1932, 34.

3. A. H. Saxon, *P. T. Barnum: The Legend and the Man* (New York: Columbia University Press, 1989), 316.

4. Beebe, "The Awful Seeley Dinner," 38.

5. Erik Larson, *The Devil in the White City* (New York: Vintage Books, 2003), 424.

6. Freiderike Melchior and Julia Haedecke, *Royal Weddings* (London: Gardners Books, 2011), 106.

7. Vicki Santillani, "How Celebrities Do Bachelor Parties," *More*, http://www.divinecaroline.com/entertainment/how-celebs-do-bachelor-parties-eight -infamous-shindigs.

8. Beth Montemurro, *Something Old, Something Bold* (New Brunswick, NJ: Rutgers University Press, 2006), 134.

9. Diane Tye and Ann Marie Powers, "Gender, Resistance and Play: Bachelorette Parties in Atlantic Canada," *Women's Studies International Forum* 21, no. 5 (1998): 551–61.

10. G. W. Titherington, "The Raik Dinka of Bahr El Ghazal Province," *Sudan Notes and Records* 10 (1927): 184.

11. Raafay Awan, "Forced Feeding and Fattening Tradition in Mauritania," *Finding Neverland Blog*, May 19, 2014, http://raafay-awan.blogspot .com/2014/05/forced-feeding-and-fattening-tradition.html.

12. Hagar Salamon and Esther Juhasz, "Goddesses of Flesh and Metal: Gazes on the Tradition of Fattening Jewish Brides in Tunisia," *Journal of Middle East Women's Studies* 7, no. 1 (Winter 2011): 7.

13. Salamon and Juhasz, "Goddesses of Flesh and Metal," 10.

14. M. Komolafe et al., "Stroke Risk Factors among Participants of a World Stroke Day Awareness Program in South-Western Nigeria," *Nigerian Journal of Clinical Practice* 18, no. 6 (November–December 2015): 808.

15. Enang Oe, "The Fattening Rooms of Calabar: A Breeding Ground for Diabesity," *Diabetes Voice* 54 (May 2009): 41, http://www.idf.org/diabetesvoice/ articles/the-fattening-rooms-of-calabar-a-breeding-ground-for-diabesity.

16. Ann M. Simmons, "Where Fat Is a Mark of Beauty," *Los Angeles Times*, September 30, 1998, 1–2.

17. Elizabeth Abbott, *A History of Celibacy* (New York: Scribner, 2000), 260.

18. Salamon and Juhasz, "Goddesses of Flesh and Metal," 24.

19. "Resolution Adopted by the General Assembly on 20 December 2012," United Nations, http://www.npwj.org/node/7462.

20. "Las Vegas Strippers," Suite Strippers, http://suitestrippers.com/party _info.htm.

21. Mario Ledwith, "What a Dignified Retirement," *Daily Globe*, November 27, 2012.

22. James Oliver Cury, *The Playboy Guide to Bachelor Parties* (New York: Fireside, 2003), 96.

23. Cury, *The Playboy Guide to Bachelor Parties*, 224.

CHAPTER 4: SHOWERS OF FOOD, SHOWERS OF GIFTS

1. Deborah Bauer, "Dowries," in *The Social History of the American Family: An Encyclopedia*, ed. Marilyn J. Coleman and Lawrence H. Ganong (Los Angeles: Sage Reference, 2014), 384.

2. Pravima Shukla, "Dowry," in *Encyclopedia of Women's Folklore and Folklife*, ed. Liz Locke, Theresa A. Vaughan, Pauline Greenhill, and Gale Group, Gale Virtual Reference Library (Westport, CT: Greenwood Press, 2009), 138–40.

3. Barbara Penner, "A Vision of Love and Luxury: The Commercialization of Nineteenth-Century American Weddings," *Winterthur Portfolio* 39, no. 1 (Spring 2004): 7.

4. Penner, "A Vision of Love and Luxury," 10.

5. Penner, "A Vision of Love and Luxury."

6. "Fashionable Table Ware: Decorated Granite and Plain China." *Decorator and Furnisher* 8, no. 6 (September 1886), 172.

7. Penner, "A Vision of Love and Luxury," 1–20.

8. *Vogue's Book of Etiquette* (Ithaca, NY: Conde Nast, 1925), 418.

9. Anna C. Mansfield, "A Merry Bundle Party," *Good Housekeeping* 49, no. 4 (October 1909), 404.

10. Mary J. Mount, "Dolls as Wedding Favors," *Good Housekeeping* 53, no. 1 (July 1911): 42.

11. "Illiteracy Rates," National Center for Education Statistics, http://nces.ed.gov/NAAL/lit_history.asp#illiteracy.

12. Michael Krondl, *Sweet Invention: A History of Dessert* (Chicago: Chicago Review Press, 2011), 333.

13. Carol Fisher, *The American Cookbook: A History* (Jefferson, NC: McFarland, 2006), 126.

14. Marion Harris Neil, *A Calendar of Dinners by Crisco* (Cincinnati, OH: Procter & Gamble, 1925), 18.

15. Cathy Luchetti, *Home on the Range: A Culinary History of the American West* (New York: Villard Books, 1993), 160. Quote from Eliza Leslie, *Miss Leslie's New Cookery Book* (Philadelphia: T. B. Peterson, 1857), 586, http://www.gutenberg.org/files/40943/40943-h/40943-h.htm#FINE_DESSERTS.

16. *Brides* 34 (June–July 1968): 89.

17. Karen M. Dunak, *As Long as We Both Shall Love: The White Wedding in Postwar America* (New York: New York University Press, 2013), 36.

18. "Julia Lee Cook Tells Brides How to Choose a Glass Wardrobe," *Brides* 30, no. 2 (Winter 1963): 53.

19. Alison Weir, Kate Williams, Sarah Gristwood, and Tracy Borman, *The Ring and the Crown: A History of Royal Weddings, 1066–2011* (London: Hutchinson, 2011), 76.

20. Marian Fowler, *In a Gilded Cage: American Heiresses Who Married British Aristocrats* (New York: St. Martin's Press, 1993), 157.

21. Carol Wallace, *All Dressed in White: The Irresistible Rise of the American Wedding* (New York: Penguin Books, 2004), 51.

22. Wallace, *All Dressed in White*, 53.

23. "Bridesmaid Luncheon," *Brides* 4, no. 3 (Spring 1937): 92.

24. Simon DeBruxelles, "Wales Sends Its Princess a Love Spoon," *Times*, November 18, 2000.

25. "Yichud Room," Chabad.org, http://www.chabad.org/library/article_cdo/aid/477338/jewish/Yichud-Room.htm.

26. Margaret Visser, *The Rituals of Dinner* (Toronto: HarperCollins, 1991), 195.

27. Wallace, *All Dressed in White*, 126.

28. Matthew Josephson, *Edison: A Biography* (New York: McGraw-Hill, 1959), 309.

29. Cora C. Klein, *Practical Etiquette* (Chicago: A. Flanagan, 1899), 53.

CHAPTER 5: TABLE MANNERS MATTER

1. P. Smiley Publishing Company, ed., *Smiley's Cook Book and Universal Household Guide* (Chicago: J. B. Smiley, 1901), 663.

2. Cathy Cuchetti, *Home on the Range: A Culinary History of the American West* (New York: Villard Books, 1993), 156.

3. Edward Sorel, "Astor vs. Astor," *Town & Country* 166, no. 538 (December 2012): 136.

4. Molly W. Berger, "'The Rich Man's City': Hotels and Mansions of Gilded Age New York," *Journal of Decorative and Propaganda Arts* 25 (2005): 47.

5. Berger, "The Rich Man's City," 57.

6. Berger, "The Rich Man's City."

7. "Daily Menu [held by] American House [at] 'BOSTON, MA, ([HOTEL])," New York Public Library, http://digitalcollections.nypl.org/items/510d47db-19ed-a3d9-e040-e00a18064a99.

8. William Grimes, *Appetite City: A Culinary History of New York* (New York: North Point Press, 2009), 54.

9. Berger, "The Rich Man's City," 52.

10. Linda Civitello, *Cuisine and Culture: A History of Food and People*, 2nd ed. (Hoboken, NJ: John Wiley: 2008), 85.

11. Berger, "The Rich Man's City," 47.

12. "Delmonico's Bill of Fare, 1830s," Food Timeline, http://www.foodtimeline.org/foodfaq5.html#delmonicos.

13. Cele C. Otnes and Elizabeth H. Pleck, *Cinderella Dreams: The Allure of the Lavish Wedding* (Berkeley: University of California Press, 2003), 32; search results for "Kennedy wedding," Library of Congress, http://www.loc.gov/pictures/search/?q=kennedy%20wedding.

14. Dennis Hall, "Modern and Postmodern Wedding Planners: Emily Post's *Etiquette in Society* (1937) and Blum & Kaiser's *Weddings for Dummies* (1997)," *Studies in Popular Culture* 24, no. 3 (April 2002): 38.

15. A Woman of Fashion, *Etiquette for Americans* (New York: Herbert Stone and Co., 1898), 95.

16. Joan Jacobs Brumberg, "The Appetite as Voice," in *Food and Culture: A Reader*, ed. Carole Counihan and Penny Van Esterik, 2nd ed. (New York: Routledge, 2008), 152.

17. A Woman of Fashion, *Etiquette for Americans*, 96.

18. A Woman of Fashion, *Etiquette for Americans*, 107.

19. George P. Monger, *Marriage Customs of the World: An Encyclopedia of Dating Customs and Wedding Traditions*, 2nd ed. (Santa Barbara, CA: ABC-CLIO, 2013), 87–88.

20. Pamela McArthur Cole, "New England Weddings," *Journal of American Folklore* 6, no. 21 (April–June 1893): 104.

21. Marion Harland and Virginia Van de Water, *Marion Harland's Complete Etiquette: A Young People's Guide to Every Social Occasion* (Indianapolis: Bobbs-Merrill Company, 1914), 70–72.

22. Emily Post, *Etiquette in Society, in Business, in Politics, and at Home* (New York: Funk & Wagnallis, 1922), 312.

23. G. R. M. Devereux, *The Etiquette of Engagement and Marriage: Describing Modern Manners and Customs of Courtship and Marriage* (London: C. Arthur Pearson, 1919), 86.

24. Lillian Eichler, *Book of Etiquette* (Oyster Bay, NY: Doubleday, 1921), 60.

25. Enid Wells, *Living for Two: A Guide to Homemaking* (New York: David Kemp and Co., 1939), 231.

26. Wylie Sypher, "Mrs. Post May I Present Mr. Eliot," *American Scholar* 54, no. 3 (Spring 1985): 251.

27. Amy Vanderbilt, *Amy Vanderbilt's Complete Book of Etiquette: A Guide to Gracious Living* (Garden City, NY: Doubleday, 1954), 628.

28. Michael Owen Jones, "Food Choice, Symbolism, and Identity: Bread and Butter Issues for Folklorists and Nutrition Studies," *Journal of American Folklore* 120, no. 476 (2007): 138.

29. Kay Corinth and Mary Sargent, "Executive's Wives," *Brides* 33 (February–March 1967): 116–17.

30. Judith Martin and Jacobina Martin, *Miss Manners' Guide to a Surprisingly Dignified Wedding* (New York: W. W. Norton, 2010), 63.

31. Martin and Martin, *Miss Manners' Guide to a Surprisingly Dignified Wedding*, 51.

32. Martin and Martin, *Miss Manners' Guide to a Surprisingly Dignified Wedding*, 270.

33. Martin and Martin, *Miss Manners' Guide to a Surprisingly Dignified Wedding*, xi.

34. Hall, "Modern and Postmodern Wedding Planners," 42.

35. Otnes and Pleck, *Cinderella Dreams*, 52.

36. "Man Flies to Wedding a Year Early," *BBC News*, July 10, 2007, http://news.bbc.co.uk/2/hi/uk_news/wales/6289770.stm.

CHAPTER 6: CHICKEN OR BEEF?

1. Rebecca Mead, *One Perfect Day: The Selling of the American Wedding* (New York: Penguin Books, 2007), 135.

2. Libby H. O'Connell, *The American Plate* (Naperville, IL: Sourcebooks, 2014), 4.

3. Genevieve Flavin, "Mud Slinging Is Just an Old Tribal Custom," *Chicago Tribune*, October 19, 1952, 198.

4. James L. Roark, ed., *The American Promise: A History of the United States* (Boston: Bedford/St. Martin's, 2003), 250.

5. Roark, *The American Promise*, 272.

6. Robert S. Fogarty, ed., *Special Love, Special Sex: An Oneida Community Diary* (Syracuse, NY: Syracuse University Press, 1994), 7.

7. David S. Reynolds, *Waking Giant* (New York: HarperCollins, 2009), 147.

8. Daniel J. Wakin, "Rev Sun Myung Moon, Self-Proclaimed Messiah Who Built Religious Movement, Dies at 92," *New York Times*, September 2, 2012.

9. Laurie Goodstein, "35,000 Couples Are Invited to a Blessing by Rev. Moon," *New York Times*, November 28, 1997.

10. "Amana Colonies Today," National Park Service, https://www.nps.gov/nr/travel/amana/amana.htm.

11. Emilie Hoppe, *Seasons of Plenty: Amana Communal Cooking* (Ames: University of Iowa Press, 1998), 181.

12. Marilyn Yalom, *A History of the Wife* (New York: HarperCollins, 2001), 253.

13. Cynthia D. Bertelsen, "Seventh Day Adventists and Food Practices," in *Sage Encyclopedia of Food Issues*, ed. Ken Albala (Thousand Oaks, CA: Sage, 2015), 1255.

14. Tanya MacLaurin, "Religion and Food Practices," in Albala, *Sage Encyclopedia of Food Issues*, 1188.

15. Leena Trivedi-Grenier, "Hindu Food Restrictions," in Albala, *Sage Encyclopedia of Food Issues*, 782–83.

16. Simran Chawla, *Indian Weddings* (Atglen, PA: Schiffer, 2010), 48.

17. Have Trunk Will Travel, Inc., http://www.weddingelephants.com/details.html.

18. "FAQ," Sikh Coalition, http://www.sikhcoalition.org/resources/about-sikhs/faq.

19. "Sikh Wedding," Sikhs.org, http://www.sikhs.org/wedding.

20. "A Sikh Wedding," SikhMuseum.com, http://www.sikhmuseum.com/vrwedding.

21. George P. Monger, "Buddhist Marriages," in *Marriage Customs of the World: An Encyclopedia of Dating Customs and Wedding Traditions*, 2nd ed. (Santa Barbara, CA: ABC-CLIO, 2013), 104.

22. Sherrie A. Inness, *Dinner Roles: American Women and Culinary Culture* (Iowa City: University of Iowa Press, 2001), 96.

23. Rachelle H. Saltzman, "Identity and Food," in Albala, *Sage Encyclopedia of Food Issues*, 822–26.

24. Bertha M. Wood, *Foods of the Foreign Born: In Relation to Health* (Boston: Whitcomb and Barrows, 1922), 89–90.

25. P. Smiley Publishing Company, ed., *Smiley's Cook Book and Universal Household Guide* (Chicago: J. B. Smiley, 1901), 89–90.

26. Linda Civitello, *Cuisine and Culture: A History of Food and People*, 2nd ed. (Hoboken, NJ: John Wiley: 2008), 274.

27. Hasia R. Diner, *Hungering for America: Italian, Irish and Jewish Foodways in the Age of Migration* (Cambridge, MA: Harvard University Press, 2001), 215.

28. *Good Housekeeping* 106, no. 6 (June 1938): 182.

29. Joellyn Zollman, "Jewish Immigration to America: Three Waves," My Jewish Learning, http://www.myjewishlearning.com/article/jewish-immigration -to-america-three-waves.

30. Laura Schenone, *A Thousand Years over a Hot Stove* (New York: W. W. Norton, 2003), 208.

31. Schenone, *A Thousand Years over a Hot Stove*.

32. Schenone, *A Thousand Years over a Hot Stove*, 229.

33. Israel Berger, "Kosher Foods," in Albala, *Sage Encyclopedia of Food Issues*, 870.

CHAPTER 7: JUMPING THE BROOM

1. Ken Albala, "Food in Time and Place," in *Food in Time and Place: The American Historical Association Companion to Food History*, ed. Paul Freedman, Joyce E. Chaplin, and Ken Albala (Oakland: University of California Press, 2014), 36.

2. James L. Roark, ed., *The American Promise: A History of the United States* (Boston: Bedford/St. Martin's, 2003), 483.

3. Frederick Douglass Opie, *Hog and Hominy: Soul Food from Africa to America* (New York, Columbia University Press, 2008), 28.

4. Cathy Cuchetti, *Home on the Range: A Culinary History of the American West* (New York: Villard Books, 1993), 223.

5. Laura Schenone, *A Thousand Years over a Hot Stove* (New York: W. W. Norton, 2003), 71.

6. Patrick W. O'Neil, "Bosses and Broomsticks: Ritual and Authority in Antebellum Slave Weddings," *Journal of Southern History* 75, no. 1 (February 2009): 40.

7. Andrew J. Cherlin, *The Marriage-Go-Round: The State of Marriage and the Family in America Today* (New York: Alfred A. Knopf, 2009), 45.

8. Cherlin, *The Marriage-Go-Round*, 46.

9. George P. Monger, "Marriage over the Broom," in *Marriage Customs of the World: An Encyclopedia of Dating Customs and Wedding Traditions*, 2nd ed. (Santa Barbara, CA: ABC-CLIO, 2013), 101.

10. O'Neil, "Bosses and Broomsticks," 46.

11. Opie, *Hog and Hominy*, 41.

12. Schenone, *A Thousand Years over a Hot Stove*, 287.

13. Opie, *Hog and Hominy*, 56.

14. Opie, *Hog and Hominy*, 104.

15. "How to Capture and Train Your Maid," *Brides* 3, no. 2 (Winter 1936–1937): 62.

16. "How to Capture and Train Your Maid," *Brides* 3, no. 2 (Winter 1936–1937): 62.

17. Karen M. Dunak, "'Ceremony and Citizenship': African American Weddings, 1945–60," *Gender and History* 21, no. 2 (August 2009): 418.

18. Cele C. Otnes and Elizabeth H. Pleck, *Cinderella Dreams: The Allure of the Lavish Wedding* (Berkeley: University of California Press, 2003), 45.

19. Kathleen Collins, *Watching What We Eat: The Evolution of Television Shows* (New York: Continuum Books, 2009), 124.

20. Opie, *Hog and Hominy*, 46.

21. Preface to Princess Pamela, *Princess Pamela's Soul Food Cook Book* (New York: Signa, 1969).

22. Cynthia M. Frisby and Erika Engstrom, "Always a Bridesmaid, Never a Bride: Portrayals of Women of Color in Bridal Magazines," *Media Report to Women* 34 (Fall 2006): 11.

CHAPTER 8: WHAT ARE YOU?

1. Sherrie A. Inness, *Dinner Roles: American Women and Culinary Culture* (Iowa City: University of Iowa Press, 2001), 89.

2. Jonathan Rees, *Refrigeration Nation: A History of Ice, Appliances, and Enterprise in America* (Baltimore: Johns Hopkins University Press, 2013), 86–95.

3. Jennifer Jensen Wallach, *How America Eats: A Social History of U.S. Food and Culture* (Lanham, MD: Rowman & Littlefield, 2013), 94.

4. Cathy Cuchetti, *Home on the Range: A Culinary History of the American West* (New York: Villard Books, 1993), 37.

5. Cuchetti, *Home on the Range*, 37.

6. Linda Civitello, *Cuisine and Culture: A History of Food and People*, 2nd ed. (Hoboken, NJ: John Wiley: 2008), 287.

7. "The Man, The Can: Recipes of the Real Chef Boyardee," *All Things Considered*, May 17, 2011, http://www.npr.org/2011/05/17/136398042/the-man-the-can-recipes-of-the-real-chef-boyardee.

8. "Chef Hector Boiardi, a True American Hero," Chef Boyardee, http://www.chefboyardee.com/articles/chef-hector-boiardi-true-american-hero.

9. Emily J. H. Contois, "Supermarkets," in *Savoring Gotham: A Food Lover's Companion to New York City*, ed. Andrew Smith (New York: Oxford University Press, 2015), 579.

10. Susan Marks, *Finding Betty Crocker: The Secret Life of America's First Lady of Food* (New York: Simon and Schuster, 2005), 164.

11. Jessamyn Neuhaus, *Manly Meals and Mom's Home Cooking: Cookbooks and Gender in Modern America* (Baltimore: John's Hopkins University Press, 2003), 181.

12. Civitello, *Cuisine and Culture*, 220.

13. Cuchetti, *Home on the Range*, 217.

14. James L. Roark, ed., *The American Promise: A History of the United States* (Boston: Bedford/St. Martin's, 2003), 541.

15. Laura Schenone, *A Thousand Years over a Hot Stove* (New York: W. W. Norton, 2003), 223.

16. "Mark Twain's Observations about Chinese Immigrants in California," Library of Congress, http://www.loc.gov/teachers/classroommaterials/presentations andactivities/presentations/timeline/riseind/chinimms/twain.html.

17. Debra M. Kawahara, "Chinese Immigrant Families," in *The Social History of the American Family: An Encyclopedia*, ed. Marilyn J. Coleman and Lawrence H. Ganong (Los Angeles: Sage Reference, 2014), 2:228.

18. Dalila Bothwell, "Weddings," in *Encyclopedia of Food and Culture*, ed. Solomon H. Katz (New York: Charles Scribner's Sons, 2003), 3:526.

19. William Grimes, *Appetite City: A Culinary History of New York* (New York: North Point Press, 2009), 131.

20. Erik Vance, "An Ocean Apart," *Virginia Quarterly Review* 91, no. 2 (Spring 2015): 46.

21. Adrian Wan, "Restaurants and Hotels Sign Up to Provide Shark-Free Banquet Menus," *South China Morning Post*, May 6, 2010.

22. Randa Serhan, "Palestinian Weddings: Inventing Palestine in New Jersey," *Journal of Palestine Studies* 37, no. 4 (Summer 2008): 27.

23. Wallach, *How America Eats*, 76.

24. Michael J. Eula, "Failure of American Food Reformers among Italian Immigrants in NYC, 1891–1897," *Italian Americana* 18, no. 1 (Winter 2000): 86–99.

25. Simone Cinotto, "Italians," in Smith, *Savoring Gotham*, 295.

26. Bertha M. Wood, *Foods of the Foreign Born: In Relation to Health* (Boston: Whitcomb and Barrows, 1922), 10.

27. Schenone, *A Thousand Years over a Hot Stove*, 208.

28. Cuchetti, *Home on the Range*, 219.

29. Ayaka Yoshimizu, "Hello, War Brides: Heteroglossia, Counter-Memory, and the Auto/biographical Work of Japanese War Brides," *Meridians* 10, no. 1 (2009): 115–16.

30. Masako Ishii-Kuntz, "Japanese Immigrant Families," in Coleman and Ganong, *Social History of the American Family*, 2:777–80.

31. Ofra Goldstein-Gidoni, "Hybridity and Distinction in Japanese Contemporary Commercial Weddings," *Social Science Japan Journal* 4, no. 1 (April 2001): 26.

32. Elise Hu, "Need Fake Friends for Your Wedding? In S. Korea You Can Hire Them." *Morning Edition*, August 5, 2015, http://www.npr.org/sections/parallels/2015/08/05/419419307/fake-wedding-guests-korea-role-players.

33. Thei Zervaki and Cathy K. Kaufman, "Diners, Restaurants, and Famous Greek Food," in Smith, *Savoring Gotham*, 245.

34. Elizabeth Rholetter Purdy, "German Immigrant Families," in Coleman and Ganong, *The Social History of the American Family*, 2:630.

35. Michael Owen Jones, "Food Choice, Symbolism, and Identity: Bread and Butter Issues for Folklorists and Nutrition Studies," *Journal of American Folklore* 120, no. 476 (Spring 2007): 136.

CHAPTER 9: DATING AND DINING

1. John P. McKay, Bennett D. Hill, and John Buckler, *History of Western Society*, 7th ed. (Boston: Houghton Mifflin, 2003), 315.

2. Warren Hollister, "Courtly Culture and Courtly Style in the Anglo-Norman World," *Albion: A Quarterly Journal Concerned with British Studies* 20, no. 1 (Spring 1988): 5.

3. Hollister, "Courtly Culture and Courtly Style in the Anglo-Norman World," 16.

4. McKay et al., *History of Western Society*, 396.

5. McKay et al., *History of Western Society*, 513.

6. Lawrence Stone, *Family, Sex, and Marriage in England, 1500–1800* (New York: Penguin, 1977), 646.

7. Stone, *The Family, Sex and Marriage in England 1500–1800*, 647.

8. "Highlights of the Percy Skuy History of Contraception Gallery: Condoms and Sponges," Case Western Reserve University, last modified 2010, http://case.edu/affil/skuyhistcontraception/online-2012/Condoms-Sponges.html.

9. Martin King Whyte, "Choosing Mates—the American Way," *Society* 29, no. 3 (1992): 71.

10. James L. Roark, ed., *The American Promise: A History of the United States* (Boston: Bedford/St. Martin's, 2003), 483.

11. Thomas R. Pegram, *Battling Demon Rum: The Struggle for a Dry America, 1800–1933* (Chicago: Ivan R. Dee, 1998), 177.

12. Amy Boesky, "Solving the Crime of Modernity: Nancy Drew in 1930," *Studies in the Novel* 42, no. 1 (2010): 186.

13. Cele C. Otnes and Elizabeth H. Pleck, *Cinderella Dreams: The Allure of the Lavish Wedding* (Berkeley: University of California Press, 2003), 38.

14. Whyte, "Choosing Mates—the American Way," 75.

15. Carol Polsky, "Marriage Traditions Changing for Indian Immigrants," *Newsday*, July 15, 2012.

16. Brittany Wong, "The 30 Most Popular Places to Take a First Date, According to Dating App Clover," *Huffington Post*, April 6, 2015, http://www.huffingtonpost.com/2015/04/06/where-to-go-on-first-dates_n_7011884.html.

17. Sherrie A. Inness, *Dinner Roles: American Women and Culinary Culture* (Iowa City: University of Iowa Press, 2001), 27.

18. Margaret Mead, "The Problem of Changing Food Habits," in *Food and Culture: A Reader*, ed. Carole Counihan and Penny Van Esterik, 2nd ed. (New York: Routledge, 1997), 21.

19. Ron Ruggless, "It's Bubble, Bubble, Toil, and Truffle for Valentine's Day," *Nation's Restaurant News*, February 7, 2005, 64.

20. "James Beard's Books," James Beard Foundation, https://www.jamesbeard.org/about/james-beard-books.

21. "James Beard's Books."

22. Ruggless, "It's Bubble, Bubble, Toil, and Truffle for Valentine's Day," 64.

23. Stephanie Tuder, "How This Restaurant Pulls Off America's Most Marriage Proposals," *ABC News*, February 27, 2015, http://abcnews.go.com/Lifestyle/restaurant-pulls-off-americas-marriage-proposals/story?id=29281652.

24. Tuder, "How This Restaurant Pulls Off America's Most Marriage Proposals."

25. Andrea Strong, "A Hallmark Moment," *Restaurant Business*, December 15, 2001, 70.

26. Tom Sietsema, "Dinner Engagements: The Perils of Popping the Question in a Restaurant," *Washington Post*, February 9, 2000, F01.

27. "Restaurant Workforce Demographics Are Shifting," National Restaurant Association, March 17, 2015," http://www.restaurant.org/News-Research/News/Restaurant-workforce-demographics-are-shifting.

28. "Marital Events of Americans: 2009," American Community Survey Reports. US Census, August 2011, http://www.census.gov/prod/2011pubs/acs-13.pdf.

29. Anthony Bourdain, *Kitchen Confidential: Adventures in the Culinary Underbelly* (New York: Bloomsbury, 2000), 61.

30. Bourdain, *Kitchen Confidential*, 62.

31. Marjorie Coeyman, "Isn't It Romantic?" *Restaurant Business* 96, no. 20 (October 15, 1997): 50.

32. Coeyman, "Isn't It Romantic?" 50.

33. Donna Castañeda, "Romantic Relationships in the Workplace," in *Gender, Race, and Ethnicity in the Workplace: Issues and Challenges for Today's Organizations*, ed. M. F. Karsten (Westport, CT: Praeger, 2006), 88–89.

34. Coeyman, "Isn't It Romantic?" 50.

35. Jean Anthelme Brillat-Savarin, *The Physiology of Taste: The Mediation on Transcendental Gastronomy*, trans. M. F. K. Fisher (Washington, DC: Counterpoint, 1994), 87.

36. Eugenia Bone, *Mycophilia: Revelations from the Weird World of Mushrooms* (New York: Rodale, 2011), 145.

37. Bone, *Mycophilia*, 144.

38. Bone, *Mycophilia*, 159.

39. Raphael Minder, "Spain Has Little Appetite for Truffles, but Plenty for the Truffle Trade," *New York Times*, December 31, 2015, http://www.nytimes.com/2016/01/01/world/europe/spain-has-little-appetite-for-truffles-but-plenty-for-the-truffle-trade.html.

40. "Auction Results," Sotheby's, http://www.sothebys.com/en/auctions/2014/white-truffle-n09231.html (accessed July 8, 2016).

41. Bone, *Mycophilia*, 161.

42. Sophie D. Coe and Michael D. Coe, *The True History of Chocolate* (London: Thames and Hudson, 1996), 94.

43. Samira Kawash, *Candy: A Century of Panic and Pleasure* (New York: Faber and Faber, 2013), 156.

44. Kawash, *Candy*, 157.

CHAPTER 10: CHAMPAGNE ANYONE?

1. Introduction to Jo Packham, *Wedding Toasts and Speeches: Finding the Perfect Words* (New York: Stirling, 2007).

2. Margaret Visser, *The Rituals of Dinner* (Toronto: HarperCollins, 1991), 258.

3. "A Foreigner's Guide to Polish Weddings," Culture.pl, July 6, 2013, http://culture.pl/en/article/a-foreigners-guide-to-polish-weddings.

4. Dan Jurafsky, *The Language of Food: A Linguist Reads the Menu* (New York: W. W. Norton, 2014), 77.

5. Eric Burns, *The Spirits of America: A Social History of Alcohol* (Philadelphia: Temple University Press, 2004), 16.

6. Alison Weir et al., *The Ring and the Crown: A History of Royal Weddings, 1066–2011* (London: Hutchinson, 2011), 36.

7. Jurafsky, *The Language of Food*, 77.

8. Burns, *The Spirits of America*, 31.

9. Visser, *The Rituals of Dinner*, 261.

10. Karen MacNeil, *The Wine Bible*, 2nd ed. (New York: Workman Publishing, 2015), 183.

11. Marcy Blum and Laura Fisher Kaiser, *Weddings for Dummies* (Foster City, CA: IDG Books Worldwide, 1997), 165.

12. MacNeil, *The Wine Bible*, 187.

13. MacNeil, *The Wine Bible*, 190.

14. Pagan Kennedy, "Who Made That?" *New York Times Magazine*, December 23, 2012, 16.

15. Kolleen M. Guy, "'Oiling the Wheels of Social Life': Myths and Marketing in Champagne during the Belle Époque," *French Historical Studies* 22, no. 2 (Spring 1999): 232.

16. Guy, "Oiling the Wheels of Social Life," 236.

17. Guy, "Oiling the Wheels of Social Life," 233.

18. Guy, "Oiling the Wheels of Social Life," 229.

19. Guy, "Oiling the Wheels of Social Life," 219.

20. Alisa Hixson-Lefils, "The Art of Champagne and Its Hispanic Connection," *Hispanic Outlook in Higher Education* 16, no. 21 (July 31, 2006): 11.

21. MacNeil, *The Wine Bible*, 176.

22. "Odette Pol-Roger, Obituary," *Telegraph*, December 30, 2000, http://www.telegraph.co.uk/news/obituaries/1379766/Odette-Pol-Roger.html (accessed July 8, 2016).

23. William Grimes, *Appetite City: A Culinary History of New York* (New York: North Point Press, 2009), 197.

24. Linda Civitello, *Cuisine and Culture: A History of Food and People*, 2nd ed. (Hoboken, NJ: John Wiley: 2008), 303.

25. Introduction to Victor Hirtzler, *The Hotel St. Francis Cook Book* (Chicago: John Wiley, 1919).

26. Frederick Kaufman, *A Short History of the American Stomach* (Orlando, FL: Harcourt, 2008), 132.

27. Kaufman, *A Short History of the American Stomach*, 132.

28. Thomas R. Pegram, *Battling Demon Rum: The Struggle for a Dry America, 1800–1933* (Chicago: Ivan R. Dee, 1998), 175.

29. Caryn E. Neumann, "The End of Gender Solidarity: The History of the Women's Organization for National Prohibition Reform in the United States, 1929–1933," *Journal of Women's History* 9, no. 2 (Summer 1997): 36.

30. Burns, *The Spirits of America*, 259.

31. Merril D. Smith, *History of American Cooking* (Santa Barbara, CA: ABC-CLIO, 2013), 9.

32. Civitello, *Cuisine and Culture*, 303.

33. Burns, *The Spirits of America*, 190.

34. Burns, *The Spirits of America*.

35. Pegram, *Battling Demon Rum*, 176.

36. "Wedding Cake," *Brides* 4, no. 3 (Spring 1937): 59.

37. Smiley Publishing Company, ed., *Smiley's Cook Book and Universal Household Guide* (Chicago: J. B. Smiley, 1901), 387.

38. Julian Street, "The Grooms Cellar," *Brides* 1, no. 1 (Autumn 1934): 31.

39. *Brides* 1, no. 4 (Summer 1935): 84.

40. Jennifer Marx et al., *PassPorter's Walt Disney World* (Ann Arbor, MI: PassPorter Travel Press, 2006), 28.

41. "Magic Kingdom," Drinking at Disney, http://www.drinkingatdisney .com/magic-kingdom.php.

42. Olive Lodge, "Wedding Customs: St. Peter's Day in Galicnk," *Slavonic and East European Review* 13, no. 39 (April 1935): 660.

43. Jurafsky, *The Language of Food*, 65.

44. Weir et al., *The Ring and the Crown*, 30.

45. *Wedding Report Quarterly*, May 2016, 9.

46. Janet Chrzan, "Alcohol: Cultural Beliefs and Practices," in *Sage Encyclopedia of Food Issues*, ed. Ken Albala (Thousand Oaks, CA: Sage, 2015), 28.

47. Sierra Clark, "Alcohol: Industry, Regulation, and Taxation of," in Albala, *Sage Encyclopedia of Food Issues*, 32.

48. Judith Martin, *Miss Manner's Guide to Excruciatingly Correct Behavior* (New York: Warner Books, 1982), 643.

CHAPTER 11: LET THEM HAVE WEDDING CAKE

1. Abbie Fentress Swanson, "Let Them Eat Sugar Sculpture! The Getty Celebrates Edible Table Art," *The Salt*, November 20, 2015, http://www.npr.org/ sections/thesalt/2015/11/20/456627679/let-them-eat-sugar-sculpture-the-getty -celebrates-edible-table-art.

2. Emily Allen, "Culinary Exhibition: Victorian Wedding Cakes and Royal Spectacle," *Victorian Studies* 45, no. 3 (Spring 2003): 464.

3. Carol Wilson, "Wedding Cake: A Slice of History," *Gastronomica: The Journal of Food and Culture* 5, no. 2 (Spring 2005): 70.

4. Allen, "Culinary Exhibition," 462.

5. Donald Bassett, "Victorian Cakes and Architecture," *British Art Journal* 11, no. 2 (2010–2011): 78.

6. Simon Charsley, "Marriages, Weddings, and Their Cakes," in *Food, Health, and Identity*, ed. Pat Caplan (New York: Routledge, 1997), 59.

7. Michael Krondl, *Sweet Invention: A History of Dessert* (Chicago: Chicago Review Press, 2011), 321.

8. Simon Charsley, *Wedding Cakes and Cultural History* (London: Routledge, 1992), 37.

9. Laura Schenone, *A Thousand Years over a Hot Stove* (New York: W. W. Norton, 2003), 39.

10. Lydia Maria Child, *The American Frugal Housewife* (1892; Mineola, NY: Dover, 1999), 126–27.

11. Hugo Ziemann and F. L. Gillette, *The White House Cook Book* (Akron, OH: Saalfield Publishing Company, 1913).

12. Susan Marks, *Finding Betty Crocker: The Secret Life of America's First Lady of Food* (New York: Simon and Schuster, 2005), 11.

13. Marks, *Finding Betty Crocker*, 24.

14. Marks, *Finding Betty Crocker*, 70.

15. Marks, *Finding Betty Crocker*, 71.

16. Krondl, *Sweet Invention*, 336.

17. Marcia Gaudet, "Ribbon Pulls in Wedding Cakes: Tracing a New Orleans Tradition," *Folklore* 117, no. 1 (April 2006): 91.

18. Gaudet, "Ribbon Pulls in Wedding Cakes," 92.

19. Marcy Blum and Laura Fisher Kaiser, *Weddings for Dummies* (Foster City, CA: IDG Books Worldwide, 1997), 154.

20. "Wedding Cake," *Harper's Bazaar* 15, no. 46 (November 18, 1882): 722.

21. Charsley, "Marriages, Weddings, and Their Cakes," 54.

22. "A History of Wilton," Wilton, http://www.wilton.com/cms-wilton -history.html.

23. "Hoenshel Fine Foods," *Brides* 16, no. 1 (Spring 1950): 159.

24. Charsley, *Wedding Cakes and Cultural History*, 96.

25. Robert Reed, "Bride and Groom Wedding Cake Toppers," *Antique Shoppe Newspaper*, June 2006, http://antiqueshoppefl.com/archives/rreed/Bride%20 and%20Groom.htm.

26. Jennifer Bihm, "New Wedding Cake Figurines Mirror Couple of the 21st Century," *Los Angeles Sentinel*, July 7, 2005, A11–A12.

27. "Easy-Bake Downloads," Hasbro, http://www.hasbro.com/en-us/brands/ easybake/printables.

28. "Easy-Bake Ultimate Oven," Hasbro, http://www.hasbro.com/en-us/ brands/easybake/videos?bctid=4371806556001.

29. Lisa Milbrand, "Cupcake Couture," *Modern Bride* (August–September 2009): 45.

30. "100-Year-Old Piece of Wedding Cake Found in Attic," WNPR, November 24, 2015, http://wnpr.org/post/100-year-old-piece-wedding-cake-found -attack#stream/0.

31. *Wedding Report Quarterly*, Q2 edition, May 2016, 85.

32. Suzanne Martinson, "Youngstown Lays Claim to the Cookie Table," *Pittsburgh Post-Gazette*, August 15, 2004, http://www.post-gazette.com/ life/food/2004/08/15/Youngstown-lays-claim-to-the-cookie-table/stories/ 200408150194.

33. "Our History," Original Maids of Honour, http://www.theoriginalmaids ofhonour.co.uk/about/history (accessed July 11, 2016).

34. Charsley, *Wedding Cakes and Cultural History*, 37.

CHAPTER 12: DO ME A FAVOR
AND GET ME SOME RICE

1. Nichola Fletcher, *Charlemagne's Tablecloth: A Piquant History of Feasting* (New York: St. Martin's Press, 2005), 179–80.

2. George P. Monger, *Marriage Customs of the World: An Encyclopedia of Dating Customs and Wedding Traditions*, 2nd ed. (Santa Barbara, CA: ABC-CLIO, 2013), 151.

3. Dalila Bothwell, "Weddings," in *Encyclopedia of Food and Culture*, ed. Solomon H. Katz (New York: Charles Scribner's Sons, 2003), 3:527.

4. John P. McKay et al., eds., *A History of World Societies*, 8th ed. (Boston: Bedford/St. Martin's, 2009), 429.

5. Lisa Bramen, "Breaking Bread (and Dancing with It) at a Macedonian Wedding," Smithsonian.com, September 14, 2010, http://www.smithsonianmag.com/arts-culture/breaking-bread-and-dancing-with-it-at-a-macedonian-wedding-99451635/#Thr01R0ozqCqmVGk.99.

6. "Against the Grain," Snopes, March 16, 2015, http://www.snopes.com/critters/crusader/birdrice.asp.

7. *Vogue's Book of Etiquette* (Ithaca, NY: Conde Nast, 1925), 59.

8. Margaret Montgomery, "A Macedonian Wedding in Indianapolis," *Hoosier Folklore* 7, no. 4 (December 1948): 101–4.

9. Martha Kohl, "And the Bride Wore . . . Montana Weddings, 1900–1960," *Montana: The Magazine of Western History* 62, no. 4 (Winter 2012), 69.

CHAPTER 13: HONEYMOONS AND FOOD

1. Abby Buchanan Longstreet, *Social Etiquette of New York* (New York: D. Appleton, 1879): 140.

2. Deborah Reed-Danahay, "Champagne and Chocolate: Taste and Inversion in a French Wedding Ritual," *American Anthropologist*. 98, no. 4 (1996): 750–61.

3. Michele Roberts, "From Gastroporn to Wedding-Night Recipes, Food and Sex Are Intimately Linked," *New Statesmen*, February 13, 2006, 60.

4. Cele C. Otnes and Elizabeth H. Pleck, *Cinderella Dreams: The Allure of the Lavish Wedding* (Berkeley: University of California Press, 2003), 140.

5. Amy Vanderbilt, *Amy Vanderbilt's Complete Book of Etiquette: A Guide to Gracious Living* (Garden City, NY: Doubleday, 1957), 105.

6. Otnes and Pleck, *Cinderella Dreams*, 135.

7. Helena Michie, "Victorian Honeymoons: Sexual Reorientations and the Sights of Europe," *Victorian Studies* 43, no. 2 (Winter 2001): 233.

8. Cas Wouters, "Etiquette Books and Emotional Management in the 20th Century: Part Two: The Integration of the Sexes," *Journal of Social History* 29, no. 2 (Winter 1995): 325–39.

9. Wouters, "Etiquette Books and Emotional Management in the 20th Century," 114.

10. Emily Post, *Etiquette in Society, in Business, in Politics, and at Home* (New York: Funk & Wagnallis, 1922), 299.

11. Vanderbilt, *Amy Vanderbilt's Complete Book of Etiquette*, 126.

12. Joan Jacobs Brumberg, "The Appetite as Voice," in *Food and Culture: A Reader*, ed. Carole Counihan and Penny Van Esterik, 2nd ed. (New York: Routledge, 2008), 150.

13. Tanfer Emin Tunc, "Ashley Wilkes Told Me He Likes to See a Girl with a Healthy Appetite," *European Journal of American Culture* 32, no. 2 (2012): 91.

14. Alison Weir, Kate Williams, Sarah Gristwood, and Tracy Borman, *The Ring and the Crown: A History of Royal Weddings, 1066–2011* (London: Hutchinson, 2011): 36.

15. Rick Archbold and Dana McCauley, *The Last Dinner on the Titanic* (Toronto: Madison Press Books, 1997), 137.

16. Rainy Clint, "The World's Most Expensive Cracker Just Sold for $23,000," *Grub Street*, October 27, 2015, http://www.grubstreet.com/2015/10/expensive-cracker-from-titanic.html.

17. Jon Wiener, "Pop and Avant-Garde: The Case of John and Yoko," *Popular Music and Society* 22 no. 1 (1998): 9.

18. Rebecca Mead, *One Perfect Day: The Selling of the American Wedding* (New York: Penguin Books, 2007), 160.

19. Elliot Partin, "Highland Beach, Maryland," BlackPast.org, http://www.blackpast.org/aah/highland-beach-maryland-1893.

20. Sam Roberts, "Morris Wilkins Dies at 90, Lured Lovers to Poconos," *New York Times*, May 29, 2015, B15.

21. Otnes and Pleck, *Cinderella Dreams*, 142–43.

22. Travis Hoke, "Honeymoons Don't Wane," *North American Review* 236, no. 3 (September 1933): 266.

23. Hoke, "Honeymoons Don't Wane," 270.

24. Andrew Jacobs, "The Thrills Are Over at Mount Airy Lodge," *New York Times*, November 2, 2001, D1.

25. Weir et al., *The Ring and the Crown*, 79.

26. "In Russia, Weddings Can Be Dangerous Affairs," NPR, September 5, 2015, http://www.npr.org/2015/09/05/437768146/in-russia-weddings-can-be-dangerous-affairs.

27. Otnes and Pleck, *Cinderella Dreams*, 156–57.

28. Jean Anthelme Brillat-Savarin, *The Physiology of Taste: The Mediation on Transcendental Gastronomy*, trans. M. F. K. Fisher (Washington, DC: Counterpoint, 1994), 87.

29. Miriam Hospodar, "Aphrodisiac Foods: Bringing Heaven to Earth," *Gastronomica: The Journal of Food and Culture* 4, no. 4 (Fall 2004): 86.

30. Sophie D. Coe and Michael D. Coe, *The True History of Chocolate* (London: Thames and Hudson, 1996), 95.

31. Michael Krondl, *Sweet Invention: A History of Dessert* (Chicago: Chicago Review Press, 2011), 338.

32. Nichola Fletcher, *Charlemagne's Tablecloth: A Piquant History of Feasting* (New York: St. Martin's Press, 2005), 96.

33. Hospodar, "Aphrodisiac Foods," 86.

34. Hospodar, "Aphrodisiac Foods," 21.

35. Fletcher, *Charlemagne's Tablecloth*, 96.

36. Hospodar, "Aphrodisiac Foods," 85.

37. Margaret Magat, "Fertilized Duck Eggs: Their Role in Filipino Culture," *Western Folklore* 61, no. 1 (Spring 2001): 64–65.

38. Associated Press, "U.S. Says 4 Died in NY Eating an Alleged Aphrodisiac," *New York Times*, November 25, 1995, http://www.nytimes.com/1995/11/25/nyregion/us-says-4-died-in-new-york-eating-an-alleged-aphrodisiac.html.

CHAPTER 14: THE BUSINESS OF LOVE

1. Margaret Visser, *The Gift of Thanks: The Roots and Rituals of Gratitude* (Boston: Houghton Mifflin Harcourt, 2009), 102–3.

2. Joseph G. Jorgensen, *Western Indians* (San Francisco: W. H. Freeman, 1980), 145.

3. Ronald L. Trosper, "U.S. Indian Business and Enterprise," in *The Native North American Almanac*, ed. Duane Champagne (Detroit, MI: Gale Research, 1994), 917.

4. Daisy Goodwin, "Cash for Titles: The Billion-Dollar Ladies," *Daily Mail Online*, August 14, 2010, http://www.dailymail.co.uk/home/you/article-1302195/Cash-titles-The-Billion-dollar-ladies.html.

5. Angela Serratore, "How American Rich Kids Bought Their Way into the British Elite," Smithsonian.com, August 13, 2013, http://www.smithsonianmag.com/ist/?next=/history/how-american-rich-kids-bought-their-way-into-the-british-elite-4252.

6. Lloyd Morris, "A Particular Form of Wisdom," review of *The Glitter and the Gold*, by Consuelo Vanderbilt Balsan, *American Scholar* 22, no. 1 (Winter 1952–1953): 118.

7. Marian Fowler, *In a Gilded Cage: American Heiresses Who Married British Aristocrats* (New York: St. Martin's Press, 1993), 156.

8. Eric D. Lehman, *Becoming Tom Thumb* (Middletown, CT: Wesleyan University Press, 2013), 117, http://site.ebrary.com/lib/citytech/reader.action?ppg=117&docID=10769728&tm=1459377857896 (accessed March 28, 2016).

9. Lehman, *Becoming Tom Thumb*, 132.

10. Karen M. Dunak, *As Long as We Both Shall Love: The White Wedding in Postwar America* (New York: New York University Press, 2013), 171.

11. Cele C. Otnes and Elizabeth H. Pleck, *Cinderella Dreams: The Allure of the Lavish Wedding* (Berkeley: University of California Press, 2003), 50.

12. Jada F. Smith, "At Federal Bridal Show, Things Old, New and Seized and Blue," *New York Times*, July 7, 2015, http://www.nytimes.com/2015/07/08/us/at-federal-bridal-show-things-old-new-seized-and-blue.html.

13. "Gay Day at the Magic Kingdom in Disney World on Saturday, June 6, 2015 Will Expose Thousands of Children to Lifestyle," Florida Family Association, http://www.floridafamily.org/full_article.php?article_no=37.

14. "A Star Trek Wedding," *People* 70, no. 13 (September 29, 2008): 158–59.

15. Vicki Howard, *Brides, Inc.: American Weddings and the Business of Tradition* (Philadelphia: University of Pennsylvania Press, 2006), 230.

16. Otnes and Pleck, *Cinderella Dreams*, 37.

CHAPTER 15: WHAT'S COOKING NOW?

1. "Say 'I Do,'" Rainbow Room, https://rainbowroom.com/weddings/#.

2. Michelle Kozin, *Organic Weddings: Balancing Ecology, Style and Tradition* (Gabriola Island, British Columbia: New Society Publishers, 2003).

3. Erin Flood, Sandra Kapoor, and Belinda De Villa-Lopez, "The Sustainability of Food Served at Wedding Banquets," *Journal of Culinary Science and Technology* 12, no. 2 (2014): 138.

4. Carol Pogash, "Offline, D.I.Y. Weddings Aren't So Picture Perfect," *New York Times*, November 19, 2015, http://www.nytimes.com/2015/11/22/fashion/weddings/diy-wedding-ideas-not-picture-perfect.html.

5. Pogash, "Offline, D.I.Y. Weddings Aren't So Picture Perfect."

6. "What's New & Hot," Pier Sixty, http://piersixty.com/gallery/whats-new-hot.

7. Laura Schenone, *A Thousand Years over a Hot Stove* (New York: W. W. Norton, 2003), 175.

8. Schenone, *A Thousand Years over a Hot Stove*, 179.

9. Adrian Miller, *Soul Food: The Surprising Story of an American Cuisine: One Plate at a Time* (Chapel Hill: University North Carolina Press, 2013), 38.

10. Rebecca Mead, *One Perfect Day: The Selling of the American Wedding* (New York: Penguin Books, 2007), 39.

11. Rebecca Leung, "The Echo Boomers," *CBS News*, October 1, 2004, http://www.cbsnews.com/news/the-echo-boomers-01-10-2004/2.

CONCLUSION

1. Michele de Certeau and Luce Giard, "The Nourishing Arts," in *Food and Culture: A Reader*, ed. Carole Counihan and Penny Van Esterik (New York: Routledge, 1997), 67.

2. De Certeau and Giard, "The Nourishing Arts," 70.

3. Marilyn Yalom, *A History of the Wife* (New York: HarperCollins, 2001), 211.

4. Yalom, *A History of the Wife*, 208.

5. Carole Counihan, *The Anthropology of Food and Body: Gender, Meaning, and Power* (New York: Routledge, 1999), 8.

6. Counihan, *The Anthropology of Food and Body*, 8.

7. Counihan, *The Anthropology of Food and Body*, 123.

8. Mira Kamdar, "The Pleasures of Excess," *World Policy Journal* 28, no. 2 (Summer 2011): 15–16.

9. Alec Luhn, "Sting and Jennifer Lopez Star in Lavish Moscow Wedding of Oligarch's Son," *Guardian*, March 30, 2016, https://www.theguardian.com/world/2016/mar/30/multimillion-pound-wedding-russia-sting-jlo-gutseriev.

10. Tyler Durden, "Russian Energy Tycoon Spends $1 Billion on Son's Wedding: Locals Dub It 'Feast in a Time of Plague,'" ZeroHedge.com, March 31, 2016, http://www.zerohedge.com/news/2016-03-31/russian-energy-tycoon-spends-1-billion-sons-wedding-locals-dub-it-feast-time-plague.

11. Ally Hickson, "Here's How Much It Costs to Get Married in 2016," *Living*, April 5, 2016.

12. "Newark, New Jersey (NJ) Poverty Rate Data," City-Data.com, http://www.city-data.com/poverty/poverty-Newark-New-Jersey.html.

Selected Bibliography

Abbott, Elizabeth. *A History of Celibacy.* New York: Scribner, 2000.

Ackerman, Diane. *A Natural History of Love.* New York: Random House, 1994.

Albala, Ken, ed. *Sage Encyclopedia of Food Issues.* Thousand Oaks, CA: Sage, 2015.

Allen, Emily. "Culinary Exhibition: Victorian Wedding Cakes and Royal Spectacle." *Victorian Studies* 45, no. 3 (Spring 2003): 457–84.

Archbold, Rick, and Dana McCauley. *The Last Dinner on the Titanic.* Toronto: Madison Press Books, 1997.

Associated Press. "U.S. Says 4 Died in NY Eating an Alleged Aphrodisiac." *New York Times*, November 25, 1995. http://www.nytimes.com/1995/11/25/nyregion/us-says-4-died-in-new-york-eating-an-alleged-aphrodisiac.html.

Awan, Raafay. "Forced Feeding and Fattening Tradition in Mauritania." *Finding Neverland Blog*, May 19, 2014, http://raafay-awan.blogspot.com/2014/05/forced-feeding-and-fattening-tradition.html.

Barthes, Roland. "Toward a Psychology of Contemporary Food Consumption." In *Food and Culture: A Reader*, edited by Carole Counihan and Penny Van Esterik, 28–36. 2nd ed. New York: Routledge, 1997.

Bassett, Donald. "Victorian Cakes and Architecture." *British Art Journal* 11, no. 2 (2010–2011): 71–81.

Berger, Molly W. "'The Rich Man's City': Hotels and Mansions of Gilded Age New York." *Journal of Decorative and Propaganda Arts* 25 (2005): 47–71.

Bhatnagar, Radhika. "Of Pomp, Pizza and Phera." *Daily News Analysis*, February 4, 2013, 1–2.

Bihm, Jennifer. "New Wedding Cake Figurines Mirror Couple of the 21st Century." *Los Angeles Sentinel*, July 7, 2005.

Blum, Marcy, and Laura Fisher Kaiser. *Weddings for Dummies.* Foster City, CA: IDG Books Worldwide, 1997.

Boesky, Amy. "Solving the Crime of Modernity: Nancy Drew in 1930." *Studies in the Novel* 42, no. 1 (2010): 185–201.

Bonds-Raacke, Jennifer. "Extended Dating Couples' Decision-Making Strategies about Eating: A Comparison to Married Couples." *Appetite* 51 (2008): 198–201.

Bone, Eugenia. *Mycophilia: Revelations from the Weird World of Mushrooms.* New York: Rodale, 2011.

Bothwell, Dalila. "Weddings." In *Encyclopedia of Food and Culture*, ed. Solomon H. Katz, 3:523–527. New York: Charles Scribner's Sons, 2003.

Bourdain, Anthony. *Kitchen Confidential: Adventures in the Culinary Underbelly.* New York: Bloomsbury, 2000.

Bove, Caron F., Jeffery Sobal, and Barbara S. Rauschenbach. "Food Choices Among Newly Married Couples: Convergence, Conflict, Individualism, and Projects." *Appetite* 40 (2003): 25–41.

Bradsher, Keith. "Chinese Delicacy Has Disney in Turbulent Waters." *New York Times*, June 17, 2005, http://query.nytimes.com/gst/fullpage.html?res=9F02E 2DC143BF934A25755C0A9639C8B63.

Bramen, Lisa. "Breaking Bread (and Dancing with It) at a Macedonian Wedding." Smithsonian.com, September 14, 2010, http://www.smithsonianmag .com/arts-culture/breaking-bread-and-dancing-with-it-at-a-macedonian -wedding-99451635/#Thr01R0ozqCqmVGk.99.

Brillat-Savarin, Jean Anthelme. *The Physiology of Taste: The Mediation on Transcendental Gastronomy.* Translated by M. F. K. Fisher. Washington, DC: Counterpoint, 1994.

Brown, DeNeen. "Oak Bluffs, Mass., Is Where the Black Elite Is at Home in the Summer." *Washington Post*, August 20, 2009, http://www.washington post.com/wpdyn/content/article/2009/08/19/AR2009081904045.html? sid=ST2009082001663.

Brownell, Ginanne. "How Segregation Created a Black Eden." *Financial Times*, August 17, 2012, http://www.ft.com/cms/s/2/6aead2f6-e554-11e1-8ac 00144feab49a.html#axzz28qJxVujz.

Brumburg, Joan Jacobs. "The Appetite as Voice." In *Food and Culture: A Reader*, edited by Carole Counihan and Penny Van Esterik, 141–61. 2nd ed. New York: Routledge, 2008.

Buchwald, Art. "Buchwald Attends Wedding at Kelly Family's Invitation." *New York Times*, April 20, 1956, http://www.nytimes.com/2013/10/14/business/ media/buchwald-attends-wedding-at-kelly-familys-invitation.html.

Burnnett, John. *Useful Toil: Autobiographies of Working People from the 1820s to the 1930s.* New York: Routledge, 1994.

Burns, Eric. *The Spirits of America: A Social History of Alcohol.* Philadelphia: Temple University Press, 2004.

Camden, Carroll. *The Elizabethan Woman.* Houston, TX: Elsevier Press, 1951.

Caplan, Pat, ed. *Food, Health, and Identity.* New York: Routledge, 1997.

Castañeda, Donna. "Romantic Relationships in the Workplace." In *Gender, Race, and Ethnicity in the Workplace: Issues and Challenges for Today's Organizations*, edited by M. F. Karsten, 83–99. Westport, CT: Praeger, 2006.

Centers for Disease Control and Prevention. "Deaths Associated with a Purported Aphrodisiac—New York City, February 1993–May 1995." *Morbidity and Mortality Weekly Report* 44, no. 26 (November 24, 1995): 853–55, 861.

Charsley, Simon. *Wedding Cakes and Cultural History*. London: Routledge, 1992.

Chawla, Simran. *Indian Weddings*. Atglen, PA: Schiffer Publishing, 2010.

Cheng, Ninette. "Marrying Two Worlds." *Northwest Asian Weekly*, August 17, 2013.

Cherlin, Andrew J. *The Marriage-Go-Round: The State of Marriage and the Family in America Today*. New York: Alfred A. Knopf, 2009.

Child, Lydia Maria. *The American Frugal Housewife*. Mineola, NY: Dover, 1999 (originally published 1829).

Civitello, Linda. *Cuisine and Culture: A History of Food and People*. 2nd ed. Hoboken, NJ: Wiley, 2008.

Coe, Sophie D., and Michael D. Coe. *The True History of Chocolate*. London: Thames and Hudson, 1996.

Coeyman, Marjorie. "Breaking Up Is Hard to Do: When the Marriage Falls Apart, What Happens to a Couple's Business Partnership?" *Restaurant Business* 95, no. 1 (January 1, 1996): 38.

———. "Isn't It Romantic?" *Restaurant Business* 96, no. 20 (October 15, 1997): 50.

Cole, Pamela McArthur. "New England Weddings." *Journal of American Folklore* 6, no. 21 (April–June 1893): 103–7.

Coleman, Marilyn J., and Lawrence H. Ganong, ed. *The Social History of the American Family: An Encyclopedia*. Los Angeles: Sage Reference, 2014.

Collins, Kathleen. *Watching What We Eat: The Evolution of Television Shows*. New York: Continuum Books, 2009.

Corinth, Kay, and Mary Sargent. "Executive's Wives." *Brides* 33 (February–March 1967): 116–17.

Costa, S. S. "Rituals of Bliss: Want More Than Cookie-Cutter Nuptials for the Most Important Day of Your Life? Here's How to Plan the Perfect Asian American Wedding!" *A_Magazine* 50, July 31, 2000, http://search.proquest .com/docview/200194277?accountid=28313.

Counihan, Carole. *The Anthropology of Food and Body: Gender, Meaning, and Power*. New York: Routledge, 1999.

Counihan, Carole, and Penny Van Esterik, eds. *Food and Culture: A Reader*. 2nd ed. New York: Routledge, 1997.

Cross, Wilbur, and Ann Novotny. *White House Weddings*. New York: David McKay Company, 1967.

Cury, James Oliver. *The Playboy Guide to Bachelor Parties*. New York: Fireside, 2003.

de Certeau, Michele, and Luce Giard. "The Nourishing Arts." In *Food and Culture: A Reader*, edited by Carole Counihan and Penny Van Esterik, 67–78. 2nd ed. New York: Routledge, 1997.

DeGouy, Louis P. *The Gold Cook Book*. New York: Greenberg Publishers, 1948.

Delineator Home Institute. *New Delineator Recipes*. Chicago: Butterick Publishing Company, 1929.

Devereux, G. R. M. *The Etiquette of Engagement and Marriage: Describing Modern Manners and Customs of Courtship and Marriage*. London: C. Arthur Pearson, March 1919.

Diner, Hasia R. *Hungering for America: Italian, Irish and Jewish Foodways in the Age of Migration*. Cambridge, MA: Harvard University Press, 2001.

Dubinsky, Karen. "Falling for Niagara." *Alternatives Journal* (Summer 2001): 21.

Dunak, Karen M. *As Long as We Both Shall Love: The White Wedding in Postwar America*. New York: New York University Press, 2013.

———. "'Ceremony and Citizenship': African American Weddings, 1945–60." *Gender and History* 21, no. 2 (August 2009): 402–24.

Durden, Tyler. "Russian Energy Tycoon Spends $1 Billion on Son's Wedding: Locals Dub It 'Feast in a Time of Plague.'" ZeroHedge.com, March 31, 2016, http://www.zerohedge.com/news/2016-03-31/russian-energy-tycoon-spends -1-billion-sons-wedding-locals-dub-it-feast-time-plague.

Earle, Alice Morse. "Old Time Marriage Customs in New England." *Journal of American Folklore* 6, no. 21 (April–June 1893): 97–102.

"The Edible Monument: The Art of Food for Festivals." Getty Research Institute, October 6, 2015, http://news.getty.edu/images/9036/ediblemonumentpress release2.pdf, 3 (accessed July 11, 2016).

Eichelberger, Ezra. *Remarkable Banquet Service*. Hoboken, NJ: Wiley, 2014.

Eichler, Lillian. *Book of Etiquette*. Oyster Bay, NY: Doubleday, 1921.

Eula, Michael J. "Failure of American Food Reformers among Italian Immigrants in NYC: 1891–1897." *Italian Americana* 18, no. 1 (Winter 2000): 86–99.

Farmer, Fannie Merritt. *The Boston Cooking School Cook Book*. 1st ed. New York: Little, Brown, 1896.

———. *The Boston Cooking School Cook Book*. 5th ed. New York: Little, Brown, 1939.

———. *The Boston Cooking School Cook Book*. 7th ed. New York: Little, Brown, 1941.

———. *The Boston Cooking School Cook Book*. 8th ed. New York: Little, Brown, 1950.

"Fashionable Table Ware: Decorated Granite and Plain China." *Decorator and Furnisher* 8, no. 6 (September 1886): 172.

"The Fattening Rooms of Calabar." *BBC News*, July 19, 2007, http://news.bbc .co.uk/2/hi/6904640.stm.

Fisher, Carol. *The American Cookbook: A History*. Jefferson, NC: McFarland, 2006.

Flavin, Genevieve. "Mud Slinging Is Just an Old Tribal Custom." *Chicago Tribune*, October 19, 1952.

Fletcher, Anthony. "Englandpast.net: A Framework for the Social History of England." *Historical Research* 75, no. 189 (2002): 296–315.

Fletcher, Nichola. *Charlemagne's Tablecloth: A Piquant History of Feasting*. New York: St. Martin's Press, 2005.

Flood, Erin, Sandra Kapoor, and Belinda De Villa-Lopez. "The Sustainability of Food Served at Wedding Banquets." *Journal of Culinary Science and Technology* 12, no. 2 (2014): 137–52.

Fogarty, Robert S., ed. *Special Love, Special Sex: An Oneida Community Diary*. Syracuse, NY: Syracuse University Press, 1994.

Fowler, Marian. *In a Gilded Cage: American Heiresses Who Married British Aristocrats*. New York: St. Martin's Press, 1993.

Fox, Minnie. *The Blue Grass Cook Book*. New York: Duffield and Co., 1917.

Frank, Robert. "The Most Expensive Wedding Ever?" *Wall Street Journal*, March 4, 2011.

Freedman, Paul, Joyce E. Chaplin, and Ken Albala, eds. *Food in Time and Place: The American Historical Association Companion to Food History*. Oakland: University of California Press, 2014.

Friedman, D. S., D. Heisey-Grove, F. Argyros, E. Berl, J. Nsubuga, T. Stiles, J. Fontana, R. S. Beard, S. Monroe, M. E. McGrath, H. Sutherby, R. C. Dicker, A. DeMaria Jr., and B. T. Matyas. "An Outbreak of Norovirus Gastroenteritis Associated with Wedding Cakes." *Epidemiology and Infection* 133, no. 6 (December 2005): 1057–63.

Frisby, Cynthia M., and Erika Engstrom. "Always a Bridesmaid, Never a Bride: Portrayals of Women of Color in Bridal Magazines." *Media Report to Women* 34 (Fall 2006): 10–14.

Ganapathy, Nirmala. "Want Not, Waste Not: India Debates Food Security as It Moves to Curb Lavish Wedding Feasts." *Straits Times*, April 21, 2011.

Garofalo, Robert, dir. *The Windsors: From George to Kate*. Classic Media Group Production, 2011.

Gaudet, Marcia. "Ribbon Pulls in Wedding Cakes: Tracing a New Orleans Tradition." *Folklore* 117, no. 1 (April 2006).

Given, Meta. *Modern Encyclopedia of Cooking*. Chicago: JG Ferguson, 1949.

Glover, Terry. "Jumping the Broom." *Ebony*, January 10, 2012, http://www.ebony.com/love-sex/jumping-the-broom#axzz4L2XVd300.

Goldstein-Gidoni, Ofra. "Hybridity and Distinctions in Japanese Contemporary Commercial Weddings." *Social Science Japan Journal* 4, no. 1 (April 2001): 21–38.

Good Housekeeping 66, no. 6 (June 1918): 65.

———. 80, no. 6 (June 1925): 80.

———. 82, no. 6 (June 1926): 69.

———. 91, no. 6 (December 1930): 18, 244.

———. 97, no. 6 (December 1933): 84.

————. 106, no. 6 (June 1938): 5–182.

————. 112, no. 3 (March 1941): 11.

————. 114, no. 3 (March 1942): 11–13.

————. 119, no. 3 (September 1944): 59.

Good Housekeeping Magazine. *Good Housekeeping's Cake Book.* Chicago: Consolidated Publishers, 1958.

Goodstein, Laurie. "35,000 Couples Are Invited to a Blessing by Rev. Moon." *New York Times*, November 28, 1997.

Greenburg, Zach O'Malley. "The Real Story behind Jay Z's Champagne Deal." *Forbes*, November 6, 2014, http://www.forbes.com/sites/zackomalleygreenburg /2014/11/06/why-jay-zs-champagne-news-isnt-so-new/#4ad55e4d45d6 (accessed July 8, 2016).

Greene, Mary. "The Other Queen Mother." *Daily Mail Online*, August 17, 2012, http://www.dailymail.co.uk/femail/article-2189197/The-Queen-mother-She -spent-years-asylum-nun-A-new-documentary-explores-unconventional-life -Queen-s-mother-law-Princess-Alice.html.

Greenhill, Pauline, and Kendra Magnusson. "Your Presence at Our Wedding Is Present Enough." *Journal of Folklore Research* 47, no. 3 (September–December 2010): 307–33.

Grimes, William. *Appetite City: A Culinary History of New York.* New York: North Point Press, 2009.

Guy, Kolleen M. "'Oiling the Wheels of Social Life': Myths and Marketing in Champagne during the Belle Époque." *French Historical Studies* 22, no. 2 (Spring 1999): 211–39.

Hagen, Shelly. *The Everything Wedding Book.* 3rd ed. Avon, MA: Adams Media, 2004.

Hall, Dennis. "Modern and Postmodern Wedding Planners: Emily Post's *Etiquette in Society* (1937) and Blum & Kaiser's *Weddings for Dummies* (1997)." *Studies in Popular Culture* 24, no. 3 (April 2002).

Harland, Marion, and Virginia Van de Water. *Marion Harland's Complete Etiquette: A Young People's Guide to Every Social Occasion.* Indianapolis: Bobbs-Merrill, 1914. http://www.gutenberg.org/files/30522/30522-h/30522 -h.htm.

Hartley, Florence. *The Ladies Book of Etiquette and Manual of Politeness.* Boston: Lee & Shepard Publishers, 1872.

Hensley, Nicole. "Historic Biscuit Salvaged from 1912 Sinking of Titanic Sells for $23G." *New York Daily News*, October 27, 2015, http://www.nydaily news.com/news/world/historic-biscuit-salvaged-titanic-sells-23k-article-1.24 12614.

"Highlights of the Percy Skuy History of Contraception Gallery: Condoms and Sponges." Case Western Reserve University, last modified 2010, http://case .edu/affil/skuyhistcontraception/online-2012/Condoms-Sponges.html.

Hirtzler, Victor. *The Hotel St. Francis Cook Book.* Chicago: John Wiley, 1919.

Hixson-Lefils, Alisa. "The Art of Champagne and Its Hispanic Connection." *Hispanic Outlook in Higher Education* 16, no. 21 (July 31, 2006): 10–12.

Hoke, Travis. "Honeymoons Don't Wane." *North American Review* 236, no. 3 (September 1933): 264–70.

Holister, Warren. "Courtly Culture and Courtly Style in the Anglo-Norman World." *Albion: A Quarterly Journal Concerned with British Studies* 20, no. 1 (Spring 1988): 1–17.

Hopkins, Martha. *Inter Course: An Aphrodisiac Cookbook.* Memphis, TN: LPC Group, 1997.

Hoppe, Emilie. *Seasons of Plenty: Amana Communal Cooking.* Ames: Iowa State University Press, 1998.

Hospodar, Miriam. "Aphrodisiac Foods: Bringing Heaven to Earth." *Gastronomica: The Journal of Food and Culture* 4, no. 4 (Fall 2004): 82–93.

"How Much Is a Scrap of Royal Wedding Toast Worth?" *Morning Edition*, July 23, 2012, http://www.npr.org/2012/07/23/157219617/how-much-is-a-scrap-of-royal-wedding-toast-worth.

Howard, Vicki. *Brides, Inc.: American Weddings and the Business of Tradition.* Philadelphia: University of Pennsylvania Press, 2006.

Inness, Sherrie A. *Dinner Roles: American Women and Culinary Culture.* Iowa City: University of Iowa Press, 2001.

Jacobs, Andrew. "The Thrills Are Over at Mount Airy Lodge." *New York Times*, November 2, 2001, D1.

Jet. "Marriage Announcements." *Jet*, http://www.jetmag.com/jet-weddings-application.

Jimenez, Mercedes Laura, Andria Apostolou, Alba Jazmin Palmera Suarez, Luis Meyer, Salvador Hiciano, Anna Newton, Oliver Morgan, Cecilia Then, and Raquel Pimentel. "Multinational Cholera Outbreak after Wedding in Dominican Republic." *Emerging Infectious Diseases* 17, no. 11 (November 2011).

Jones, Michael Owen. "Food Choice, Symbolism, and Identity: Bread and Butter Issues for Folklorists and Nutrition Studies." *Journal of American Folklore* 120, no. 476 (Spring 2007): 129–77.

Jorgensen, Joseph G. *Western Indians.* San Francisco: W. H. Freeman, 1980.

Jurafsky, Dan. *The Language of Food: A Linguist Reads the Menu.* New York: W. W. Norton, 2014.

Kamdar, Mira. "The Pleasures of Excess." *World Policy Journal* 28, no. 2 (Summer 2011): 15–19.

Kander, Mrs. Simon, ed. *The Settlement Cook Book.* Milwaukee, WI: Settlement Cook Book Co., 1947.

Kaufman, Frederick. *A Short History of the American Stomach.* Orlando, FL: Harcourt, 2008.

Kawash, Samira. *Candy: A Century of Panic and Pleasure.* New York: Faber and Faber, 2013.

Kennedy, Pagan. "Who Made That?" *New York Times Magazine*, December 23, 2012, 16.

Klein, Cora C. *Practical Etiquette*. Chicago: A. Flanagan, 1899.

Klein, Erica. "Four Seasons of Fun in the Poconos." *Modern Bride* 52, no. 6 (December 2000): 558.

Kohl, Martha. "And the Bride Wore . . . Montana Weddings, 1900–1960." *Montana: The Magazine of Western History* 62, no. 4 (Winter 2012): 69.

Kolpan, Steven, Brian H. Smith, and Michael A. Weiss. *Wine Wise: Your Complete Guide to Understanding, Selecting, and Enjoying Wine*. New York: John Wiley and Sons, 2008.

Komolafe, M., Mob Olaogu, A. Abembe, M. Fawale, and A. Adebowale. "Stroke Risk Factors among Participants of a World Stroke Day Awareness Program in South-Western Nigeria." *Nigerian Journal of Clinical Practice* 18, no. 6 (November–December 2015): 807–10.

Kozin, Michelle. *Organic Weddings: Balancing Ecology, Style and Tradition*. Gabriola Island, British Columbia: New Society Publishers, 2003.

Krondl, Michael. *Sweet Invention: A History of Dessert*. Chicago: Chicago Review Press, 2011.

Kurlansky, Mark. *The Food of a Younger Land*. New York: Penguin, 2009.

Lane, John. *A Taste of the Past: Menus from Lavish Luncheons, Royal Weddings, Indulgent Dinners and History's Greatest Banquets*. Cincinnati, OH: F&W, 2004.

Larson, Erik. *The Devil in the White City*. New York: Vintage Books, 2003.

Leslie, Eliza. *Miss Leslie's New Cookery Book*. Philadelphia: T. B. Peterson, 1857. http://www.gutenberg.org/files/40943/40943-h/40943-h.htm#FINE_DESSERTS.

Leung, Rebecca. "The Echo Boomers." *CBS News*, October 1, 2004, http://www.cbsnews.com/news/the-echo-boomers-01-10-2004/2.

Locke, Liz, Theresa A. Vaughan, Pauline Greenhill, and Gale Group. *Encyclopedia of Women's Folklore and Folklife*. Gale Virtual Reference Library. Westport, CT: Greenwood Press, 2009.

Lodge, Olive. "Wedding Customs: St. Peter's Day in Galicnk." *Slavonic and East European Review* 13, no. 39 (April 1935): 650–73.

Longstreet, Abby Buchanan. *Social Etiquette of New York*. New York: D. Appleton, 1879.

Luchetti, Cathy. *Home on the Range: A Culinary History of the American West*. New York: Villard Books, 1993.

Luhn, Alec. "Sting and Jennifer Lopez Star in Lavish Moscow Wedding of Oligarch's Son." *Guardian*, March 30, 2016, https://www.theguardian.com/world/2016/mar/30/multimillion-pound-wedding-russia-sting-jlo-gutseriev.

MacNeil, Karen. *The Wine Bible*. 2nd ed. New York: Workman Publishing, 2015.

Magat, Margaret. "Fertilized Duck Eggs: Their Role in Filipino Culture." *Western Folklore* 61, no. 1 (Spring 2001): 63–96.

Marks, Susan. *Finding Betty Crocker: The Secret Life of America's First Lady of Food.* New York: Simon and Schuster, 2005.

Marshall, D. W., and A. S. Anderson. "Proper Meals in Transition, Young Married Couples on the Nature of Eating Together." *Appetite* 39 (2002): 193–206.

Martin, Judith. *Miss Manners' Guide to Excruciatingly Correct Behavior.* New York: Warner Books, 1982.

Martin, Judith, and Jacobina Martin. *Miss Manners' Guide to a Surprisingly Dignified Wedding.* New York: W. W. Norton, 2010.

Martinson, Suzanne. "Youngstown Lays Claim to the Cookie Table." *Pittsburgh Post-Gazette,* August 15, 2004, http://www.post-gazette.com/life/food/2004/08/15/Youngstown-lays-claim-to-the-cookie-table/stories/200408150194.

Marx, Jennifer, et al. *PassPorter's Walt Disney World.* Ann Arbor, MI: PassPorter Travel Press, 2006.

McKay, John P., Bennett D. Hill, and John Buckler. *History of Western Society.* 7th ed. Boston: Houghton Mifflin, 2003.

McKay, John P., Bennett D. Hill, John Buckler, Patricia Buckley Ebrey, Roger B. Beck, Clare Haru Crowston, and Merry E. Weisner-Hanks, eds. *A History of World Societies.* 8th ed. Boston: Bedford/St. Martin's, 2009.

Mead, Margaret. "The Problem of Changing Food Habits." In *Food and Culture: A Reader,* edited by Carole Counihan and Penny Van Esterik, 17–28. 2nd ed. New York: Routledge, 1997.

Mead, Rebecca. *One Perfect Day: The Selling of the American Wedding.* New York: Penguin Books, 2007.

Melchior, Freiderike, and Julia Haedecke. *Royal Weddings.* London: Gardners Books, 2011.

Michie, Helena. "Victorian Honeymoons: Sexual Reorientations and the Sights of Europe." *Victorian Studies* 43, no. 2 (Winter 2001): 229–51.

Miller, Adrian. *Soul Food: The Surprising Story of an American Cuisine One Plate at a Time.* Chapel Hill: University of North Carolina Press, 2013.

Minder, Raphael. "Spain Has Little Appetite for Truffles, but Plenty for the Truffle Trade." *New York Times,* December 31, 2015, http://www.nytimes.com/2016/01/01/world/europe/spain-has-little-appetite-for-truffles-but-plenty-for-the-truffle-trade.html (accessed July 8, 2016).

Mintz, Sidney W. *Sweetness and Power: The Place of Sugar in Modern History.* New York: Penguin Books, 1985.

Monger, George P. *Marriage Customs of the World: An Encyclopedia of Dating Customs and Wedding Traditions.* 2nd ed. Santa Barbara, CA: ABC-CLIO, 2013.

Montgomery, Margaret. "A Macedonian Wedding in Indianapolis." *Hoosier Folklore* 7, no. 4 (December 1948): 101–4.

Morris, Lloyd. "A Particular Form of Wisdom." Review of *The Glitter and the Gold,* by Consuelo Vanderbilt Balsan. *American Scholar* 22, no. 1 (Winter 1952–1953): 118–20.

Moyer, Justin William. "Anthony Bourdain Defends Immigrants, Shreds Trump and Lazy Culinary School Kids." *Washington Post*, October 30, 2015, https://www.washingtonpost.com/news/morning-mix/wp/2015/10/30/anthony-bourdain-defends-immigrants-shreds-trump-and-lazy-culinary-school-kids.

Moynihan, Susan. "10 Ways to Get Romantic in the Poconos." *Modern Bride* 54, no. 1 (February 2002): 652.

Murphy, Brian. *The World of Weddings: An Illustrated Celebration.* New York: Paddington Press, 1978.

Naylor, Sharon, ed. *Wedding Report Quarterly*, 2016, http://www.theweddingreport.com.

Neil, Marion Harris. *A Calendar of Dinners by Crisco.* Cincinnati, OH: Procter & Gamble, 1925.

Neumann, Caryn E. "The End of Gender Solidarity: The History of the Women's Organization for National Prohibition Reform in the United States, 1929–1933." *Journal of Women's History* 9, no. 2 (Summer 1997): 31.

O'Neil, Patrick W. "Bosses and Broomsticks: Ritual and Authority in Antebellum Slave Weddings." *Journal of Southern History* 75, no. 1 (February 2009): 29–48.

Oe, Enang. "The Fattening Rooms of Calabar: A Breeding Ground for Diabesity." *Diabetes Voice* 54 (May 2009): 40–41.

Opie, Frederick Douglass. *Hog and Hominy: Soul Food from Africa to America.* New York: Columbia University Press, 2008.

Otnes, Cele C., and Elizabeth H. Pleck. *Cinderella Dreams: The Allure of the Lavish Wedding.* Berkeley: University of California Press, 2003.

Packham, Jo. *Wedding Toasts and Speeches: Finding the Perfect Words.* New York: Stirling, 2007.

Parry, Tyler D. "Married in Slavery Time: Jumping the Broom in Atlantic Perspective." *Journal of Southern History* 81, no. 2 (May 2015): 273.

Partin, Elliot. "Highland Beach, Maryland." BlackPast.org, http://www.blackpast.org/aah/highland-beach-maryland-1893.

Paul, Gill. *Titanic Love Stories: The True Stories of 13 Honeymoon Couples Who Sailed on the Titanic.* East Sussex, UK: Ivy Press Limited, 2011.

Pegram, Thomas R. *Battling Demon Rum: The Struggle for a Dry America, 1800–1933.* Chicago: Ivan R. Dee, 1998.

Penner, Barbara. "A Vision of Love and Luxury: The Commercialization of Nineteenth-Century American Weddings." *Winterthur Portfolio* 39, no. 1 (Spring 2004): 1–20.

People 70, no. 13 (September 29, 2008): 158–59.

Phillip, Abby. "Jay Z's Gold Champagne and the Murky Story behind His Latest Business Deal." *Washington Post*, November 6, 2014.

Pogash, Carol. "Offline, D.I.Y. Weddings Aren't So Picture Perfect." *New York Times*, November 19, 2015, http://www.nytimes.com/2015/11/22/fashion/weddings/diy-wedding-ideas-not-picture-perfect.html.

Pogrebin, Robin. "Goodbye Quaint, Hello, Poconos!" *New York Times*, February 2, 1996.

Post, Emily. *Etiquette in Society, in Business, in Politics, and at Home*. New York: Funk & Wagnallis, 1922.

Pottker, Jan. *Janet and Jackie: The Story of a Mother and Her Daughter, Jacqueline Kennedy Onassis*. New York: St. Martin's Press, 2001.

Price, Sean. "What Made the Twenties Roar?" *Scholastic Update* 131, no. 10 (February 22, 1999): 18.

Purdy, Ken W. "Prince Phillip: England's Most Misunderstood Man." *Look*, April 7, 1964.

Rainy, Clint. "The World's Most Expensive Cracker Just Sold for $23,000." *Grub Street*, October 27, 2015, http://www.grubstreet.com/2015/10/expensive-cracker-from-titanic.html.

Randall, Joe, and Toni Tipton-Martin. *A Taste of Heritage: The New African American Cuisine*. Hoboken, NJ: Wiley, 2002.

Reed-Danahay, Deborah. "Champagne and Chocolate: Taste and Inversion in a French Wedding Ritual." *American Anthropologist* 98, no. 4 (1996): 750–61.

Rees, Jonathan. *Refrigeration Nation: A History of Ice, Appliances, and Enterprise in America*. Baltimore: Johns Hopkins University Press, 2013.

Reynolds, David S. *Waking Giant*. New York: HarperCollins, 2009.

Roark, James L., ed. *The American Promise: A History of the United States*. Boston: Bedford/St. Martin's, 2003.

Roberts, Michele. "From Gastroporn to Wedding-Night Recipes, Food and Sex Are Intimately Linked." *New Statesmen*, February 13, 2006, 60.

Roberts, Sam. "Morris Wilkins Dies at 90, Lured Lovers to Poconos." *New York Times*, May 29, 2015, B15.

Rombauer, Irma S., and Marion Rombauer Becker. *Joy of Cooking*. New York: Signet, 1973.

Ronald, Mary. *The Century Cook Book*. New York: The Century Company, 1899.

Ruggless, Ron. "It's Bubble, Bubble, Toil, and Truffle for Valentine's Day." *Nation's Restaurant News*, February 7, 2005, 64.

Salamon, Hagar, and Esther Juhasz. "Goddesses of Flesh and Metal: Gazes on the Tradition of Fattening Jewish Brides in Tunisia." *Journal of Middle East Women's Studies* 7, no. 1 (Winter 2011): 1–30.

Schenone, Laura. *A Thousand Years over a Hot Stove*. New York: W. W. Norton, 2003.

Schomburg Center for Research in Black Culture, Jean Blackwell Hutson Research and Reference Division, New York Public Library. "The Negro Motorist Green Book: 1948." New York Public Library Digital Collections, http://digitalcollections.nypl.org/items/6fa574f0-893f-0132-1035-58d385a7bbd0 (accessed May 10, 2016).

———. "The Negro Travelers' Green Book: 1953." New York Public Library Digital Collections, http://digitalcollections.nypl.org/items/2bc86d90-92d0-0132-e771-58d385a7b928 (accessed May 10, 2016).

Serhan, Randa. "Palestinian Weddings: Inventing Palestine in New Jersey." *Journal of Palestine Studies* 37, no. 4 (Summer 2008): 21–37.

Shepard, Alexandra. "Family and Household." In *The Elizabethan World*, edited by Susan Doran and Norman Jones. London: Routledge, 2010.

Sietsema, Tom. "Dinner Engagements: The Perils of Popping the Question in a Restaurant." *Washington Post*, February 9, 2000, F01.

Simmons, Amelia. *The First American Cookbook*. New York: Dover Publishing, 1984 (originally published 1796).

Simmons, Ann M. "Where Fat Is a Mark of Beauty." *Los Angeles Times*, September 30, 1998, 1–2.

Smiley Publishing Company, ed. *Smiley's Cook Book and Universal Household Guide*. Chicago: J. B. Smiley, 1901.

Smith, Andrew F., ed. *Savoring Gotham: A Food Lover's Companion to New York City*. New York: Oxford University Press, 2015.

Smith, Jada F. "At Federal Bridal Show, Things Old, New and Seized and Blue." *New York Times*, July 7, 2015, http://www.nytimes.com/2015/07/08/us/at -federal-bridal-show-things-old-new-seized-and-blue.html.

"So You're Going to Be Married." *Brides* 3, no. 1 (Autumn 1936) and 3, no. 2 (Winter 1936–1937).

Steinberg, Ellen F., and Jack H. Prost. "A Menu and a Mystery: The Case of the 1834 Delmonico Bill of Fare." *Gastronomica: The Journal of Food and Culture* 8, no. 2 (Spring 2008): 40–50.

Stone, Lawrence. *Family, Sex, and Marriage in England, 1500–1800*. New York: Penguin, 1977.

Strong, Andrea. "A Hallmark Moment." *Restaurant Business*, December 15, 2001, 70.

Sturgis, Ingrid. *The Nubian Wedding Book*. New York: Three Rivers Press, 1997.

Theophano, Janet. *Eat My Words: Reading Women's Lives through the Cookbooks They Wrote*. New York: Palgrave, 2002.

Thompson, Joyce, and Phyllis Bridges. "West Texas Wedding Cars." *Western Folklore* 30, no. 2 (April 1971): 123–26.

Titherington, G. W. "The Raik Dinka of Bahr El Ghazal Province." *Sudan Notes and Records* 10 (1927): 184.

Trosper, Ronald L. "U.S. Indian Business and Enterprise." In *The Native North American Almanac*, edited by Duane Champagne, 915–24. Detroit, MI: Gale Research, 1994.

Tshumi, Gabriel. *Royal Chef: Recollections of Life in Royal Households from Queen Victoria to Queen Mary*. London: W. Kimber, 1954.

Tuder, Stephanie. "How This Restaurant Pulls Off America's Most Marriage Proposals." *ABC News*, February 27, 2015, http://abcnews.go.com/Lifestyle/ restaurant-pulls-off-americas-marriage-proposals/story?id=29281652.

Tunic, Tanfer Emin. "Ashley Wilkes Told Me He Likes to See a Girl with a Healthy Appetite." *European Journal of American Culture* 32, no. 2 (2012): 85–107.

Twain, Mark. *Roughing It*. Hartford, CT: American Publishing Co., 1872.

Vance, Erik. "An Ocean Apart." *Virginia Quarterly Review* 91, no. 2 (Spring 2015): 40.

Vanderbilt, Amy. *Amy Vanderbilt's Complete Book of Etiquette: A Guide to Gracious Living*. Garden City, NY: Doubleday, 1957.

Visser, Margaret. *The Gift of Thanks: The Roots and Rituals of Gratitude*. Boston: Houghton Mifflin Harcourt, 2009.

———. *The Rituals of Dinner*. Toronto, ON: HarperCollins, 1991.

Vogue's Book of Etiquette. Ithaca, NY: Conde Nast, 1925.

W. H. Mansfield and Co. *The Mansfield Cook Book*. Putnam CT: Patriot Press, 1890.

Wakin, Daniel J. "Rev Sun Myung Moon, Self-Proclaimed Messiah Who Built Religious Movement, Dies at 92." *New York Times*, September 2, 2012.

Wallace, Carol. *All Dressed in White: The Irresistible Rise of the American Wedding*. New York: Penguin Books, 2004.

Wallach, Jennifer Jensen. *How America Eats: A Social History of U.S. Food and Culture*. Lanham, MD: Rowman & Littlefield, 2013.

Wan, Adrian. "Restaurants and Hotels Sign Up to Provide Shark-Free Banquet Menus." *South China Morning Post*, May 6, 2010.

Weatherford, Doris. *American Women and World War II*. Edison, NJ: Castle Books, 2008.

Weir, Alison, Kate Williams, Sarah Gristwood, and Tracy Borman. *The Ring and the Crown: A History of Royal Weddings, 1066–2011*. London: Hutchinson, 2011.

Wells, Enid. *Living for Two: A Guide to Homemaking*. New York: David Kemp and Co., 1939.

Whyte, Martin King. "Choosing Mates—the American Way." *Society* 29, no. 3 (1992): 71–77.

Wiener, Jon. "Pop and Avant-Garde: The Case of John and Yoko." *Popular Music and Society* 22 no. 1 (1998): 1–13.

Wilson, Bee. "Gulp Fiction." *New Statesman*, February 5, 1999, 42.

Wilson, Carol. "Wedding Cake: A Slice of History." *Gastronomica: The Journal of Food and Culture* 5, no. 2 (Spring 2005): 69–72.

Wiswell, Joyce. "Las Vegas: The Ultimate Over-the-Top Honeymoon." *Modern Bride* 53, no. 2 (April 2001): 644.

Wong, Brittany. "The 30 Most Popular Places to Take a First Date, According to Dating App Clover." *Huffington Post*, April 6, 2015, http://www.huffington post.com/2015/04/06/where-to-go-on-first-dates_n_7011884.html.

Wood, Bertha M. *Foods of the Foreign Born: In Relation to Health*. Boston: Whitcomb and Barrows, 1922.

Wouters, Cas. "Etiquette Books and Emotional Management in the 20th Century: Part Two: The Integration of the Sexes." *Journal of Social History* 29, no. 2 (Winter 1995): 325–39.

Yalom, Marilyn. *A History of the Wife*. New York: HarperCollins, 2001.

Yoshimizu, Ayaka. "Hello, War Brides: Heteroglossia, Counter-Memory, and the Auto/biographical Work of Japanese War Brides." *Meridians* 10, no. 1 (2009): 111–36.

Ziemann, Hugo, and F. L. Gillette. *The White House Cook Book*. Akron, OH: Saalfield Publishing Company, 1913.

Zollman, Joellyn. "Jewish Immigration to America: Three Waves." My Jewish Learning, http://www.myjewishlearning.com/article/jewish-immigration-to -america-three-waves.

Index

About the Author

Claire Stewart graduated from the Culinary Institute of America, and was executive chef at the Continental Club in New York City, as well as executive sous chef at the Yale Club of New York City. She worked as chef tournant at Gee's Brassiere in Oxford, England, and as chef poissonier at the Rainbow Room. Stewart was banquet chef at Highlawn Pavilion and a chef at Gracie Mansion in New York City. In her native California, she worked as chef tournant at Delta King in Sacramento and as a chef garde manger at the Hyatt Regency.

Stewart lives with her husband and teenage son, and she teaches culinary arts and restaurant management at City University of New York in Brooklyn.